CONTENTS

From Don Overstreet:

This book is dedicated to

LEESA

My beloved wife,
my best friend, the love of my life
and the ROCK of our family.
Thank you for walking alongside me through
this church planting journey.

From Dr. Mark Hammond:

I'm dedicating this book to my mother Tina,
the eighty nine year young city dweller
that lives in New York City and raised me
to love the sounds and atmosphere of city life.

YOU'RE THE GOD OF THE CITY

You're the God of the city
You're the King of these people
You're the Lord of this nation
You are
You're the light in the darkness
You're the hope of the hopeless
You're the peace for the restless
For there is no one like our God
There is no one like You God

— by Chris Tomlin

CHAPTER ONE

CITITES: A BLESSING OR A CURSE?

"If what GOD is doing in the world at large means anything to the church today, it should be clear that the phenomenon of urbanization is the work of God in preparing great multitudes of people for evangelization and the planting of tens of thousands of new churches." ROGER GREENWAY[1]

"Should I not care about the great city of Nineveh, which has more than 120,000 people who cannot distinguish between their right and their left, as well as many animals?" JONAH 4:11

It was the summer of 2005 and the Los Angeles Baptist Association was conducting a tour of some suburbs of Los Angeles where we needed to start churches. We stopped the bus and all the pastors and leaders of the local churches got off. They went on a walking tour of the city of Artesia. Artesia is not ghetto, it is in a well developed but multi-ethnic community of 45,000 people, 20 miles from downtown Los Angeles. It is a very diverse community. It is made up of people from North and South India, Nepal, China, Korea, Philippines, Mexico blended in with African Americans and Anglo. A really blended community. The pastors were sent out to ask some information gathering questions of people on the streets of Artesia. Nothing hard, nothing too difficult and definitely something doable.

Soon one of the pastors came running back to the bus muttering," I have been in a foreign country, I have been in a foreign country."

What he was really saying is that this multi-cultural world is too overwhelming. This is a world that I do not feel comfortable in. This is a world that I have not been trained for. I do not know how to handle it. It is outside my comfort zone. I did not sign up 30 years ago to minister in this environment. The sad but also comical thing was his church was just one mile away from this multi-cultural world that he did not know existed!

As the Church of the 21st Century looks at the great cities of the world the majority of the Christians are saying the same thing. This is <u>not</u> the world that we signed up to minister to when we first became Christians, when we first started this church forty years ago, when we first moved to this city.

As God looks at the great cities of the world, He says that He loves each and every one of the people crammed into the crowded slums of Calcutta. He loves all the homeless children sleeping in the garbage dump in Rio de Janeiro. He loves the thousands of people living in the multi-million dollar homes of Beverly Hills as well as the homeless of Skid Row in downtown Los Angeles. He also loves His church and expects them--no commands them to -- love each and every one in the great cities. So, the question before the Church is:

WHAT IS THE CHURCH GOING TO DO WITH THE CITY?

With the mega cities of the world – that are multiplying at an extraordinary rate and at an extraordinary pace. The Church cannot ignore the cities of the world. The city is here to stay. For the first time in history, as of 2008, the majority of the world's population lives in the urban centers of the world.

A quick look at history shows that the city has been around for a long time and is here to stay. The city has grown, declined, and grown again over the years, but the city has always survived and prospered.

"The explosion of cities has taken place largely in the twentieth century, but cities themselves are not new. In the middle of the third millennium B.C., cities such as Eridu and Thebes emerged along the Tigris-Euphrates and Nile rivers. In the second millennium B.C., they appeared in North India at Harappa and Mohenjodaro and in Cheengchou, China. In the first millennium B.C Teotihuacan and other cities appeared in Central America. Cities emerged in West Africa after the coming of Christ.

Most of the ancient cities were not large by modern standards. Ur had a population of about 24,000 in 2000 B.C. and Athens about 180,000 in 300 B.C. Rome emerged as the first great city in Europe. It had about one million people in New Testament times. When Rome fell to the invading barbarians from Inner Asia, Europe reverted to peasantry with small Episcopal cities rarely larger than 3,000 people with their lords and bishops, walls, cathedrals, and religious institutions.

In North India, the cities of Harappa and Mohenjo-Daro were destroyed about 1500 B.C. Large cities re-emerged in South Asia only a few hundred years before the coming of Christ. In China, cities have flourished and decayed, but urban life never collapsed as completely as it did in Europe or North India.

Modern cities emerged about 1000 A.D. They were centers of economic activities such as trade and manufacturing. Business, not government or religion was the driving force. They were not refuges in times of war. They thrived in times of peace and walls became hindrances. These cities emerged in northern Europe but they soon spread around the world as commerce and manufacturing increased.

In our century, modern cities have exploded. In 1900 only one city, London, had more than a million people. Today there are more than 380 cities larger than that, including little-known urban areas such as Ibadan and Lagos in Nigeria, Nagpur in India, Belo in Japan, Mashed in Iran, and Omsk and Kuybyshev in the former U.S.S.R. There are now at least 15 cities with more than a population of 10 million people.

The massive flow of people from the countryside to cities continues. Never before in history have so many people moved from one place to another. In 1800, less than 3 percent of the world's people lived in towns of more than 5,000 people. By the end of this century, more than 55 percent will do so. More than 48 percent will live in cities of more than 100,000 people. Today urbanization is taking place faster in China, India, Africa, and Latin America than in Europe and North America. By the end of this century only three out of the 10 largest cities will be in North America (including Mexico City), none in Europe.

The sheer size of the modern cities makes it difficult for us to understand them. The population of Tokyo is more than five times as large as Papua Guinea with the nearly one thousand tribes. One high-rise in Bombay may have more people than 10 Indian villages."[2]

Before we look at the vast growth and the domination of the city in the world we live in today, let's take a step back, and put a definition of the city on the table. I am using as the definition of the city one that Donald McGavran used. He writes, "I classify as rural all those who earn their living from the soil, dwell in village, and eat largely what they raise. All those who live in market centers and live by trade or manufacture, I classify as urban. Some will live in towns of less than ten thousand; others live in towns of ten to ninety thousand, and still others in great manufacturing cities of a hundred thousand and up. The huge metropolises – Tokyo, Osaka, Calcutta, Bombay, Kinshasa, Mexico City, Sao Paulo, and others – present special problems, but for the time being we shall consider them also as simply urban populations."[3]

Robert Redfield developed a chart that shows the differences between rural and urban living clearly. It is very helpful in clarifying the difference. They are:

REDFIELD'S RURAL-URBAN CONTINUUM

RURAL	URBAN
Established tradition	mobile, free
Homogeneous	heterogeneous
Group-orientated	individualistic
Ascribed roles	achieved roles
Community	intersecting communities
Harmonious	managed conflict
Status quo, little change	rapid change
Egalitarian	hierarchical
Holistic life	segmented life
Human in scale	impersonal
Sacred cosmos	secular cosmos[4]

Now, let us remind ourselves the importance of the city. Cities are a key component of life, for you see, "cities are centers of service and dominance. That is to say, cities arise and grow because they serve the towns, villages, and farms that surround them. This activity takes various forms; some cities emphasize one more than the other. As a city grows larger, however, it tends to serve and influence its hinterlands in at least eight major areas. People who live in towns and villages expect cities to render these services and would be disappointed if cities failed to provide them. Note that each of these services requires personnel to run them, and therefore each contributes to urban growth.

The eight services are:

1. *Government.* Many ancient cities began as centers of government. All modern nations need not only national capitals, but they also need regional government centers.

2. *Education.* Most schools of higher education are in cities, which offer libraries, part-time work for students, and easy access from the local regions. This is especially important in developing nations.

3. *Health care.* Big, diversified hospitals are found in large cities. This is especially true in the developing nations. Throughout the world, therefore, the health care industry promotes urbanization.

4. *Information.* People, even those who are illiterate, want to be informed about the world, and especially about their own nation. Radio, television, newspapers, magazines, and books provide information. All these avenues of information are provided best in the city. The sphere of influence of a given city often extends as far as its radio waves. Radio and television place virtually everyone in immediate contact with the city.

5. *Entertainment.* Whether it's through the fine arts, museums, popular music, sports, movies, or eating out, people go to the city to enjoy themselves. They expect the city to provide this type of cultural leadership.

6. *Trade.* In the days when people were dependent on shipping goods by water than they are today, cities grew by the riverside or where

there were deepwater harbors. Later, cities grew where railroad lines and roads intersected. Now airports (or the lack thereof) affect urban growth. Commerce and the transportation that it includes contribute mightily to the growth of cities.

7. *Industry*. Manufacturing has given tremendous impetus to the growth of western cities and some cities of the developing world.

8. *Warfare*. Some cities have started as military camps. The need to set up military camps and defense plants encourage urbanization during wartime. After the war efforts are ended, people stay in the urban centers where they had moved to and the urban center continues to expand.[5]

To continue to emphasize the importance of the city in today's world, let me share how Paul G. Hiebert and Eloise Hiebert Menses identify six general characteristics of all cities. "They are: scale, centers, diversity, specialization, hierarchy, and change.

First, cities are of great scale. The size of cities is generally much larger than most towns and villages, with inhabitants organizing themselves in various ways. Second, cities are centers of significance. The urban areas are centers of leadership, power, and authority. Third, cities are generally represented by a great amount of cultural, spiritual, political and economic diversity. Even within ethnic enclaves (e.g. Little Havana in Miami), there is great diversity. Fourth, cities are usually categorized by specialization. Cities are able to function, in large part, because of the various specializations, which come together to create an overarching economic system. The general store of the small town seems to vanish in the cities and is replaced by numerous specialty stores. The local hospital in a small community may have a few general practioners but generally does not provide a multitude of specialists (e.g., endocrinologists, neurologist) who are more likely to be found in cities. Fifth, hierarchy also defines cities. The gap between the rich and the poor, the powerful and powerless, and the educated and uneducated is much wider in the cities. Finally, in contrast to rural communities, change occurs in cities at a regular and rapid rate. Cities are constantly evolving, reorganizing and restructuring, growth and declining."[6]

The reasons for the city are valid ones. Each of the functions of the city are important to everyday life and the existence of a thriving nation and world.

The city is here to stay. The city cannot be ignored nor can the city be thrown away.

In A.D. 374, Jerome, scolding a monk for having abandoned the desert for the world of the city, wrote these words: 'O wasteland bright with the spring flowers of Christ! O solitude out of which comes these stones that build the city of the great king in the Apocalypse! O desolate desert rejoicing in God's familiar presence! What keeps you in the world, o brother? You are above and beyond the world. How long is the shade of the house going to conceal you? How long shall the grimy prisons of those cities intern you?'"[7]

Too many times, as Christians, we act like it is better to run away from the city. I believe the Lord would be running <u>into</u> the city.

So, *WHAT ARE WE GOING TO DO WITH THE CITIES?*

What is the Church going to do with the mega cities of the world?

It is a well-known fact that if the Church captures the cities for Christ, it will grow. If it loses the cities, it will become a movement on the margins of modern life. The early church understood that fact. The early church was an urban movement. It began in Jerusalem. God blessed the work there. Through persecution the church expanded to the cities of Samaria (Acts 8:5), Damascus (9:2), Caesarea (10:1), and Antioch (11:19). Antioch became the missionary sending center for the urban expansion of Christianity:

> *In the church of Antioch there*
> *were prophets and teachers: Barnabas,*
> *Simeon called Niger, Lucius of Cyrene,*
> *Manaen (who had been brought up with*
> *Herod the tetrarch) and Saul. While*
> *they were worshiping the Lord and*
> *fasting, the Holy Spirit said,*
> *'Set apart for me Barnabas and Saul*
> *for the work for which I have called*
> *them', so after they had fasted and*
> *prayed, they placed their hands on*
> *them and sent them off. (Acts 13:1-3)*

As they were sent out to the Gentile world, Paul saw the importance of the city. His strategy was an urban strategy. He did not go to the many small villages in Asia Minor but to the cities. As he ministered in the major cities and finished his work in each region, he could declare: "But now that there is no more place for me to work in these regions, and since I have been longing for many years to see you. I plan to do so when I go to Spain."(Romans 15:23-24) Was every person in the region a Christian? NO. Were the Christian workers finished working the harvest fields? NO. But Paul's strategic work of targeting the major cities, training workers and sending them out into the villages was finished. The work continued, but Paul's work was done. Throughout history the Christian movement has been predominately urban.

Then along came population explosion and the city got away from the Church's understanding as well as its control.

Let's look at some population growth statistics to see where the city is and where it is going.

Robert Neuwirth shares some extraordinary facts, when he writes, "Every year, close to 70 million people leave their rural homes and head for the cities. That's around 1.4 million people a week, 200,000 a day, 8,000 an hour, 130 every minute." [8]

The lists of the top largest cities in the world will give one numbers that are mind-boggling. The 10 top urban areas by population in the world are:

1.	TOKYO	34,997,269
2.	MEXICO CITY	18,660,221
3.	NEW YORK	18,252,339
4.	SAO PAULO	17,857,001
5.	MUMBAI (Bombay)	17,431,305
6.	DELHI	14,145,956
7.	CALCUTTA	13,805,681
8.	BUENOS AIRES	13,047,115
9.	SHANGHAI	12,759,367
10.	JAKARTA	12,295,516

In the United States the top 10 cities are:

1.	NEW YORK	8,143,197
2.	LOS ANGELES	3,844,829
3.	CHICAGO	2,842,518
4.	HOUSTON	2,016,582
5.	PHILADELPHIA	1,463,281
6.	PHOENIX	1,461,575
7.	SAN ANTONIO	1,256,509
8.	SAN DIEGO	1,255,540
9.	DALLAS	1,213,825
10.	SAN JOSE	912,332 [9]

Then add to these statistics, facts that the United Nations has presented relating to the present world population growth and the cities. Consider the following facts:

- The urban population passed the 1 billion mark in 1961. It took 25 years to add another billion urban dwellers and just 17 years more to add a third billion. The urban population reached 3 billion in 2003 and is projected to increase to 4 billion in 2018, 15 years later. By 2030, it is expected to be about 5 billion.

- The urban population in the less developed regions will increase from 2.3 billion to 3.9 billion over the next 25 years.

- Urbanization is very far advanced in the more developed regions where in 2005 the percent of the population that lived in urban settings was 74 percent. The urban population in the more developed regions is projected to increase to 81 percent by 2030. In the less developed regions, the urban population was 43 percent in 2005 and is projected to rise to 56 percent by 2030.

- Africa and Asia were the least urbanized areas in the world in 2005, just 38 percent and 40 percent respectively. By 2030, Asia will rank first and Africa second in terms of number of urban dwellers.

By 2030 almost seven out of every 10 residents in the world will be living in Africa and Asia.

- The region of Latin America and the Caribbean is already highly urbanized, with 77 percent of the population living in cities in 2005. By 2030, that proportion is projected to reach 84 percent.

- In Europe, the proportion of the population residing in urban areas is expected to rise from 72 percent in 2005 to 78 percent in 2030. In North America the increase in the proportion of urban population is projected to be from 81 percent in 2005 to 87 percent in 2030. In Oceania, the equivalent rise from 71 percent in 2005 to 74 percent in 2030.

- The twentieth century witnessed the emergence of megacities, that is, with 10 million inhabitants or more. Since 1950, the number of megacities has risen from 2 to 20 in 2005. Two additional megacities are projected to emerge over the next decade, to reach 22 by 2015, among which 17 are located in developing countries.

- With 35 million residents in 2005, the metropolitan area of Tokyo was by far the most population urban agglomeration in the world. After Tokyo, the next largest urban agglomerations are Cuidiad de Mexico (Mexico City) and the urban agglomeration of New York-Newark, with 19 million inhabitants each, followed by Sao Paulo and Mumba (Bombay) with 18 million people each.

- In 2015 Tokyo will still be the largest urban agglomeration with 35 million residents, followed by Mumbai (Bombay) and Cuidad de Mexico (Mexico City) with 22 million people each, and Sao Paulo with 21 million people.

- Small cities, that is those with a population of fewer than 500,000 people, were the place of residence of about 51 percent of all urban dwellers in the world in 2005.

- By 2030 three out every five people on earth will likely reside in urban centers, and nearly half the world's population will live in the cities of developing countries.[10]

The growth of the cities of the world has been overwhelming at times. The speed and size of the growth has been hard to keep up with and definitely not able to be controlled. "Sociologists have had to invent a whole new vocabulary to describe the changing city. From *village* to *city* to *dynapolis* to *metropolis* to *dynametropolis* to *megalopolis* and presently *dynamegalopolis*."

"The cities of the past were built to human scale. With few exceptions a man could walk from the wall to the center of town in 15 minutes. In today's cities, the dimensions have become non-human. Los Angeles is already an unofficial supercity sprawling over 100 miles with a population larger than all states in the United States except California, New York and Texas. Cities used to be contained by counties, now the Los Angeles metroplex includes five different counties."[11]

The massive numbers of people in the cities of the world are overwhelming. If one is to look from the outside, the city can only look like a "curse" instead of a blessing. "The city's bewildering diversity, high crime rate, pollution, congestion, poverty, and squalor have created a kind of anti-urban prejudice that makes people view cities with undisguised antagonism, and in some cases, self-righteous contempt. Everyone recognizes that the progenitors of new lifestyles and communication centers of the world are in the cities. Cities are places where new and exciting things happen everyday. Yet city lovers are hard to find, and worldwide anti-urban bias is growing everywhere."[12]

I live in Los Angeles – a place you either hate or love. There are no in-betweens. If you only watched the evening T.V. news reports or just read the newspapers one could easily come to see Los Angeles as a place to fear and to be afraid to come to visit. But, Los Angeles is a massive spread-out geographical area where ordinary people live. Los Angeles is full of people that Jesus loves and gave His life for on the Cross. The Church needs to see Los Angeles, as well as the other major cities of the world, as an exciting, outstanding harvest field.

John Dawson wrote, "Many Christians think cities are by nature evil places. If asked, they would say the city is a curse, not a blessing. However, that is not God's view. After all the human story begins in a garden and ends in a city." Dawson goes on to say, "I believe God intends the city to be a place of shelter, a place of communion, and a place of personal liberation as its citizens practice a division of labor according to their own unique gifts."[13]

The last church that I pastored was located in Pomona, CA, an inner-city community connected to Los Angeles. It was full of gangs, crime and was usually second or third with the most murders per year in Los Angeles County. I had to drive 450 miles one way to Sacramento (that means 900 miles round trip for those who are mathematically challenged), to sit down with the church and parents of the youth group members that wanted to help our church minister in a summer mission project. They were all afraid of what they heard on the news. The church and the parents reluctantly agreed to allow the youth group to come to Pomona.

In the 10 days that the youth group spent with us, conducting Backyard Bible Clubs and helping us in Vacation Bible School, one hundred children and adults accepted Christ. Not one member of the youth group was hurt or scared – just extremely blessed as they saw precious souls come into the Kingdom.

Another sad fact of American Christianity is that because of crime, because of the changing world around it, inner city churches moved out of the city. The churches fled to the suburbs. The suburbs were safer places. The suburbs were full of people just like people in the churches that were fleeing the cities. The suburbs were full of warmth and beauty, full of new things and new opportunities. The suburbs were just a safer place to live, to raise children and to grow old in together. The suburbs were a better place to do church.

Early this year, I spent some time with the church-planting specialists for the Southern Baptist denomination in Atlanta. Here are some facts that they shared with me:

Approximately 878,000 people live "inside the perimeter," which is equivalent to the inner city section of Atlanta. Over 500,000 of the population have no religious affiliation; over 600,000 people are not church members, and over 700,000 people do not attend church. Of the 166 Southern Baptist congregations that existed in the 1960s in the area, only 39 are still in existence, yet the area has grown 24 percent during that time period. Other interesting facts are: In the late 1990s to early 2000s this area was a very crime-ridden community. Projects for lower income families dominated the area. They have all been torn down and bulldozed away. Now the community "inside the perimeter" is an "up and coming community."

An amazing 75 percent of the population do not have children. Presently 69 percent of the adult population is not married and single parents are the fastest growing people group in that area. The median age of people living in the area is 36.1 years of age. This is considerably less than those attending the Baptist churches in the area.

This leads to the conclusion that many of the Baptist church members do not live in their church neighborhood, do not reflect the "people groups" living in their church neighborhoods, do not impact their church neighborhoods, do not penetrate the lostness in their neighborhoods, and do not know or relate to those persons who make the decisions that affect the neighborhood.

Many of the churches are dying, declining, or just holding their own. Before one says, "How could that happen? Those Baptists are not very spiritual" this is happening across denominational lines and it is happening in all major cities in the United States!

One thing that needs to be noted about the situation in Atlanta is that the inner city has gotten better, not worst. Regenification is working. Many cities in the United States are attempting to revive its downtown districts. The living conditions are now inviting, as many old structures have been torn down and attractive lofts and condominiums have been built. They are built to please the young professionals that want to move back into the city. The young professionals want to move into the city, where they can shop, live and work in a connected lifestyle and where there is an intentional "energy flow" that attracts the young adults.

God's Church must address this phenomenon in the cities. The young professionals are a "people group" that needs to be reached for Christ.

Better living conditions in the city, especially third-world cities are not yet a reality. Patrick Johnstone says it well when he writes, " The massive urbanization of the past century has occurred in the midst of and even because of terrible desolations through wars, earthquakes, ecological degradation through population growth and human sinfulness. It is the desolations due to the sins of society today that need the healing of the gospel. The crime, drug trade and abuse, alcohol, prostitution and the desolations they have caused that only can have a spiritual solution."[14]

So, *WHAT ARE WE GOING TO DO WITH THE CITIES?* What is the church going to do with the mega cities of the world?

Then added to all the other elements that have profounded the church and its attempt to impact the city is the element of DIVERSITY.

DIVERSITY of race, culture and life styles now dominate the mega cities of the world. The city is a conglomeration of the mixture of the world populations. The whole world has moved to the cities.

Let me share some facts about the Los Angeles urban metro-area that Jack Rager, director of Mobilize L.A., has put together. They are:

- The total population of the Los Angeles-Long Beach-Santa Ana Metropolitan Statistical Area is 12,818,132. Of that, 4,394,068 or 34 percent are foreign born.

- The Caste Hindu community cluster are people primarily from the Indian Sub-Continent and includes several language groups, such as Punjabi, Gujarati and Hindi that still practice Hinduism in its many forms. There are approximately 70,000 Indian born Hindus in the metro-area.

- The Muslim community cluster is comprised of people from Pakistan, Bangladesh, and other Southern Asian countries. There are about 17,000 foreign born in the Metro-Area.

- The Persian community cluster includes people from Iran, Afghanistan, Tajikistan, Uzbekistan, and Turkey. This community is also diverse in the religious mix, including Sunni Muslim, Shia Muslims, and Jews. The population is approximately 150,000 foreign born in the metro area.

- The South East Asia community cluster includes Thai, Vietnamese, Cambodian, Korean and Chinese Buddhist worldview and Japanese Shinto worldview. The total non-Christian foreign-born population is about 670,000.

- South Asia Buddhist community cluster includes people from Nepal, Tibet and Sri Lanka. We estimate the community to be about 20,000 foreign born in the metro area.

- There are about 80 Buddhist Temples and meditation centers of various traditions and practices and approximately 50 Mosques and Islamic Centers in the metro area of Los Angeles.

All those numbers of various people groups are just to show that we live in a very diverse and wonderful world. There are places in Los Angeles where you will never have to speak English and those places will blend from one people groups/ language group to another within a few city blocks.

It is amazing how GOD has brought the world to us in the form of the massive cities of the world. There are at least 242 least evangelized people groups living in Los Angeles County. Over 500 people groups need to be reached for Christ in the New York/Newark metropolis. GOD has brought the world to the cities so that the Christian Church can evangelize them. Will the Church rise up to the challenge?

Another aspect of diversity is the diversity of life-styles and world-views. One can find any and every life-style in the world right in the middle of the world-class city. Chinese may be spoken in the home, English in the classroom and work place, but Hip-Hop street language is what the American born third generation teenager lives in and understands the best. The major issue is the worldview issue – so many variation and mixed blends of worldviews, which cause a very confused and mixed-up worldview and lifestyles.

"Not only is the city of necessity a place of diversity, but also its people relish difference. They try different ethnic restaurants, look for new kinds of cars, visit other lands, and try new fashions. The enjoyment of variety is characteristic of the urban mindset."[15]

Another issue in the realm of diversity is the global connectedness that has emerged in the electronic world that we live in now. "Today, cities are also part of a growing global order. They are centers of business, education, research, travel, communication, and religion, having networks and organizations that reach around the world. It is impossible to understand Los Angeles, for instance, without understanding not only its city organization and national ties, but also its links to Japan, Korea, Southeast Asia, and the rest of the world."[16]

Every major city in the world can claim diversity as one of its strong points, as well as one of its struggle points. Massive populations that are spread out and very diverse are an "animal" that the Christian Church has not been able to put its arms around. If Christianity is going to have a short term as well as long term affect on the cities, the diversity issue must be addressed. Diversity must not be only talked about, but intentionally and aggressive attacked. We must see diversity of culture, life styles and world-views as a blessing instead of a curse.

So, *WHAT IS THE CHURCH GOING TO DO WITH THE CITY? WHAT ARE WE GOING TO DO WITH THE MEGA CITIES OF THE WORLD?*

The last issue that needs to be addressed as we look at the Mega cities of the World is the issue of poverty, the homeless and the hopelessness found among the inner city poor. Patrick Johnstone wrote, "Over the past 60 some years the urban poor in decaying inner cities and massive encircling squatter settlements has risen to about one billion people – almost as large as the entire Muslim population of the world. Of the two billion people living in Third World cities, it is reckoned that 40 percent are the very poor. Patrick Johnstone also writes, "A vast, receptive, desperate, barely surviving people need help, and the Christians are not there to offer hope with a vital spiritual message and a future as an alternative community. In the past, middle and upper classes often targeted, and most of the churches were planted among these upper mobile people. The theory was that as the movers and shakers came to Jesus, the gospel would trickle down to the poorer people. It rarely happened. Wealthy Chinese Christians in Bangkok, Thailand or prosperous Ghanaian Christians in Accra were no more willing to welcome poor urban migrants into their churches than middle class Victorian Methodists welcomed the converts from William

Booth's labors among the down-and-outs of London a century before." Johnstone goes on to write, "The urban poor are the most receptive, but also the most under evangelized. It is strategic to reach them, for the gospel has an uplifting effect when the gospel takes hold of individuals and communities. The great people movements into the Kingdom have started among the poor. This was true from the time of Acts, in the Roman Empire, the people movements in India and Pakistan over the past two centuries, the turning to God through the Pentecostal movement in Latin America, and so on. The pattern has generally been first the outcasts and the downtrodden, but that has percolated up through society until eventually impacting the structures of society. The cutting edge and spirituality of the Church is often blunted when the rich and powerful become Christians!" [17]

Viv Grigg, truly an Apostle to the poor and outcast challenges us by writing, "God is offering Western missionaries the chance to return to a biblical commitment to the poor and to incarnation as the primary missionary model. The need is urgent: several thousand catalysts in the slums of scores of third-world cities who can generate movements in each city. Two billion cry out."[18]

With all this information and a whole lot more information available the same question is still before us:

WHAT IS THE CHURCH GOING TO DO WITH THE CITY? WHAT IS THE CHURCH GOING TO DO WITH THE MEGA CITIES OF THE WORLD?

If we are going to get serious about reaching the cities, we will need to do some changing of our strategy to reach the World for Christ. Patrick Johnstone writes, "The last two centuries of mission activity have, to a great measure, been a rural success story, but a partial failure in the cities of Africa and Asia – the areas that most need pioneer evangelism. We have been winning the countryside and losing the cities, and all the time our rural constituency has been draining away to the cities." He goes one to write, "The glamour and romanticism associated with the jungles, mountains, deserts and remote islands seem like 'real' missionary work to the home constituency, but living in a concrete jungle, or squalid slum is far less attractive, and undesirable as a place of ministry. The developing world has 55 percent of the mega cities of the world in 1980, but by 2050 this will have risen to 81 percent of the cities."[19]

For a church planter strategist, living and working in Los Angeles, one of the mega-cities of the world the bottom line is, "whatever else we see, we see the city as *more of everything* – more people, more buildings and expanding neighborhoods."[20] And, I must add, *more* opportunity to reach *more* people for Christ. This opportunity is *more* urgent than ever!

Donald McGavran saw this in 1970, when he wrote "Discipling urban populations is perhaps the most urgent task confronting the Church. Bright hope gleams that now is precisely the time to learn how it may be done and to surge forward to do it."[21]

The church needs to remember the history of our faith. "The Christian religion was born in the city of David and grew to manhood in the great cities of Caesar. Unlike Islam, which became powerful in the small towns and oasis of the Arabic hinterland, the expansion of Christianity is inextricably associated with centers of power in the ancient world: Antioch, Ephesus, Corinth, Alexandria, Carthage, and Rome. St. Paul, evangelizing a receptive population – the synagogue communities, which lived by commerce in the cities – traveled from urban center to urban center to which they were directed. Eight of the epistles are titled by the name of the urban centers to which they were directed. Cities and large towns had great meaning for the Early Church and have even more significance for Christian missions in the next half century."[22]

The church of God MUST go to the cities of the World because the *World* is there.

Our marching orders were given to us in Matthew 28: 18-20, "Then Jesus came to them and said, 'All authority in Heaven and on earth has been given to me. Therefore go and make disciples of all nations, baptizing them in the name of the father and of the Son and of the Holy Spirit, and teaching them to obey everything I have commanded you, And surely I am with you always, to the very end of the age.'" It was given not as a suggestion, or a "whenever you get around it."

The Commander of the Lord's army – the Lord Jesus Christ, gave it as a command! And those orders, that command, have not changed yet. He told us to go to every ethane, or people group. Two thousand years after His command, the Church has not fulfilled His command.

The command to go to all the ends was not given to a mission board or denomination. It was not given to a para-church organization. It was given to God's Church. The Great Commission was given to each and every born-again believer in the Lord Jesus Christ. Literally, His command is "as you are going" – to the gas station, to the grocery store, to see friends, to school, work or play – "make disciples." It is a 24/7 command for every Christian! It is a command that we must obey!

In God's grace and mercy, He has even made it easier for today's Church. He has brought the world to us in the form of the great populations of the world cities.

In every major city of the world the Church can find a multitude of unreached people groups. Migration, immigration, desperation and a search for a better life have brought millions of people to the cities. For example, in the Los Angeles metro-complex, the city of Long Beach is the second largest city of Cambodians next to the Capital of Cambodia. With four and a half million Hispanics, Los Angeles is now the second largest Hispanic city. It is also the second largest Chinese city outside of Asia and the second largest Japanese city outside of Japan. The list goes on. It is the largest Korean city outside of Korea, the largest Vietnamese city outside of Vietnam and the largest Philippine city outside the Philippines. The world has come to the mega cities of the World!

CAN THE CHURCH AFFORD TO MISS THE OPPORTUNITY? CAN WE AFFORD TO IGNORE THE CITIES?

The mission minded local church will be very generous in sending money to support the work of missionaries in other countries among unreached people groups. That is a good thing to do. The Church must continue to give and send. But, so often Christians miss the fact that the same unreached people group has moved in next door to them on their own city block. The average Christians just recognizes that their neighbors look different and act different. They recognize that different smells are coming from their neighbor's kitchen and their neighbors look like "foreigners." (Whatever that means.)

We must understand that when people make major moves or changes in their lives they are more "open" to the Gospel than any time before or possibly after the move to the cities. They face new values, new ways of doing things, possibly a new language. At the same time they have left behind a large portion of their former support system. For the first time in their lives, immigrants are separated from their friends and family. It is a hard time in their lives.

As Donald McGavran says, "Immigrants and migrants have been so pounded by circumstances that they are receptive to all sorts of innovations, among which is the Gospel. They are in a phase of insecurity, capable of reaching out for what will stabilize them and raise their spirits."[23]

A recent report from the Migration Information Source, whose primary source is the worldwide Refugee Application Processing System (WRAPS), obtained from the US Office of Refugee resettlement (ORR) states that: "About 2 percent of refugees were resettled in nonmetropolitan areas, and less that 2 percent were no identifiable. The remaining 95 percent were resettled in the cities and suburbs of the 331 metropolitan areas in the United States. In total 1,575,925 refugees were resettled in metropolitan areas during the period of 1983 to 2004. The three largest metro-complexes received:

New York	186,522
Los Angeles	114,606
Chicago	63,322 [24]

Those numbers do not include all the refugees that came into one location and have moved to another later. Also all the illegal immigrants are not in this count. These numbers are larger than 50 percent of the communities in America. The majority of the immigrants are coming from countries where the Gospel is not preached freely!

The time to reach out to the various people groups that have moved to the cities is NOW! The Church needs to get serious about the multitude of people groups: linguistic, cultural, life-styles and worldviews that have moved to the cities of the world. It is time that we step up and apply the words of Jesus in John 4: 34-35:

> 'My food is to do the will of
> Him who sent me and to finish His
> work,' Jesus told them. 'Don't you
> say, 'There is still four months,
> and then comes the harvest? Listen
> to what I am telling you: Open your
> eyes, and look at the fields, for
> they are ready to harvest.

God in His wonderful grace has brought the people of the world to the major cities of the world. Now, the church MUST go to the cities to reach the peoples of the world!

We also need to remember that the One who sent Jesus, as the first apostle/ missionary into this world is the One who is so very patient with us, "not wanting any to perish, but all to come to repentance" (2 Peter 3:9) This brings up the *lostness* that is found in the cities.

Conservatively, the percentage of people who are *lost* in the cities of the world would be 95 percent. In so many of the 10/40 window cities the name of Jesus is never mentioned. The Gospel message has never been proclaimed to millions that reside in so many of the major cities of the world. That is <u>not</u> right. That is <u>not</u> from God! The Church must do something about it.

The *lostness* in our cities is multifaceted. The *lostness* of human dignity is still raging in the cities. Human slavery, human trafficking, child prostitution, starvation and disease surround and engulf the cities of the world. Precious souls in God's eyes are being *lost* in the engulfing crime and decay of the cities. Most of all precious souls are *lost* and going to hell without the saving knowledge of Jesus Christ. Should this be happening?

Robertson McQuikin asks a question to get our attention, He asks: "Have you ever experienced the terror of being lost – in some trackless mountain wilderness, or in the labyrinth of a great, strange city? Hope of finding your way out fades and fear begins to seep in. You have likely seen that fear of lostness on the tear-streaked face of a child frantically screaming or quietly sobbing because he is separated from his parent in a huge shopping center. Lost. Alone." McQuikin goes on to say, "Equally terrifying and more common is the feeling of being hopelessly entangled or trapped in a frustrating personal condition or circumstance: alcoholism, cancer, divorce. Incredibly alone! Lost. Worst than being trapped and not knowing the Way out is to be lost and not even know it, for then one does not look for salvation, recognize it when it comes, nor accept it when it is offered. That's being lost."[25]

The Church has made it "EASY TO GO TO HELL FROM THEIR CITIES!"

The Church has made it easy because so many Christians have gotten wrapped up in their own empire building instead of Kingdom building.

We have gotten wrapped up in our own selfishness– what can God and what can the Church do for me? Western Christianity is a very self-centered Christianity.

My wife and I have a bunch of kids – six by birth and ten foster children. Every once in a while I have to take one of the teenage girls aside- the one who is all freaked out because she has a pimple, or a boy did not say hello to her at school – to remind her that the world does not revolve around her. (Yes, teenage boys are also very self absorbed)

Could it be said of the average Christian church in America that it is also self-absorbed? That everything must revolve around the church members of that Church? I believe as never before the Lord God Almighty is also shouting to His people, "The World does not revolve around you" Will we listen?

GOD, in His grace and mercy did not save you and me, and keep us here on earth, so that our world could revolve around our wants and our needs. He made us, saved us, keeps us by grace, so that we could be used by God to minister to others. Most Christians know Ephesians 2:8-9, "For by grace you are saved through faith, and this is not from yourselves; it is God's gift – not from works, so that no one could boast." We praise God for the fact that we are saved by grace. But, most Christians do not go on to read Ephesians 2:10,

"For we are His creation – created in Christ Jesus for good works, which God prepared ahead of time so that we should walk in them."

In the 21ˢᵗ Century, the good works that Paul is writing about is to reach people, love people and go after the lost and perishing people of the World.

God in His grace has placed the major cities of the world close enough and available to each and every Christian. The Church of Jesus Christ <u>MUST</u> step up and be aggressive to the extent of taking back the "territory" of our cities from the control of the enemy.

How do we make it HARD to go to HELL from OUR CITIES?

First, the Church of Jesus Christ MUST make an intentional effort to reach the major cities of the world. Small efforts and token attempts will not make any impact on the mass populations.

A few dedicated ladies at a large church not too far from downtown Los Angeles had a concern for the homeless people. Because of their concern, every Saturday morning they would pack sack lunches and drive down to Skid Row, where the majority of the homeless live in downtown Los Angeles. They would roll down their car windows and hand out the sack lunches - real quick - and then drive off as fast as they could. Were they meeting a need? Yes. Were they helping a few people? Yes. Were they covering their guilt for not doing more among the poor? Yes. Were they making themselves feel good for their acts of kindness? Yes. Were there Eternal results, or changed lives? No!

Sad to say, most of the Christian churches in America approach the needs of the city in the same manner. The Church has tried to do just enough to get the guilt off their backs, to make themselves look good, and to show a little effort without getting their hands dirty. Eternal results – NONE!

That is not good enough! GOD expects more from His people than just a little. The Church of the Lord Jesus Christ needs to be reminded of God's Master plan for His Church.

Robert Linthicum writes some profound words that we need to apply more than ever today!

He writes:

> The whole world belongs to God –
> including the city. It was made
> by God's hand, for God placed in
> humanity the capacity to create
> the city. And no matter how big
> it may be or how overwhelming its
> needs – even though it may have to
> absorb ten thousand new refugees
> every day as does Bombay, even
> though it may have grown from nine
> million to nineteen million people
> in just seven years as ha Mexico City,
> even though it may have the largest
> Asian population of any city outside
> of Asia as does Los Angeles – God is
> bigger than that city and its needs.
> That city cannot contain God, and God
> is in control!
>
> But what God wants most for the
> city is that God's people – the
> church – will be humble of heart,
> contrite, and cognizant of their
> own sins and therefore not
> condemning of those in the city
> who are marginalized, who are poor
> or powerless or without hope. God
> wants a people who can tremble in
> awe both at the work of God would
> do in the city and at the recognition
> that they are called to be a part of
> that great work.[26]

So, WHAT ARE WE GOING TO DO WITH THE CITIES OF THE WORLD?

QUESTIONS:

1. WHY are we AFRAID to GO to the CITY?

2. CAN we get serious about being intentional about targeting the LOSTNESS of the City?

3. CAN we adapt to the DIVERSITY of the City?

4. WILL we CATCH UP with GOD is doing in the City

FOOTNOTES:

1. Roger S. Greenway, "Urbanization and Missions," <u>CRUCIAL DIMENSIONS IN WORLD EVANGELIZATION,</u> editors, Arthur F. Glasser, Paul G. Hiebert, C. Peter Wagner and Ralph D. Winter, Pasadena: William Carey Library, 1976, p. 222.

2. Paul G. Hiebert and Eloise Hiebert Meneses, <u>INCARNATIONAL MINISTRY: PLANTING CHRUCHES IN BAND, TRIBAL, PEASNT, AND URBAN SOCIEITES,</u> Grand Rapids: Baker Book House, 1995, pgs. 257-260.

3. Donald McGavran, <u>UNDERSTANDING CHURCH GROWTH,</u> Grand Rapids: William B. Eerdmans, 1970, p. 278.

4. Paul G. Hiebert and Eloise Hiebert Meneses, p. 262.

5. Timothy M. Mornsma, <u>Cities: Mission's New Frontier, Second Edition,</u> Grand Rapids: Baker Book House, pgs. 14-16.

6. Paul G. Hiebert and Eloise Hiebert Menses, pgs. 263-273.

7. Harvie Conn, "The Kingdom of God and the City of Man: A history of the City Church Dialogue," in <u>DISCIPLING THE CITY" THEOLOGICAL REFLECTIONS ON URBAN MISSIONS,</u> Grand Rapids: Baker Book House, 1979, p. 9.

8. Robert Neuwirth, <u>SHADOW CITIES: A BILLION SQUATTERS, A NEW URBAN WORLD,</u> London: Routhledge Publications, 2006.

9. Largest Cities in the United States and the World, www.sittercity.com.

10. United Nations, "World Urbanization Prospects: The 2005 Revision," New York: United Nations, 2006, pgs. 3-5; http://www.un.org/esa/populations/publications/ WUPHighlands_Final_Repoet.pdf.

11. John Dawson, <u>TAKING OUR CITIES FOR GOD: HOW TO BREAK SPIRITUAL STRONGHOLDS</u>, Lake My, Florida: Creation House, 1989, p. 48.

12. Roger S. Greenway, <u>APOSTLES TO THE CITY: BIBLICAL STRATEGIES FOR URBAN MISSIONS</u>, Grand Rapids: Baker Book House, p.15.

13. John Dawson, p.39.

14. Patrick Johnstone, <u>THE CHURCH IS BIGGER THAN YOU THINK: THE UNFINISHED WORK OF WORLD EVANGELIZATION</u>, London: Christian Focus Publications/WEC, 1998, p. 241.

15. Paul Hiebert and Meneses. p. 265.

16. Paul Hiebert and Meneses, p. 267.

17. Johnstone, p. 244.

18. Viv Grigg, <u>CRY OF THE URBAN POOR</u>, Monrovia: MARC. 1992, p. 19.

19. Johnstone, pgs. 242-243.

20. Harvie Conn and Manuel Ortiz, <u>URBAN MINISTRY: THE KINGDOM, THE CITY AND THE PEOPLE OF GOD</u>, Downers Grove, Illinois: InterVarsity Press, 2001, p. 17.

21. Donald McGavran, <u>UNDERSTANDING CHURCH GROWTH</u>, Grand Rapids: WILLAM B. Eerdmans, 1970, p. 295.

22. McGavran, p. 278.

23. McGavran, p. 219.

24. Report of *Migration Information Source,* Los Angeles, 2010.

25. Robertson McQuilkin, <u>THE GREAT OMISSION</u>, Grand Rapids: Baker Book House, 1984.

26. Robert C. Linthicum, <u>CITY OF GOD CITY OF SATAN: A BIBLICAL THEOLOGY OF THE URBAN CHURCH</u>, Grand Rapids: Zondervan Publishing House, 1991, p. 39.

CHAPTER TWO

JONAH'S JOURNEY

"But the Jonah story should cause us to adjust our maps and take the gospel beyond the safety of our class and race. The whole gospel for the whole city is what is required." RAY BAKKE[1]

"The Word of the Lord came to Jonah, son of Amittai, 'Get up! Go to the great city of Nineveh and preach against it, because their wickedness has confronted Me." JONAH 1:1-2

"Calcutta is the city that Rudyard Kipling described almost a century ago as the 'city of dreadful night'. It is now a city of sprawling vastness, gray, and smokey along banks of the swirling Hooghly River, the western-most tributary of the sacred Ganges. Calcutta is so lost in everything big, crowded and old that its misery defies human description. It is one of the puzzles of history that God has allowed Calcutta to exist for so long. It is estimated that 80 percent of Calcutta's families live in single rooms. This leaves two hundred thousand people for whom the pavement is the only home they know. As many as thirty persons share a single water tap and twenty a single latrine. Rats eat one-fourth of Calcutta's food supply. Some 40 percent of the students at Calcutta University, which has an enrollment of over one hundred thousand, suffer from mal-nutrition. Major diseases are endemic. Suffering is beyond description. Calcutta's 8 million people are packed eighty thousand to the square mile-hell on earth, vision of the Apocalypse, and the ultimate urban degradation in contemporary society."[2]

This is where Sister Teresa spent forty years serving the poorest of the poor. Why? Because she was following Jesus! "Why risk her life and the few human comforts to begin a life of greater sacrifice and ignominy? Because she felt a special calling from God to reach out to 'love the unloveable'."[3] *Where did He lead her? It was to the city – the city of Calcutta.*

Where is God calling His church today? He is calling them to people without Jesus. He is calling the Church to the city, because that is where the majority of the people live! The city is where Jesus would be TODAY!

GOD'S CALL to the cities of the world comes from a heart that loves everyone in the whole world. God loves even the thousands and millions that seem to get lost in the vastness of our modern city structures.

W.O. Carver reminds us that the origin of *missions* starts with God. He wrote, "The origin of missions is *ultimately* to be found in the heart of God. No thoughts of God is true to His revelation of Himself that does not rest on the fact that He 'so loved the World that He gave His only begotten Son'(John 3:16). It was God that was 'in Christ reconciling the world unto Himself, not reckoning their trespasses unto them' (2 Corinthians 5:19); and not so reckoning for the reason that this love-sent Son 'is the propitiation for the whole world' (I John 2:2). This attitude of God is eternal is determinative in all His dealings with men. He is even working towards the end that 'they who have not heard' may have 'the glad tidings preached unto them'; that 'they who were no people may come to be a people of God's own possession.' (2 Corinthians 5:20)[4]

God's Church needs to catch up with the heart of God on this matter. God loves everyone in the slums of Calcutta, as well as the high-rise in downtown Manhattan, New York City. He loves everyone who slept on the streets of Skid Row, Los Angeles as well as those who slept in the mansions of Beverly Hills. The Church of Jesus Christ needs to catch up with the passion God has for the cities of the world.

God's heart for the people in the cities is shown by the amount of reference one can find in the Bible. "The Bible contains fourteen hundred references to the city, and there are at least twenty-five examples of what can be called urban ministry in the historical books alone. With this amount of scriptural data before us, it is not surprising that both the Old and New

Testaments provide examples of outstanding urban ministries which give us important insights into God's will for cities."⁵

One of the books in the Old Testament that challenges us to go to the cities with a Divine mandate is the Book of Jonah. In this little book, we see the *first* call to urban missions,

> The word of the Lord came to Jonah,
> son of Amittai: Go to this great city
> Nineveh and preach against it, because
> its wickedness has come up before me.
> (Jonah 1:1)

I want to use this precious book as a *framework* for the challenge for the Church today to accept God's call to the cities.

Before I do that, there are some wonderful practical truths that one can learn from the Book of Jonah. They must be looked at first. So let's dig into the Book of Jonah.

The Book of Jonah is a small book (just 48 verses), but it contains a big message for God's church today from a great big GOD.

There are great truths and challenges presented in the Book of Jonah that transcends time and place, and that cannot be ignored by today's Church.

As we look through this book, we first see the major truth that flows throughout the Old and New Testaments – that the GOD of all eternity loves and cares for everyone. He loves them even when they are wicked and rotten to the core. We see a GOD who will go to extreme lengths to warn a people, a city, a nation, to repent before it is too late. The very first statement of the book challenges Jonah:

> "The Word of the Lord came to Jonah
> son of Amittai: Go to the great city
> of Nineveh and preach against it;
> because its wickedness has come up
> before me." (Jonah 1:1-2)

He is challenged to go to a wicked people in a wicked city to proclaim GOD is love to them one more time, or maybe for the very first time, before it is too late!

In a world where wickedness and sin seems to be on the increase and love for GOD is on the decrease it is always encouraging to read Jonah. The story of GOD who sent Jonah to that wicked city of Nineveh to tell the people one more time and, yes, one last time to repent before it is too late is always encouraging. Nineveh was notorious throughout the known world of Jonah's time for their wickedness, for their unmerciful torturing and killing of their enemies. That is why God Almighty sent Jonah, the prophet to Nineveh – to share the Good news with them!

John E. Kyle writes, "I believe God calls us to go where people need him. Most of these people are in the cities. In the cities we have grinding poverty, a lot of disease, severe overcrowding, millions of people in a homeless condition. Some of the world's worst conditions are in the cities. Cities are where many hurting people live, and they need to hear the healing gospel of Jesus Christ. Whether it is in the U.S. in the slums of Harlem or Bedford-Stuyvesant, New Delhi, Manila, Tokyo or Mexico City, these major cities of the world are becoming increasingly populated and for the most part, have never heard the gospel of Jesus Christ. These people need to be told. They need to hear, and they cannot hear without a messenger."[6]

Will the Church step up to the needs of the cities and the *lostness* of the cities? Will the Church go to the major cities of the world and tell them about JESUS before it is too late?

Secondly, the God of all grace and mercy loves to call out average people to do extraordinary work in the power of an extra-ordinary God – so that only He will get the Glory, honor and praise! GOD picked Jonah to go – to a far distant land, to a wicked city, to proclaim "Repent, or else"! He picked Jonah.

"Who is this man Jonah? He lived at the time in the Jewish nation when it was divided into two groups. In the North was Israel, and in the South was the kingdom of Judah. Jonah was from the Northern Kingdom. He lived about the eighth century before Christ. He is mentioned in 2 Kings 14:25, as a prophet from Gath Hepher, who prophesied that Jeroboam the king of Israel would restore the boundaries of Israel, and it was fulfilled during his own lifetime. So, obviously Jonah was a person with some respect in society. Incidentally Gath Hepher is in Galilee, so when the Pharisees aid no prophet comes from Galilee, they were wrong because Jonah had come from Galilee."[7]

Who is this man Jonah? Probably just an ordinary country preacher/prophet who had his 5 minutes of fame when his prophesy about King Jeroboam came true. Yet, God saw something in him so that He called him out to be the second world missionary! JESUS was the first missionary. "Therefore, holy brothers, who share in the heavenly calling, fix your thoughts on Jesus, the apostle and high priest whom we confess. He was faithful in all God's house." (Hebrew 3:1-2) Jesus was the first apostle/missionary to our world. He came proclaiming the Good News to those who were perishing. The first time he stood up to preach to the people in Nazareth he said,

> The Spirit of the Lord is on me,
> because he has anointed me to preach
> good news to the poor. He has sent
> me to proclaim freedom for the prisoners
> and recovery of sight for the blind,
> to release the oppressed, to proclaim
> the year of the Lord's favor.
> (Luke 4:18-19)

"Now this is a very hard commission. No prophet before this had been sent to the streets of another nation to preach judgment. Elijah was sent to the nations but never with a message like this."[8]

Who is this man Jonah? He was just an ordinary man of God who was called out to do the impossible task – reach a city for Christ. Today, God is calling out ordinary people to reach the cities of the World for Christ. The excuse that "I am just an ordinary regular kind of person – nothing special, just does not cut it as an excuse." Why? Because that is the kind of people who God uses best! Remember what Paul wrote to the saints at Corinth.

> Brothers, think of what you when
> you were called. Not many were wise
> by human standards; not many influential;
> not many were of noble birth. But God
> chose the foolish things of the world
> to shame the wise; God chose the weak
> things to shame the strong. He chose
> the lowly things of the world and
> the despised things – and the things
> that are not! – to nullify the things
> that are, so that no one may boast
> before him. It is because of him that
> you are in Christ Jesus, who has
> become for us wisdom from God – that
> is our righteousness, holiness and redemption.
> Therefore, as it is written;' Let him who boasts boast
> in the Lord. (1 Corinthians 1:26-31).

God chose twelve men. Today, most churches would not consider any of them to be on their pastoral staff. God saw – not what they were – but who they could become under the Mighty Hand of God. The Lord God Almighty chose 120 disciples. Starting with those few people, God turned the world upside down for Christ. Within the life times of the early Christians, 25 to 30 percent of the world population became Christians. There was no explanation for this amazing growth except what was written by Luke-

> When they saw the courage of Peter
> and John and realized that they were
> unschooled, ordinary men, they were
> astonished and they took note that these
> men had been with Jesus. (Acts 4:13)

When history is written about the 21st Century, my prayer is that the same thing would be written about today's Church – that we have been with Jesus, and because we had spent time with Jesus the world has never been the same! I pray that the 21st Century church will step up to be with Jesus in such a close intimate life-changing way, that the cities will never be the same again.

One of my favorite missionaries is John Hyde. It was said of John that he could not speak in public well. He struggled with the languages of India. But, he could PRAY. That is why he is known as "Praying" Hyde. When he caught up with God's power source in prayer, things and people were changed. He first prayed everyday that God would allow him to see one soul saved each day. At the end of the year exactly 365 people's names were recorded in his record book of those who had accepted Christ. He prayed that for several years, "Lord give me a soul for each day" Many days, as the day was almost over and there was no soul to record for that day, he would pray and then go out into the streets to witness. God was always faithful, as he was faithful in prayer. Then he started praying for two souls a day. God faithfully honored his prayers of faith. He continued to pray. After several years Praying Hyde's health began to fail. It is recorded of his death that he died of an enlarged heart. Enlarged because of the countless hours in earnest prayer and supplication for the people of India. Oh, how we need more of praying men in the major cities of the world today!

Today, God is calling out ordinary people to go to the major cities of the world in order that the Gospel can be shared there through them. The wonderful thing is that: He chooses to choose ordinary people to go to the cities to make a difference. Baker James Cauthen wrote so beautifully, "He choose you, not because he considered you to be superior, but because he loves you and desired to extend his mercy to others through you. He called you, knowing all your limitations, assets, strengths and weaknesses. Definitely, personally, clearly, he called you. You belong to him, and He is your Lord and Master."[9]

When God called me to preach at eighteen years of age I could not believe it. I was so bashful that I did not even take a speech class in high school. So, when he called me, I said, "Here am I send my brother." Yes, I knew what Isaiah 6:8 says, "Here am I, send me." But, I was hoping God would let me slip by, slip through without obeying. That did not work and it never will. Because if God in his sovereign grace calls us to go to the cities we must go!

Who is this man Jonah? Or, better yet, who is Jonah made to be and be used for God's Kingdom? Names are important in the Middle Eastern culture. Jonah means "dove". It is a name for someone you love. The beloved in the Song of Solomon is called "my dove" (Song 2:14). We must not forget through all his troubles and failings, flight and disobedience,

Jonah is the beloved of God. Like Israel herself, it can be said of him: "Whoever touches you touches the apple of God's eye." (Zechariah 2:8)

JONAH is also a sign of peace, like the dove that comes back to Noah with an olive branch, signifying the end of God's wrath and the subsiding of the water that for a time overcame the earth. (Genesis 8:10-11) When the Holy Spirit descended on the Lord Jesus coming up from the waters of baptism, it takes the form of a dove as a reminder of this Noachic sign of peace on earth to the one in whom God is well pleased (Matthew 3:161-7; Mark 1:10-11; Luke 3:21-22)

Despite himself, Jonah becomes a sign of peace to those voyaging on dangerous waters and to those in the evil city who, one might have thought, had no prospect but destruction on the last day. Surrounded by chaos and evil, bearing a message that breathes condemnation, desiring only destruction, Jonah is nonetheless by God's appointment the dove of peace.

The name "Amittai" is related to the word "amen" and means "truth." So Jonah is the dove of truth, sign of a love that is just warm and soft like a dove but also faithful and reliable as a rock, founded on the truth. One could hardly choose a better name for a prophet of the Lord than "Jonah, son of Amittai." [10]

Today, God's sent out servants to the cities need to go as "doves." They need to go as doves caring the leaf of peace into places where there has been no peace for years. As we pray the promises of Philippians 4:

> "Rejoice in the Lord always, I will
> say it again: Rejoice! Let your
> gentleness be evident to all.
> The Lord is near. Do not be
> anxious about anything, but
> in everything, by prayer and
> petition, with thanksgiving,
> present your requests to God.
> And the peace of God which
> transcends all understanding.
> Will guard your hearts and minds
> in Christ Jesus." (Verses 4-7)

As we apply these verses to our personal life and ministry we find peace. Then the Apostle/ missionary can go into the war zones of war-torn cities, into the angry and rebellious parts of our major inner cities, and into the gang infested streets of Los Angeles with God's peace. Because we have God's peace in us and wrapped around us, we can be the peacemakers in the troubled lives, homes and cities of the World.

Thirdly, we see the wonderful truth that GOD calls out His servants to go to the tough places, the worst places and the one place you would never want to go – so that we can share the Good News with the people before it is too late (Jonah 1:1-10).

The city of Nineveh was one of those tough places. Jonah did not want to go there because it was wicked. GOD wanted him to go because of that very reason, "Because its wickedness has come before me" (Jonah 1:2). It was a downright rotten bunch of sinners. I love the way the TLB says it, "it smells to high heaven". As God's people we want to run away from the wickedness, from the stench of *lostness*.

We have taken that spiritual truth - that we are not of this World any longer and tried to stay out of this messy World. We missed the point. Yes, we are not of this world, but God has called us back into the world, so that His glory may be seen. We are sent to share the light of the World in the very darkest places!

But, the city is where GOD would go so that He could, as the songwriter wrote, "rescue the perishing, care for the dying. Jesus is merciful, Jesus will save." Or so that He can do, as Jude tells the early Church. He can "snatch others from the fire and save them" (vs.23a). Oh by the way, He wants you and me to be the instruments He uses to snatch the people of this world out of the fire.

One Friday night, Pastor Willie Dalgity and a team from Set Free Church of Yucaipa, CA, was doing an outreach in a very tough part of San Bernardino, CA. San Bernardino is a city of 200,000 people with 60 percent living below the poverty level, full of gangs and crime. A police officer walked up to Pastor Willie and asked him, "What the Hell are you doing out here. Don't you know there was a big gang shootout the night before, right here!?!" He then showed him the bullet holes in the wall behind where the band was setting up. The only answer Pastor Willie could give the officer was, "This is where JESUS would be." That night 70 people got saved and a new church was started – Set Free Church of San Bernardino. There are a million more spots in the cities of the world that the Church must go to because that is where JEUS would be. Will you go?

The fourth lesson that we can learn from the Book of Jonah is: you can try to run, but you cannot hide, and you will always end up right where GOD wanted you in the first place (Jonah 1:3-17; 2: 10; 3:1-2).

> And the Lord commanded the fish, and
> it vomited Jonah onto dry land. Then
> the Word of the Lord came to Jonah a
> second time,' Go to the great city of
> Nineveh and proclaim to it the message
> I give you. (Jonah 2:10, 3:1-2)

Jonah tried to run away from God's call on his life by going the opposite direction. "In verse 3 we are told that Jonah ran away from the Lord and headed for Tarshish. Tarshish is probably Tartessus, a town in Spain. It was a town far west of Palestine, on the western edge of the world they knew about. Nineveh was on the eastern edge of the world, but he went to the far west."

"Now you might ask, 'Why didn't Jonah stay in the comfort of his home in Palestine? If he wanted to disobey God, why did he have to go all the way to Tarshish?' Well, Tarshish was a place where you would least expect a revelation from God. The people there did not know the Lord. Being disobedient to God is extremely uncomfortable, and when you disobedient to God and meet God's people, you become even more uncomfortable. So Jonah wanted to be a safe distance from anything that reminded him of God."[11]

Do not Christians do the same thing today? If a Christian is being disobedient, they start missing the small group meetings where there is accountability. When they are not walking with God, as they should they slip into Church quietly and slip out as fast as they can after the services are finished. They stop going to church as often, and before we know and they know it they have stopped attending church and associating with other

Christians. Does all that "moving away" from God and His people help the spiritual conditions of the disobedient saint? No, it just makes it harder and more painful. I personally believe that the most miserable person in the world is the back-slidden Christian. He knows what he should be doing, he knows he is not doing it; he knows God knows he is not doing it, which makes one miserable back-slidden Christian.

Jonah did not reject God. He did not become a heathen. As Ajith Fernando writes, "he did not discard his belief; he did not commit any great sins, but he did not do what God wanted him to do. And to disobey God is to run away from God! Not only that, to run away from the will of God is to run is to run away from the presence of God, God was there, but Jonah closed the door to experiencing the presence of God in his life."[12]

Ajith Fernando writes, "David Livingstone, who went as a pioneer missionary to what was known as the dark continent of Africa, was once asked what kept him going amid all the struggles he faced. And what struggles they were! He was attached and maimed by a lion. His body was often racked by fever and dysentery. The one home he built was burned down during the Boar War. His wife died on the field, and most of the time he was all alone. When he was asked what kept him going, he said that the word of Christ kept ringing in his ears, "Lo. I am with you always, even to the end of the World." He goes on to write, "David Livingstone also said, 'Without Christ not one step.' We are told that once, when he was asked about the sacrifices he made, he became angry and said, 'Sacrifice? The only sacrifice is to be outside the will of God!' When you do that you forfeit the presence of God and the peace that endures. That was what was happening to Jonah."[13]

Are you right in the middle of God's perfect will? Are you being the witness that God has called you to be? Have you heard the call to the cities as Jonah did? Are you being obedient to that call?

He went <u>down</u> to Joppa, paid his fare and then went <u>down</u> inside the boat, <u>down</u> into the depths of the ship and went into a <u>deep</u> sleep. (Jonah 1: 3-6)

When we run away from GOD it is never to a higher, better way of life.

It is never to an enlightened life, where all is rosy and sweet. I believe that the most miserable person in the world is the backsliding Christian. He knows what God wants him to do, but chooses to go the opposite direction and finds himself in the bottom of the sea of despair and in the belly of the big fish – a place of death. In the Bible the word death always represent separation from God. That is where Jonah found himself.

Jonah went down to Joppa, found a boat and paid his fare. (Jonah 1:3). It always *cost* to disobey God. It almost cost Jonah his life. He told the sailors to throw him overboard. (Jonah 1:12, 14-16) He ended up in the belly of a fish. That cost him dearly.

Notice also that when we are disobedient we are not the only ones affected. The seaman was scared to death. They lost the cargo on the ship. They almost lost their lives. (Jonah 1:4-5)

When the Church ignores and even runs away from the call to the cities of the world, I wonder how many people are affected? In the 1960's when it was easier for the Church to run to the suburbs than to stay in the city, I wonder if many of the social evils of the cities could have been avoided if we would have had a strong Christian witness in the city. How many fewer children would have died from neglect and hunger? How many teenage pregnancies could have been avoided? How many fewer young men would be dead? In prisons?

David Platt, pastor of The Church on Brook Hills in Birmingham, Ala., tells this story, "Just a few months before becoming a pastor, I stood a top of a mountain in the heart of Hyderabad, India. This high point in the city housed a temple for Hind gods. I smelled the offerings that had been given to the wooden gods behind me. I saw teaming masses in front of me. Every direction that I turned, I glimpsed an urban center filled with millions upon millions of people."

"And then it hit me. The overwhelming majority of these people had never heard the gospel. They offer religious sacrifices day in and day out because no one has told them that, in Christ, the final sacrifice has already been offered in their behalf. And as a result they live without Christ, and if nothing changes, they will die without him as well."

As I stood on that mountain, God gripped my heart and flooded my mind with two resounding words: 'Wake up.'"

Wake up and realize that there are infinitely more important things in your life than football and a 401(k). Wake up and realize there are real battles to be fought, so different from the superficial, meaningless 'battles' you focus on. Wake up to the countless multitudes who are currently destined for a Christless eternity.

"The cost of our nondiscipleship is high for those without Christ. It is also high for the poor of the world.

"Consider the cost when Christians ignore Jesus' commands to sell all their possessions and give to the poor and instead choose to spend their resources on better comforts, larger homes, nice cars, and more stuff. Consider the cost when these Christians gather in churches and choose to spend millions of dollars on nice buildings to drive up to, cushioned chairs to sit in, and endless programs to enjoy themselves. Consider the cost for the starving multitude that are outside the gate of contemporary Christian affluence."[14]

GOD has many methods and modes of operations to get His work done in His way and in His time. He used a burning bush to get Moses' attention. He used the cloud by day and a cloud of fire by night to lead the Israelites out of Egypt toward the Promised Land. He even used a donkey to speak to the prophet. Here GOD chooses to use a big fish to grab hold of Jonah, keep him in his belly, so that Jonah can finally get desperate enough to surrender to God, and then spits him on the ground – real close to Nineveh! Wow! GOD works in a very cool way – in spite or more like despite ourselves. Now, the question is – is it not better to obey Him the first time? To obey is better than going through all the mess – seaweed, slimy fish in the belly and a strong dose of stomach acid to digest the fish. There were probably several more gross things that Jonah experienced in those three days.

Here is the lesson we need to learn: No matter how many times it takes, the GOD who loves us will keep bringing us back to the place of our disobedience, until we obey. From life experience I highly recommend Lets OBEY the FIRST TIME!

The fifth lesson that we can learn from Jonah's experience is: One can rejoice, even in the struggles, on the way to the place where God has called you (Jonah 2: 1-9). Jonah could sing a song of praise in the fish's belly:

> But, I with a song of thanksgiving,
> will sacrifice to you. What I have
> vowed I will make good. Salvation
> comes from the Lord. (Jonah 2:9)

Yes, preparation time for serving the Lord can be painful. It can be difficult as you are learning a new language, a new culture, studying, ministering and attempting to minister to people in Jesus' Name. But, in the middle of it all, you can still praise Him. Some of the best and most meaningful prayer time you will experience will be in the time of uncertainty and even discouragement. You may even feel like you have ended up in the belly of a big fish, as you are attempting to discern and obey God's perfect will. It is in those times that GOD will show Himself and you will be humbled and amazed by His grace.

After spending seven of the most painful years of ministry helping turn an older, dying church around the Lord called me out. He had called me out to minister to the poor in the Pomona Valley of Southern California. We had turned the church around, started ten churches out of that church and impacted many lives, but it had taken a toll on our lives. In the new calling came excitement and adventure. We were stepping out in faith to trust GOD to start a whole new ministry. Then all hell broke loose! I had to kick my 18-year-old son out of the house because he was doing heavy drugs. That was the hardest thing I ever did as a dad. I hoped it would wake him up and shake him up. But it did not. He kept doing his drugs. Our 16-year-old daughter was dating a young man who said he was taking a break from attending USC. We found out he had just gotten out of prison and was a gang member. We told him that he could no longer see our daughter. He threatened to kill us. When we stepped out by faith with no salary, I still had my security blanket – my wife was a schoolteacher. We could afford to live on her salary. Then Leesa, my wife, hurt her back so bad she had to have a herniated disc removed. She could not work for 6 months. There went her salary. There were times when we were broke. No food in the house and we still had six kids at home at that time. All we knew to do was trust God! Every morning I would get up and go out on the porch to pray and share our needs with our Lord and Master. I claimed the promise of Philippians 4:19. "But, my God shall supply all of your needs according to His riches in glory, through Christ our Lord." GOD in His loving kindness provided for us – our needs – every time. A check would come in the mail unexpectedly. Somebody would bring bags of food over, just because GOD had laid it upon their hearts to do it.

My son, after two years, went to the Set Free Church Discipleship Ranch. He got clean up and quit using drugs. He felt a call to the ministry and is now serving as a youth pastor and has started churches many times over. He has taken missionary teams to more countries than I ever could have thought possible. My wife is healthy. Our daughter went in the Navy, got married and has three precious children. Yes, GOD turned it all around and made good out of it all so that he could be glorified and honored! The lesson we learned, more than once, is that we could praise Him through the times of pain and through the times of maturing in the trials, and in the sweet times of victory. We learned that GOD is faithful all the time!

Yes, in the belly of the fish –in the belly of preparation we can praise Him! We can honor Him! He will use all that time to refine and mature you for greater service. He got Jonah ready to do what He had already planned for him from the beginning of the Ages – then he had the fish spit him out right where he needed to be!

The sixth lesson that we need to be reminded of is that: "the Lord is not slow in keeping His promise as some understand slowness. He is patient with you, not wanting anyone to perish, but everyone to come repentance." (2 Peter 3: 9.) Dr. Hugh Martin says it well when he writes, "Nineveh has had a long day of grace, a long period of forbearance, an unmerited respite and reprieve, slighted also and utterly abused. The Lord sits down at last on His tribunal. The case is to be called and judged. And Jonah is sent forth as God's pursuivant to summon the culprit to the bar, to be the King's Counsel also to plead against Him." [15]

But, our wonderful loving and merciful God had to give them one more chance. One more chance to repent and to turn from their wicked ways before judgment came! "Then the word of the Lord came to Jonah a second time. Go to the great city of Nineveh and proclaim to it the message I gave you." (Jonah 3:1-2) The GOD of the second chance poured out His grace on Nineveh and the people repented.(Jonah 3: 3-9) I love what God says next in Jonah 3:10 because it applies to all of us.

> When GOD saw what they did and
> how they turned from their evil
> ways, he had compassion and did
> not bring upon them the destruction
> he had threatened.

Can we not take a moment to thank Almighty God for His mercy and grace for all sinners? Yes, even for us sinners! If we got what we deserved, it would be Hell! "All we like sheep have gone astray, each of us has turned to our own way," but in God's wonderful grace," the Lord has laid on Him the iniquity of us all."(Isaiah 53:6) Yes, all of us have, "sinned and fall short of the glory of God." (Romans 3:23) and "the wages of sin is death, but the gift of GOD is eternal life through Jesus Christ our Lord." (Romans 6:23). I have been a Christian for over 50 years, but that wonderful grace still thrills my soul – everyday!

Yet, there are over 3 billion people in the world that have never heard the name of Jesus. Because the populations of the world are moving to the cities, the majority of those who have never heard are living in the cities. That is why we must go to the Cities of our world! Missionary Gary Smith gives a profound statement about ministering to French speaking Canadians, "If you're under 40 years old and living in Quebec, you probably don't know who Jesus Christ is. I've had some people literally tell me, 'Oh, that's a curse word.' That is all they know about Jesus. And this is why we are trying to evangelize witness and plant churches."[16] A profound but sad statement that should challenge God's people to go to the cities of the World to share the Good News of Jesus Christ to those who have never heard.

Finally, the truth that transcends the Book of Jonah and yet engulfs the book comes from the mouth of our Lord Jesus Christ. After being constantly harassed by the religious leaders for a "sign" to prove that He was the Messiah, Jesus turns to them and tells them there will only be one sign. Jesus tells them:

A wicked and adulterous generation
asks for a miraculous sign. But none
will be given it except the sign of
the prophet Jonah. For as Jonah was
three days and three nights in the
belly of a huge fish, so the Son of
Man will be three days and three nights
in the heart of the earth. The men of
Nineveh will stand up at the judgment
with this generation and condemn it;
for they repented at the preaching of
Jonah, and now one greater than Jonah
is here. The Queen of the south
Will rise at the judgment with this
generation and condemn it; for she
came from the ends of the earth to
listen to Solomon's wisdom, and now
one that is wiser than Solomon is here.
(Matthew 12:39-42)

As Jonah was in the belly of the fish for three days, so will Jesus be buried in the grave and He will rise on the third day – victorious, triumphant over the grave, death and the devil.

That fact was what transformed a small band of discouraged disciples into bold witnesses for Christ and turned Jerusalem and then the rest of the world of their day upside down for Christ. The Resurrected living reigning King is the One who must challenge us and empower us to go the Cities of the world in these later days!

What a beautiful picture of the death and resurrection of Jesus Christ! That is why the Book of Jonah is a great book to read and meditate on in our walk with God. Jonah is a great Old Testament Challenge to take serious the Great Commission of our Lord Jesus Christ, "Then Jesus came to them and said, 'All authority in Heaven and on earth has been given to me. Therefore go and make disciples of all nations, baptizing them in the name of the Father and of the Son and of the Holy Spirit, and teaching them to obey everything I have commanded you. And surely, I am with you always, to the very end of the age." (Matthew 28:18-20, NIV)

This essay on the necessity to go to the Cities of our world is not written as a Commentary on the Book of Jonah. I am using the truths found in the Book of Jonah as a framework for a modern day challenge to agree with GOD ALMIGHTY when He says to Jonah, "should I not be concerned (have compassion, have a deep love for)about this great city?" (Jonah 4: 11, added words is my on understanding as to what God is saying to Jonah and to us today)

Should not GOD who, "so loved the World that He gave His only begotten Son, so that whosoever should believe in Him should not perish but have everlasting life." (John 3:16), the God who is "not willing that any should perish, but is long suffering, not willing that any should perish" (2 Peter 3:9), not be concerned for the Cities of our World? Should not the Messiah, the One who was to be the Lamb of God which takes away the sins of the world have compassion over the cities of the World, as He did on His last trip into Jerusalem?

> O Jerusalem, Jerusalem you who kill
> the prophets and stone those sent to you,
> how often I have longed to gather your
> children together, as a hen gathers her
> chicks under her wings, but you were
> not willing. Look, your house is left
> to you desolate. For I tell you, you
> will not see me again until you say,
> 'Blessed is he who comes in the name
> of the Lord. (Matthew 23:37-39)

If our Lord and Master has such great compassion over the Cities of the World should we not also have a compassion and love that compels to go to the cities of the World to tell them that Jesus loves them very much and lay down our lives for the people of the cities?

Johannes Verkuyl challenges today church with these words: "The New Testament church must pay close heed to the message of Jonah's book. Jesus Christ is 'One greater than Jonah' (Matthew 12:39-41, Luke 11:29-32). His death on the cross with its awful cry of God-forsakenness and the resurrection with its jubilant shout of victory are signs of Jonah for us, pointing to the profound meaning of his whole life and clearly attesting that that God loved the whole world so much. If a person draws his lifeblood from the one greater than Jonah and yet declines to spread the good News among others, he in effect is sabotaging the aims of God himself. Jonah is father to all those Christians who desire the benefits and blessings of election but refuses its responsibility. Thomas Carlisle's poem, "You Jonah" closes with these lines:

> And Jonah stalked
> To his shaded seat
> And waited for God
> to come around
> to his way of thinking.
> And God is still waiting for a host of
> Jonahs in their comfortable houses
> to come around
> to His way of loving.[16]

QUESTIONS:

1. HAS GOD CALLED YOU TO GO TO THE CITY?

2. WHAT IS HOLDING YOU BACK FROM GOING WHERE HE HAS CALLED YOU TO GO? YES, GOD HAS CALLED <u>ORDINARY</u> YOU! And He has called you to the greatest adventure of your life!

3. WHAT IS THE ONLY ANSWER YOU CAN GIVE THE LORD? IT is YES LORD!

FOOT NOTES:

1. Ray Bakke, <u>A THEOLOGY AS BIG AS THE CITY</u>, Downers Grove, Illinois: InterVarsity Press, 1997, p. 100.

2. Roger S. Greenway, <u>APOSTLES TO THE CITY: BIBLICAL STRATEGIES FOR URBAN MISSIONS</u>, Grand rapids: Baker Book House, 1978, pgs. 17-18.

3. Jim Cymballa, <u>FRESH FAITH</u>, Grand Rapids: Zondervan, 1999, pgs. 39-40.

4. William O. Carver, <u>MISSIONS IN THE PLAN OF THE AGES</u>, Nashville: Broadman Press, 1909

5. Roger S. Greenway, p.11

6. John E. Kyle, editor, <u>URBAN MISSION: GOD'S CONCERN FOR THE CITY,</u> Downers Grove: InterVarsity Press, 1988, page 8.

7. Ajith Fernando, "Running away from God," Jonah 1:1-16, in <u>URBAN MISSIONS: GOD'S CONCERN FOR THE CITY</u>, P. 25.

8. Fernando, p. 26.

9. Baker James Cauthen, <u>BEYOND CALL</u>, Nashville: Broadman Press, 1973, p. 35.

10. Phillip Cary, <u>JONAH</u>, Grand Rapids: Brazo Press, 2008, p. 30.

11. Fernando, p. 27.

12. Fernando, p. 28.

13. Hugh Martin, <u>THE PROPHET JONAH: THE CHARACTER AND MISSION TO NINEVEH</u>, London: The Banner of Truth Trust, 1958, p. 30.

14. David Platt, <u>RADICAL: TAKING BACK YOUR FAITH FROM THE AMERICAN DREAM</u>, Colorado Springs: Multnomah Books, 2010, ppgs. 14-15.

15. Gary Smith, quote from *On Mission Magazine*, Summer, 2009, p. 6.

16. Johannes Verkuyl, <u>CONTEMPORARY MISSIOLOGY</u>, Grand Rapids: William B. Eerdmans, 1978.

CHAPTER THREE

GOD CALLING

"This is the God who personally calls His servants: Abraham, Moses, the prophets, the disciples, Martin Luther, John Wesley. Hudson Taylor – and you and me. We do not deserve it, nor are we capable to handle such a calling. Our call affects others – even to the nations and history itself. The one God calls, He enables by His presence to fulfill completely His call. Any other assignment offered by the world will always be a huge step down!" Henry Blackaby[1]

"And the word of the Lord came to Jonah, son of Amattai, saying, Go to the great city of Nineveh and preach against it, because their wickedness has come against me."
Jonah 1:1-2

In 1958, David Wilkerson was pastoring a church in the small mountain town of Phillipsburg, Pennsylvania. God was blessing the church. He and his wife were happy there. One night as he was in prayer, David felt a discontentment in his spirit.

He picked up the latest LIFE magazine and saw a story about a murder case in New York City. Seven boys, members of a gang called the Dragons, had brutally killed a fifteen-year old polio victim. As he looked at the drawings of the boys on trial, he heard these words from God, "Go to New York City and help those boys." That did not make sense to him. The boys in question were members of a violent gang, and on trial for murder. He on the other hand was a country preacher settled comfortably in a little mountain church in Pennsylvania. What could God possibly expect him to accomplish – in New York City, of all places? He struggled with that thought for several days. Finally he went. Through that experience he started ministering to the gangs in New York City on a part time basis. Two years later, he and his family moved to New York City. There they started Teen Challenge to minister to the gangs of New York City. Today, after leading Teen Challenge for years, starting World Challenge to minister to drug addicts around the world, God is still using David Wilkerson. He is pastor of the Times Square Church in New York City.

The word of the Lord came to David Wilkerson and told him to go to New York City. Because he was obedient, hundreds of thousands of people are now in the Kingdom of God.

GOD is calling you – to go to the cities. Will you obey and go? Cannot the God of David Wilkerson do something special through you – to reach thousands for the Kingdom in that special city God is calling you to go?

Why would God call a country preacher like Jonah to go to one of the largest and wickedest cities of his day? Why would God call a country preacher like David Wilkerson to New York City, one of the largest and wickedness cities in the world today? One reason and one reason only – because HE is GOD and He is sovereign!

Why would God call out a murderer of Christians, a hater of the church to be the Apostle to the Gentiles? Look what God told Ananias:

"Go, for he is a chosen instrument of mine, to bear My Name before the Gentiles and kings and the sons of Israel; for I will show him how much he must suffer for my name's sake." Acts 9:15-16

GOD is sovereign and He had a plan for Saul changed and transformed into Paul, the first missionary to the rest of the world.

Why would GOD in all his love and mercy call you and me to go to the cities of the world? Because he is LOVE. Because He is sovereign!

Let's go back to Jonah and get the right perspective on just how God works in His redemptive plan of the ages. Phillip Cary in his commentary on Jonah says it well,
"The book of Jonah does not begin with Jonah but with something better – the word of the Lord. It all begins with the word of him who began everything by saying, 'Let there be light,' and there was light. This is the same word that was with God in the beginning, as the gospel testifies (John 1:1)"

Cary goes on to write, "This is a story originated, enfolded, and driven by God's address to his creatures. It begins with the word of the Lord, and in the end, this same Lord has the last word. In the middle his word moves events forward, telling the fish to vomit up Jonah, sending him over to Nineveh with a message, then arguing with the distraught prophet when Nineveh is spared."

Cary sums it up by writing, "So the whole story is initiated and moved along and shaped by the word of the Lord, without which there would be no story, no movement, no tension, no flight, and no rescue. There is no meaning to the story, and the events of the story are inconceivable, without this word and without the particular deity whose word this is."[2]

He is the Lord God Almighty, ruler of Heaven and earth!

The call of Jonah, the ministry of Jonah and even the book of Jonah starts and finishes with the word of the Lord! That is the way it ought to be. That is the way your life and ministry should be.

Our life starts with God, it has an *encounter* with God, it is *enthused* with God – to go and to be and to do – what God has called us and told us to do!

For you see, God has always chosen to work that way. As Henry Blackaby writes, "God has chosen to reveal Himself, His purpose and His ways, involving His people with Him as He invites all the world's peoples to know and worship Him."

Look at a short list of how He has chosen and used His people:

- Through Abraham, God revealed Himself as the Lord, the Almighty and the Provider, who wants to bless all the people of the world through His people.

- Through Moses, God revealed Himself as the I AM THAT I AM, whose plan is to show His glory to the world through His people, who are to be a kingdom of priests to all peoples.

- Through David, God revealed that his Seed would rule all nations and His kingdom would be for all peoples.

- Through Jesus, God revealed His love and His purpose to reconcile the world to Himself through Christ's incarnation, crucifixion, resurrection and ascension.

- Through Paul, God revealed that the mystery of the ages is that He includes all peoples in His redemption.

- Through John, God revealed that some from every nation, tribe, tongue and people will worship Him forever.

"He is at work all the time to the very end of time, bringing about this revelation, for all peoples' reconciliation. When this mission is fulfilled, it will not only be the fullest expression of earth's praise, it will be the fullest revelation of God's love."[3]

So let us go back to this wonderful, Almighty, Majestic God who calls us out of ourselves to go to the world's cities. He is Lord!

"The Lord is not just any lord, nor is he merely 'God' in general. He is all together different from the gods of the nations. He declares in Isaiah: "I am the Lord, that is My name; I will not give My glory to another, nor my praise to graven images." (42:8)

"So the God whose words sets this story in motion is not just any God. He has a proper name, and it is not enough to describe him as God in general, as if he was nothing but the Supreme Being, the first principle of all things, and the ultimate Good. He is indeed all those things, but we will miss the point if we do not recognize from the beginning that he is first and foremost the Lord, the God of Israel."[4]

The Lord is Almighty God, the Great I AM. "This is the Lord, the God of Israel, the God of Abraham, Isaac, and Jacob who revealed his name to Moses as I AM or (perhaps more accurately) I AM WHO I AM or (perhaps more accurately yet) I WILL BE WHO I WILL BE (Exodus 3:14) Like Exodus, the book of Jonah is a story showing us who he will be, and thus at bottom it is about the proclamation of the name of the Lord."[5]

It is just simply amazing that the God of All creation, the LORD of Heaven and Earth, the great I AM would in his loving kindness call out to Jonah and tell him that he has a plan, a purpose for him to fulfill. That purpose was to go to Nineveh.

It is simply amazing and very humbling that the great I AM would bend down, from Heaven above, and speak my name and speak to you by name, and then to call us out to the great task of reaching the cities of the world for Christ! Amazing grace – that is what it is all about!

As Herbert Kane says, "If God were any other kind of God, there would be no Christian mission. The revelation of God in the Scriptures is not confined to his existence, it includes the *kind* of God He is. Indeed, the Scriptures are not concerned to prove the existence of God; that is taken for granted. What the Bible reveals is the *character* of God. His person can never be divorced from His character."[6]

As he examined the character of God that operates out a missionary heart, John makes two great declarations concerning the character of God. In his first epistle he declares, "God is light" (1:5) and "God is love" (4:16). After spending three wonderful years in the company of the Son of God, John expresses it well in these beautiful words,

"This is the message that we have heard from Him and proclaim unto you, that God is light and in Him there is no darkness at all." I John 1:5)

The same is true of the other attribute, love. John says, "In this the love of God was manifest among you that God sent His only Son into the world, so that we might live through Him. In this is love, not that we loved him, but that he loved us and sent His Son to be the expiation for our sins." (I John 4:9-10)

GOD IS LOVE – that is amazing truth that humbles and amazes me everyday. The more you dwell in that love the more you know it is true.

"God's love like Himself, is eternal, inscrutable, and immutable, He loves mankind with an everlasting love (Jeremiah 31:3); and having once set His love on man, He can never let him go. No matter how long the prodigal has remained in the far country, he is always free to return to his Father's house; and on his return he will find the door open, the lamps burning, and the feast spread. This indestructible, all-inclusive love of God prompted Him to send Jesus Christ to be the Savior of the world. (I John 4:9). This is the Good News that constitutes the Gospel. This great, glorious fact is the foundation of all missionary endeavor. Without it there would be no missionary mandate."[7]

GOD IS LIGHT – God is light as well as love. "Light" in scripture is a symbolic term standing for three things. Physically it stands for splendor or glory (2 Corinthians 4:6; Revelation 21:23). Intellectually, it stands for truth (Psalm 43:3). Morally it stands for holiness (Romans 13:11-14) God is light; God is love. The two statements belong together.

God's love is a holy love. That is what makes it unique. It can never be compared with man's love. The difference between the two is not simply one of quantity, but one of quality as well. God's love is as white as snow and pure as sunshine. Man's love on the other hand, a debased, corrupted form of love, streaked with selfishness and tinted with pride. This is why man has so much difficulty in understanding the true nature of love.

God's love makes it possible for the repentant sinner to be saved; God's holiness makes it inevitable that the unrepentant sinner will perish. Both are part of the gospel; both are part of the mandate. Without the love of God, we would have no gospel. Without the wrath of God, there would be no need for the gospel. Therefore, the missionary mandate is rooted in the character of God, who is light and who is also love.[8]

George W. Peters summarizes it all up this way, "Looking back over the qualitative statements concerning the being of God – Spirit, light, love –

the missionary implications are obvious. God is an outgoing God who, because He is light and love, wills the benevolence of mankind and even seeks to impart Himself to man."⁹

The mandate to go to the great cities of the world comes out of the heart of God who, "So loved the world that He gave His only begotten Son, that whosoever believes in Him, should not perish, but have ever lasting life." (John 3:16) The call to "be my witness in Jerusalem, Judea, and Samaria and unto the uttermost parts of the world," (Acts 1:8) comes out of the character of God who is not "willing that any should perish, but all comes to repentance." (2 Peter 3:9)

The next amazing things is that the God of All creation, ruler of Heaven and earth chooses to come to you and me and "calls" us to be a part of the missionary mandate.

God in his grace called me to be a part of the missionary mandate forty-six years ago, and I am still humbled and amazed by that call everyday. We need to take time to look at that call.

The call is imitated by and verbalized by GOD Himself. It starts from His heart. The call will come in many different and various ways. God called Abram after his father had passed. He called Moses out of a "burning bush." He knocked Paul off his donkey with a bright shining light from Heaven. He calls each one of us individually so that it is special to our individual needs. But, it will come to you and it will be your call. In your spirit you will know that it is from God – the One that loves you. He will call you in His own special way.

It will be a three-fold call. The call will consist of:

1. A CALL TO SALVATION

Because God loves you He made you special. But, just like Adam and Eve, we have sinned against God. Sin is simply disobeying God. God told Adam and Eve not to eat of the fruit of the tree of the Knowledge of good and evil. The serpent lied to Eve, while he was tempting her to eat of the fruit. It goes like this: "The serpent said to the women. 'You surely will not die!

For God knows that in that day you eat from it your eyes will be opened and you will be like God, knowing good and evil." (Genesis 3:4-5)

That is been our problem ever since – we want to be like God – no, we really want to take God's place. There can be only one God. Yet, we keep trying to take God's place. There has to be consequences for our actions. This is what the book of Romans tells us, "For all have sinned and fall short of the glory of God" (3:23). And, then, "For the wages of sin is death, but the gift of God is eternal life in Christ Jesus our Lord" (6:23). Here, is the greatest gift on earth,

"But, God demonstrates His own love toward us, in that while we were yet sinners, Christ died for us. Much more then, having now been justified by His blood, we shall be saved from the wrath of God through Him" (5:8)

I accepted that FREE GIFT fifty-five years ago, and I still stand amazed in the presence of the One who loves me that much! Aren't you amazed that God would save you also?

If there is only one reason needed to go and fulfill the Great Commission – this would be it – God loves me so much that he saved me from death and Hell and gave me eternal life. What about you? Don't you want to go and tell someone about how much God loves you and how much God loves her or him? Dr. Sam Simmons writes, "All who are grateful for their salvation will inevitably be motivated to join God in his missionary enterprise. To do less is nothing more than spiritual selfishness. To discuss mission strategy without seeing at the core of missions, God's redemptive act through Jesus Christ is spiritual oversight. Salvation is not just at the heart of missions; salvation is the heart of mission."[10]

2. A CALL TO HIMSELF

For God to save my soul is fantastic, but that is not the end. Salvation starts a love relationship between our Heavenly Father, who adopted us, "For you have not received a spirit of slavery leading to fear again, but you have received a spirit of adoption as sons by which we cry out, 'Abba Father!'" (Romans 8:15)

Because, He has adopted us, we have the privilege to have a personal love relationship with God. That is why the second call from God to each of His children is to Himself.

Jesus called the twelve disciples to come and follow Him, to have a three-year journey with Him in developing and growing a godly character. He called them to be disciples. His ultimate goal was to make them to be apostles – "sent out" ones – to go out to the rest of the known world and share the Good News of Jesus Christ.

Jesus, in His wonderful grace and mercy has also called us to "come follow me." His call upon our lives is to make us disciples and then to make us fishers of men. He knows it is a process – sometimes fast and at other times slower process. In His loving patience, He has wrapped His loving arms around us and whispered in our souls, "Come follow me and I will guide you to places you have never been and you will grow spiritually in ways you never thought and I will make you into ALL that I intended you to be from the time I made you. Wow! Lets get on board and follow Him! Let's stop a minute and catch up with what God, in love, wants you to do. He is calling you:

> Then He said to them all, 'If
> anyone wants to follow Me, he
> must deny himself, take up his
> Cross daily and follow Me.'
> (Luke 9: 23)

He is calling you to:

A. *DENY YOURSELF* – He knows that the one thing that will get in our way the most and the fastest is out PRIDE. Pride is just another way of saying that I know as much as God and I can handle my life and my calling pretty good all by myself. (Remember Genesis 3:4-5) He also knows that pride will only tie us down to our own abilities and expectations. GOD has more than that for us. Self will not give up or give in easily. That is why we must:

B. *TAKE UP YOUR CROSS* – The Cross in the scriptures is always a place of death. The Cross in our lives represents a place of death for us. Our old man, our sinful nature needs to die! We need to stop producing the works of the flesh. Galatians 5: 19-21 reminds us what they are: " Now the works of the flesh are obvious: Sexual immorality, moral impurity, promiscuity, Idolatry, sorcery, hatreds, strife, jealousy, outbursts of anger, selfish ambitions, dissensions, factions, envy, drunkenness and carousing, and anything similar"

The only way that the victory can be won is to say as Paul says:

> I have been crucified with Christ, and I no longer live, but Christ lives in me. The life I now live by faith in the Son of God, who loved me and gave Himself for me. (Galatians 2:20)

The dying to self is a day-by-day, moment-by-moment process, DAILY DYING to self.

If we do not die daily – the old nature, our flesh will jump up and attempt to take over. Attempting to do God's mission in the "flesh" gets to be real ugly, real quick.

We are servants of the King of Kings and Lord of Lords, but when we are doing the work "for" God we can quickly give a false impression of who God really is. John Piper is correct when he says, "It is possible to be distracted from God in trying to serve God. Martha-like, we neglect the one thing needful and soon begin to present God as busy and fretful as we are."[11]

A.W. Tozer warned us about this: "We commonly represent God as a busy, eager, somewhat frustrated Father hurrying about seeking help to carry out His benevolent plan to bring peace and salvation to the world... Too many missionary appeals are based upon fancied frustration of Almighty God."[12]

C. ABIDING IN CHRIST – The one thing that is easy to neglect is ABIDING IN CHRIST, as John tells us so powerfully, "I AM the vine; you are the branches. The one who abides in Me and I in him, produces much fruit, because you can do nothing without Me."(15:5) And again, "If you abide in Me and My words in you, ask whatever you want and it will be done for you. My Father is glorified by this: that you produce much fruit and prove to be my disciples."(15:7)

To abide in Christ simply means to rest in, rely on and let God do what he does best – His Kingdom's work – in you and through you.

I have been a church planter most of my ministry years, which means our family didn't always have a lot of money. I had an old worn-out recliner chair. On Friday nights I would pop a big bowl of popcorn and sit in that chair and watch the good old family shows like the original "Dukes of Hazard" and "Knight Rider." Kirk, my son, was 6 or 7 years old. As the family watched T.V., he would climb up in my chair with me, most of the time on my lap, and watch T.V. with me.

I think in pictures so as I dwell on the practice of abiding in Christ, I can picture, spiritually, climbing up into ABBA Father's lap, like my son used to do and letting Him put His loving arms around me, as I rest in Him. As I do that, I gain a peace, strength from above, and the joy of the Lord's presence fills and renews my soul. I do not know about you, but I need to do that a lot! I also know that that is ABBA Father's desire for us.

He desires us to climb up in His lap, lean on Him, listen to his heartbeat and gain strength and purpose. Then we can go back out into the Harvest field of the major cities of the world.

We abide in Him, through prayer. We abide in Him through "casting all your cares on Him, because He cares for you" I Peter 5:7). And I mean, ALL of them. Letting go and letting God take charge and glorify Himself. Baker James Cauthen, speaking to newly appointed missionaries said it well: "Whatever grace is needed - cleansing grace, fruit-bearing grace, the grace of patience, or the grace of courage – God has it. Your value on the mission field will in direct proportion to your coming to the throne of grace and receiving from him who pours his grace into your heart in order that He may communicate it through you to a world that needs to know."[13]

As we abide in Him through prayer and Bible study, through surrender, then we can apply Psalm 37:4, everyday:

> Delight yourself in the Lord,
> and he will give you the desires
> of your heart.

This verse teaches us two important lessons: "One is that the source of the desires in the heart of a person who is delighting himself in the Lord is God Himself. When we re-delight in Him, He places desires in our hearts that He wants to fulfill. When our hearts are right, He guides us by giving us godly desires. The second truth is that God gave us the desire because He wants to fulfill it." [14]

Therefore we can ask the question, what do you desire?

Do you desire to delight yourself in Hi m? If you do, then when He places the desire in your heart to go to the cities of the world do not be afraid to obey or fulfill those desires that come from God.

3.   SERVICE -

As, God has called you to salvation, and to Himself in discipleship. He has one more calling – to service. In His wonderful plan of the Ages, God knew that we would be alive and called out. At this time in history He has a plan for you. He has a special ministry for you to do. A ministry in the City, that only you can fulfill.

Let me show you, from David Wilkerson's life as he shared in THE CROSS AND THE SWITCHBLADE, a book about the starting of Teen Challenge, how God works. God had called him to salvation when he was young. He had called him to the pastoral ministry. He was pastoring a church in Pennsylvania. But God had something more in store for him.

Here is his story of how God works:

"It was February 9, 1958. On that night I decided to sell my T.V."

"How *much time do I spend in front of that screen each night? What would happen?* I wondered. *A couple hours at least. What would happen, Lord, if I sold that TV and spent that time – praying?* I was the only one in the family who ever watched TV anyway."

"What would happen if I spent two hours every single night in prayer? It was an exhilarating idea. Substitute prayer for television, and see what happened."

"My life has never been the same since. Every night at midnight, instead of flipping some dials, I stepped into my office, closed the door and started to pray. At first the time seemed to drag and I grew restless. Then I learned to make systematic Bible reading a part of my prayer life. I would never before read the Bible through including all the begets. And I learned how to balance prayer of petition and prayer of praise. What a wonderful thing it is to spend a solid hour just being thankful. It throws all of life into a new prospective.

It was during one of these late evenings of prayer that I picked up *Life* magazine.

I'd had been strangely fidgety all night. I was alone in the house; Gwen and the children were in Pittsburgh visiting grandparents. I had been at prayer for a long time. I felt particularly close to God, and yet for reasons I could not understand I also felt a great, heavy sadness. It came over me all at once and I wondered what it could possibly mean. I got up and turned the light on in the study. I felt uneasy, as if I had received orders but could not make what they were.

What are you saying to me, Lord?

"I walked around the study, seeking to understand what was happening to me. On my desk lay a copy of *Life*. I reached over to pick it up, and then caught myself. No, I wasn't going to fall into the trap: reading a magazine when I was supposed to be praying.

I started prowling around the office again, and each time I came to the desk my attention was drawn to that magazine.

"'Lord is there something in there you want me to see?' I said aloud, my voice suddenly booming out of the silent house.

I sat down in my brown leather swivel chair and with a pounding heart, as if I was on the verge of something bigger than I could understand, I opened the magazine. A moment later, I was looking at a pen drawing of seven boys and tears were streaming down my face.

"What is the matter with me!" I said aloud, impatiently brushing away a tear. I looked at the picture more carefully. The boys were all teenagers; they were members of a gang called the Dragons. Beneath their picture was a story of how they had gone into Highbridge Park in New York and brutally attacked and killed a fifteen-year-old polio victim named Michael Farmer. The seven boys stabbed Michael in the back seven times with their knifes. Then they beat him over the head with garrison belts. They went away wiping blood through their hair, saying, 'We messed him good.'

"The story revolted me. It turned my stomach. In our little mountain town such things seemed mercifully unbelievable.

"That's why I was dumbfounded by a thought that sprang suddenly into my head – full-blown, as though it had come into me from somewhere else.

"Go to New York City and help those boys."

I thought aloud. 'Me? Go to New York? A country preacher barge into a situation he knows less than nothing about?'

"Go to New York City and help those boys. The thought was still there, vivid as ever, apparently completely independent of my own feelings and ideas.

"It is no use. The idea would not go away. I was to go to New York, and furthermore I was to go at once, while the trial was still in progress."[15]

David Wilkerson went to New York City. He was never able to meet with those seven gang members, but God used that encounter in his prayer time to get him to New York City. God was not done with David Wilkerson yet:

"It was a hot August night, a year and a half after my first timorous trip to New York. I was standing in the pulpit at the Wednesday evening prayer service, when suddenly my hands began to tremble. The thermometer read 85 degrees but now I was shaking as if I had a chill. Instead of feeling troubled or sick. I felt a tremendous exhilaration. It was as if the Spirit of the Lord was drawing near, in that room."

After the prayer service, David walked out in to the church's backyard. David continues his story: "And then I turned and looked at the church and the parsonage where Gwen and the three children were safe, happy, secure in their life in a country parish. However, as I stood and looked at them, a quiet inner voice spoke to me as clearly as if a friend had been standing nearby. *The church is no longer yours, you are to leave.*

"I looked at the parsonage, and the same inner voice said, *This home is no longer yours, you are to leave.*

"And, in the same still, slow and inner voice, I answered. 'Yes, Lord, I shall go.'

"I walked over to the parsonage after that, and there was Gwen, waiting up. She was dressed for bed, but I could tell from looking at her that something had been happening to her too.

"What is it, Gwen?"
"How do you mean?"
"There is something different about you,"
"David," Gwen said, "you don't have to tell me. I know already. You're going to leave the Church, aren't you? You've got to leave."

I looked at Gwen a long time before I answered her. In the moonlight that flowed into the parsonage bedroom, I could see the glint of a tear in the corner of her eye.

"I heard it too, David," said Gwen, "We're going, aren't we?"

In the darkness I put my arms around her, "Yes my dear one. We're going." [16]

Do you see the process that God used to get David Wilkerson to New York City? To get him to a place where he would develop a passion to reach troubled drug addicts and gang members. Where he would be able to start the world-wide ministry of Teen Challenge?

God called him to salvation when he was a young boy. Then He started the process of getting him closer to Himself. As David started having a prayer time each night and he drew closer to God he learned to abide in Him, he learned to listen to the heart of God. Then God could call him to his life-long ministry.

God is so amazing in the way He works in His people. Each one of us who have been called into the ministry can testify how God has patiently, lovingly called each one of us to the place of service we are in right now. Each one has a different story, but all of the stories display the Lord's amazing grace and eternal love.

David Sills shares his own experiences, "I have traveled around the world and known many missionaries, taught many mission students, spoken at many missions conferences, and counseled many people seeking God's will for their life regarding missions. I have never heard two calls to gospel ministry that identical or two calls to missionary service that are the same. God seems to call some to a particular kind of mission service, others to a people group, others, to a region, others to a country, others to a city, and others to a life purpose (such as rescuing young girls from prostitution)) or some combination of these. With married couples, rarely does God call both spouses at the same time and they frequently consider the missionary call because of completely different motivations." [17]

How has He called you to the City that he has you serving in now? How is He drawing you to minister to the millions of people in the major cities in our cities?

GOD CALLS – WILL WE HEAR AND OBEY?

Is GOD calling you because…?

1. The City is where the MAJORITY of the World lives. It just makes sense to go to where the Gospel can make the greatest *impact* on the greatest amount of people at one time. God called Jonah to Nineveh because it was a GREAT city. It had the people there that needed to hear the Gospel.

It just makes sense to go to the MAJOR Cities of the world where there are ten million people massed in one of the major cities. To go to the cities where there are 250 or 500 different people groups and language groups melted together in one big metropolitan area just makes sense.

We need to go to the cities and observe the multitudes as Jesus did.

"When He saw the crowds, He felt compassion for them, because they were weary and worn out, like sheep without a shepherd." Then we need to pray as Jesus told His disciples, "The harvest is abundant, but the workers are few. Therefore, pray to the Lord of the harvest to send out workers into the harvest" (Matthew 9:36-38). But, watch out, if you pray that prayer, He may be sending you into the harvest fields of the cities!

2. The LOSTNESS of the Cities is overwhelming.

God called Jonah to Nineveh because the wickedness of that city had come up to Him and that wickedness "stunk to high heavens." Does the *lostness* of your city bother you? Does the *lostness* of Calcutta, of Bombay, of Tokyo, of Mexico City, of Los Angeles bother you at all?

I was born, raised and lived most of my life in Los Angeles. There are still areas of the city I have never been involved in as a minister. As I drive the streets of L.A. I see all the people, from all over the world – the little children, the young people, the senior citizens and everyone in between, and it breaks my heart. Many times, I have to stop and pull my car over to the side of the road because I am so heavily burdened, tears are flowing and my prayers for my city is being lifted up to God, who wept over Jerusalem.

Is your heart broken over the *lostness* of our cities? That is a good enough reason to go to the great cities of the World.

But, the greatest reason and the long lasting reason is because GOD has called you to go to the cities.

He has called you deep down in your soul. You know it and God knows it, and you cannot get away from it. It is eating on your soul; the passion of your life is to go to the city. And you will never be satisfied until you go.

David Sills admits that the call is a combination of things that come together in a special way. He writes, "We should understand the missionary call as a combination of all these aspects: an awareness of the needs and commands, a passion for the lost, a commitment to God, the Spirit's gifting, and you church's affirmation, blessing, and commissioning."

He goes on to say, "In addition, one must include another essential aspect of the missionary call: an indescribable yearning that motivates beyond all understanding. Defining this yearning is virtually impossible. It is tantamount to describing how you know that you are in love. How would you explain it to an eight-year-old the difference between liking someone a lot, loving someone, and being 'in love'? To make the definition even more elusive, the truth is that no two calls are exactly the same."[18]

I like the way David Sills explains the beauty of God's call to go to the nations and the cities, "Missionary callings, like snow flakes, are each unique and when combined with others, cover the land as the waters cover the sea. Amazingly, God uses people like us to take His saving gospel message to a lost world and is pleased to save souls through our preaching."19

P.J. Tibayan grew up in a comfortable suburb of Los Angeles. After attending seminary and a six-month intern at Capital Hills Church in Washington, D.C., he felt called to the inner city of Los Angeles. His family and friends told him not to go, the mentors and advisors were recommending him to other places. I heard of his desire to plant a church in 2008. I called him and set up an appointment. We talked about planting a church in inner city Los Angeles. After the meeting, I was not sure. I called and talked to him again. I heard his heart. He has planted a church in the Mid-Wilshire District of Los Angeles. It is an area where I had been praying over for years. It is an area where there was no evangelical witness. At his ordination service, he shared this testimony: He was starting to think maybe he was wrong. Maybe everyone else was right. He asked the Lord to give him a sign if he was to start a church in Los Angeles. And he gave God a deadline. That happened to be the day I called him to make an appointment to talk about church planting. He heard the call and he obeyed it. His church is starting to grow and they have even started a Spanish church in the same community center that he uses for church. God called and he obeyed.

IS GOD CALLING YOU TO THE CITY? Is God calling you TO ONE OF THE GREAT CIIES OF THE WORLD? Will you GO? Will you say as Isaiah? "Then I heard the voice of the Lord saying: Who should I send? Who will go for us? I said, "Here I am. Send me." (6:8)

One more important and exciting truth wrapped up in God's call to the cities is that:
"Then the word of the Lord came to Jonah a second time. Get up! Go to the great city of Nineveh and preach the message that I tell you. So, Jonah got up and went to Nineveh according to the Lord's command." (Joan 3:1-3)

Our GOD is a GOD of a second chance! And often a third and fourth and hundredth chance! That is so great and wonderful to know!

Phillip Cary says, "It all starts again, just as before, with the very same words we read at the beginning except the added phrase reminding us that it is the second time. The Lord is nothing if not persistent, always ready to begin again. But this time things should be different. For Jonah is not just starting over; he has been given a new life out of the depths of Sheol, like Israel freed from exile in Babylon; like a man buried with Christ in baptism and raised to newness of life."[19]

Is it not fantastic that God gave Jonah a second chance? He will also give you a second chance, or a third, or hundredth chance. He who called you will never let you go. He will keep bringing you back to the calling. The call to the city will never be able to leave you – until you simply "trust and obey, for there is no other way to be happy in Jesus, but to trust and obey."

I know this truth from personal experience. God has been so good to me over the last 46 years of ministry. He called me to preach at 18 years of age. I obeyed. God called my family to St. Vincent, an island in the Caribbean. God blessed our effort to start Southern Baptist work on the island. People came to the Lord almost every week. I felt like I had arrived. That this is where I was supposed to be.

But, sometimes circumstances, events, and people affect and change our plans. After four years, I found myself a single, divorced dad raising three children.

I felt like my ministry was over. Because of the stigma of divorce, I did not think I would ever pastor a church or plant a church again. But, God in His grace is a forgiving God and a God of restoration.

I went to a little church in South Sacramento to supply preach one Sunday. It was in a multiracial, multicultural community. It was in an unsafe place, with lots of gangs, drugs and crime. When I walked in the building I knew I was home. They called me as their "permanent part-time pastor."

God blessed the church and they were able to make me a full-time pastor. We were able to start five churches out of that church. After seven years, God brought Leesa across my path and we have been married for 23 years. She had two children, I had three and we have had one together. We have also raised ten foster children. It has been a blessing.

We then moved to Pomona, an inner city suburb of Los Angeles. I pastored there for seven years. God blessed. We were able to start ten churches out of that inner city church.

Through all those years I had dreams of attending the Southern Baptist Convention annual meeting, and I always had a big "D" on my back. I felt shame and that I was worthless.

In the early '90s, God did a deeper work among the pastors in the Inland Empire area of Southern California through Pastor Prayer Summits. It was a time when pastors went away in a retreat setting. We just praised and prayed. No preaching, no bragging, or postulating – just prayer and praise. One time, in a small group, I shared my dreams with the group. The leader of the group said, "Don, from now on that 'D' will represent 'Delivered' instead of Divorce, as the group prayed over me. That time set my spirit free to believe that God could use me again in a greater way than I had expected.

A few years later, Phil Langley, the director of English speaking church starting for the California Southern Baptist Convention called me and asked if I would consider being a Church Start Strategist. When I got off the phone with Phil, I turned to my wife and said, "That won't happen, I've been divorced." Leesa gave me a Godly answer, "God is bigger than the system." Three months later, I was appointed as a Church Start Strategist for the North American Mission Board of the Southern Baptist Convention. The area where I have the privilege to help start churches is Los Angeles, San Bernardino and Riverside counties in Southern California. There are approximately 20 million people in those three counties. God has blessed our efforts with hundreds of new churches and thousands of new believers in the Kingdom of God.

I thought God could never use me again. I thought God was finished with me. But, praise God! He is a God of the SECOND CHANCE! He proved it to me. I cannot thank Him enough for His kindness!

He is a God of the second, third and hundredth chance for you too! Your responsibility is: To accept His forgiveness and cleansing as a free gift, and humbly surrender to His perfect will for you.

GOD is calling His people – you and me- to the major cities of the world. It is a divine calling that comes from the heart of our Sovereign God. He is Lord! He is the missionary God who sends. As He calls us to the cities, we need to respond to that call as pastor Manaseh Mutsoli of Kenya responded:

"HERE AM I SEND ME"

Here am I,
I give my spirit
And service to you.
I will go where you want
Me to go, Father.
I will go to the countryside,
To the city, to the valley
Or to the mountain.
Here am I, send me.
I will go and tell
All the tribes.
I will go to the lost
Wherever you wish, Father,
I will go. Here am I,
Send me."[20]

QUESTIONS:

1. Do you really KNOW how much GOD loves you?

2. Can you share your Salvation experience?

3. How is your Love relationship with JESUS?

4. Are you OBEYING the Call to the City?

FOOT NOTES:

1. Henry Blackaby and Henry Brandt, <u>THE POWER OF THE CALL,</u> Nashville: Broadman and Holman, 1997, p. 28.

2. Phillip Cary, <u>JONAH</u>, Grand Rapids: Brazos Press, 2008, p. 27.

3. Henry T. Blackaby, <u>EXPERIENCING GOD</u>, Nashville: LifeWay Press, 1990.

4. Cary, p. 28.

5. Cary, p. 29.

6. J. Herbert Kane, <u>CHRISTIAN MISSIONS IN BIBLICAL PERSPECTIVE</u>, Grand Rapids: Baker Book House, 1976, p. 141.

7. J. Herbert Kane, p. 142.

8. J. Herbert Kane, pgs. 142-144.

9. George W. Peters, <u>A BIBLICAL THEOLOGY OF MISSIONS</u>, Chicago: Moody Press, 1972, p. 60.

10. Sam Simmons, *"Salvation and Missions"*, found in <u>MISSIOLOGY</u>, edited by John Mark Terry, Ebbie Smith and Justice Anderson, Nashville: Braodman and Holman, 1998, p. 129.

11. John Piper, <u>LET THE NATIONS REJOICE! THE SUPREMACY OF GOD INMISSIONS</u>, Grand rapids: Baker Book House, 1993, 2003, p. 18.

12. Quoted in John Piper, p. 19.<u>LET THE NATIONS REJOICE!</u>

13. Baker James Cauthen, <u>BEYOND CALL</u>, Nashville: Broadman Press, 1973, p. 28.

14. M. David Sills, <u>THE MISSIONARY CALL: FIND YOUR PLACE IN GOD'S PLAN FOR THE WORLD</u>, Chicap: Moody Press, 2008, p. 28.

15. David Wilkerson, <u>THE CROSS AND THE SWITCHBLAD</u>, Grand Rapids: Baker Book House, 1963, 2008.

16. Wilkerson, pgs. 124-126.

17. M. David Sills, p. 29.

18. David Sills, p. 30.

19. David Sills, p. 30

20. Cary, p. 105.

21. Manasheh Mutoshi, "Nitume: Here am I, send me", *Your Church On Mission,* Richmond: International Mission Board, SBC, September 2000.

CHAPTER FOUR

HOW WICKED ARE THE CITIES?

"In the Bible, urban mission began with the story of Jonah, the Old Testament prophet whom God called to preach to the wicked in the city of Nineveh."[1]
Roger S. Greenway

"Get up! Go to the great city of Nineveh and preach against it, because their wickedness has confronted ME" JONAH 1:2

In 2006, a mission team from the island of St. Vincent in the West Indies came to Los Angeles. St. Vincent is a beautiful tropical island in the Caribbean. It is one of the poorer islands. The majority of the population does not have jobs. The family income averages about $100 U.S. a month or less. I had started the Southern Baptist work on that island in 1976. Many of the team members were teenagers when I was a missionary in St. Vincent. I baptized most of them. As they arrived in Los Angeles, all of them said, "Now pastor, the circle is complete. You came to minister to us, now we have come to minister to you and your people."

As they spent time with us in Los Angeles, they sang and ministered in some of the churches that had sent mission teams to St. Vincent. God blessed their time with us!

One afternoon, I took them to downtown Los Angeles. We went to minister in the Skid Row area of downtown Los Angeles. Skid Row is famous and *notorious at the same time for the high density of homeless people, drugs and crime. There are more homeless people in Los Angeles County than the whole population of St. Vincent.*

As the team ministered at our SET FREE CHURCH in Skid Row, they were amazed and challenged by the homelessness and hopelessness of the community. As they walked the streets around the church, they saw drug deals going down, prostitutes working the streets and homeless people stacking out their squats for the night. They were deeply touched by what they saw on the streets of Los Angeles. They were so touched that when they started to sing, they broke down crying. They could not continue because they were so touched by what they saw on the streets.

The choir director of the team, with tears streaming down his face, asked me: "Pastor, how can this be? How can this be in the richest country in the world?"

I did not have a good answer. The only answer I could give him is – the sins of the people have caused the brokenness, the suffering that we find in so many of the major cities in the World.

Is the city so wicked? Is the city so sinful and wicked that it is a hopeless situation?

GOD called Jonah to the great city of Nineveh, to preach against the wickedness found in that city. "Nineveh was a great city in many ways. It was a world metropolis and capital of a powerful empire. The city lasted for fifteen hundred years, making most modern cities look like adolescent upstarts by comparison. Nineveh was famous for its beauty, and many considered it the fairest city built since Cain founded Enoch. Militarily, Nineveh stretched for sixty miles; its inner walls were a hundred feet high. Horse-drawn chariots, three abreast, could ride the battlements. It took ten thousand slaves twelve years to build the king's house, and the city's parks and public buildings were praised throughout the world."[2]

Thought the city of Nineveh was beautiful, its foundations were built on wickedness. Nahum called her the "city of blood" in Nahum 3:1, we read:

> Woe to the city of blood,
> totally deceitful,
> full of plunder,
> never without prey.

"It was a cruel and wicked city built on the foundation of witchcraft and a capital of vice. Her artistic achievements were fouled by obscenities, her culture by idols. And her beauty by violence."[3]

Ray Bakke explains the culture of Nineveh in these terms, "The Assyrians were the Nazis of the ancient world. They were the most violent culture in the Middle East. The Assyrian army would raid a village, put out the eyes of the oldest men and murder the women and children in front of them, so the blinded victims could hear the death cries of their families. After stacking the bodies in the street like cordwood, the army would move to the next village. The Assyrians spread terror through the Middle East for hundred of years."[4]

"Nineveh's wickedness provoked God's wrath. God knew precisely what was going on. He said to Jonah that '*their* wickedness' had come up before him. The sin of the city was personal, for it was committed personally by Nineveh's thousands of inhabitants. It was also collective, for when it was all added up, the sum total for Nineveh's life, culture, and achievements had *wickedness* written across it. When judgment fell, everyone would be affected. The warp and woof of Ninevitish life was depraved, and the city's only hope consisted in a repentance as wide and complete as the sin that stained it."[5]

The great cities of the world are the greatest mission field of the 21st Century! Why? The city is a great mission field, because that is where the majority of the world live now. The city is a great mission field because of the great *lostness* found in the city.

Saint Augustine wrote that in every city there were two cities, the *City of God* and the *City of Satan* and they are in conflict with one another. Roger Greenway states, "It is undeniable that cities contain strongholds of satanic power that resists the spread of the Gospel and promotes unrighteousness in society." Greenway goes on to say, "There is much that is beautiful and good in cities. By their schools, hospitals and productivity, cities enhance the quality of human life. But at the same time, the power of evil is evident. Sin expresses itself not only in the wrong doing of individuals, but also in institutions whose policies and actions exploit and oppress, as well as in the wrong use of the systems by which cities are managed."[6]

The wickedness in our cities is caused by a combination of factors: growth of population in our cities, immigration, poverty, drugs and alcoholism, homelessness, and sinful mankind.

The problem is not that this issue is one problem after the other, or one problem added to another, but it is all of them added together and multiplied or magnified, whichever you prefer, by each other.

Let's look at each of these factors:

1. The LARGENESS OF THE CITIES – The number of people in the world cities are staggering. Looking at just an overview of our world cites will stagger your mind:

PROJECTED POPULATION FIGURES

(Projected for 2015)

1.	TOKYO, JAPAN	28.7
2.	MUMBAI, INDIA	27.4
3.	LAGOS, NIGERIA	24.4
4.	JAKARTA, INDONESIA	21.2
5.	SAO PAULO, BRAZIL	20.8
6.	BEIJING, CHINA	19.4
7.	MEXICO CITY, MEXICO	18.8[7]

Here is the problem: The larger the cities, the larger the needs, and the easier for confusion and the heartache to come pouring out of the hearts of the masses. If the Church is not careful the people in these major cities will just be a number in the crowd. We need to keep in mind that every one of those millions of people is a human being made in God's image. Each one has many needs and above all else, needs Jesus Christ and salvation through Him. What a tremendous missionary challenge awaits us in the cities!

Instead of looking at the major cities with the concept that it is an overwhelming task to reach the city, we need to look at the great opportunities that we have in the cities. As Roger Greenway says, "the massive migration to the cities that is occurring around the world may be, in God's providence, a key to world evangelization. Through urbanization, God is drawing people of every race, tribe and language to places where they can be reached with the gospel."[7]

2. IMMIGRATION – Migration from rural areas to urban centers explains about half of the growth of cities. The movement of more than a billion people to the cities over the last two decades is the largest population movement in history.

As of 2008, 38 million immigrants lived in the United States, or 12.5 percent of the population, a rising share but still lower than in the early part of the 20th Century. Again, by 2008, the dramatic transformation in opportunities across the world are apparent in the composition of the 38 million U.S. foreign born; only 13 percent are from Europe; Mexican immigrants comprise fully 30 percent of the total with another 23 percent from other Latin American and Caribbean countries; 27 percent are from Asia; Africans represent nearly 4 percent of the total; only 2 percent are from North America."[9]

The shift from the immigration majority being European based, or Northern Hemisphere based to Southern Hemisphere based is a significant factor. The Asian immigrants are coming from oppressed countries such as Vietnam and Cambodia. There is also a larger number of Asian immigrants from Mainland China.

"New York and Los Angeles top the list of metropolitan areas with the largest number of immigrants, with 5.3 and 4.4 million, respectively, followed by other well-established destination areas including Miami and Chicago. However, when metro areas are ranked by the percentage of foreign born, nine of the top 10 are the in the Sun Belt states, all with long-standing immigrant populations. Six are in California; two lie along the Texas border; and Miami and New York round out the top 10."[10]

LARGEST NUMBER OF IMMIGRANTS

Rank	Metro area	Immigrants
1.	New York-Newark, NY-NJ-PA	5,328,033
2.	Los Angeles-Long Beach-Santa Ana	4,374,583
3.	Miami-Ft. Lauderdale	1,995,037
4.	Chicago-Naperville-Joliet	1,689,617
5.	San Francisco-Oakland-Fremont	1,258,324
6.	Houston	1,237,719
7.	Dallas-Ft.Worth-Arlington	1,121,321
8.	Washington-Arlington-Alexandria	1,089,950
9.	Riverside–San Bernardino-Ontario	894,527
10.	Boston-Cambridge, MA-NH	731,960
	ALL LARGE METRO AREAS	32,425,888

HIGHEST FOREIGN-BORN POPULATION SHARE

Rank	Metro Area	%Foreign Born
1.	Miami-Ft. Lauderdale	36.8
2.	San Jose-Sunnyvale-Santa Clara	36.4
3.	Los Angeles-Long Beach-Santa Ana	34.0
4.	San Francisco-Oakland-Fremont	29.4
5.	McAllen, TX	29.2
6.	New York-Newark	28.0
7.	El Paso, TX	27.3
8.	Stockton, CA	22.8
9.	Oxnard-Thousand Oaks-Ventura	22.3
10.	San Diego	22.1
	ALL LARGE METRO AREAS	16.3[11]

Another important factor in the immigration issue is the "second generation" development. The "second generation" presents a large share of the child population in several established metropolitan gateways. In the Los Angeles, Miami, San Francisco metro areas, more than half of children have at least one foreign born parent or are themselves foreign born. The New York area has 1.8 million such children, 44 percent of all children metro-wide."[12]

The immigration movement to the United States is toward a better life. The people on the whole do have a better life than where they came from in Third world countries. The people have a good chance to improve their life and the life of their children. In the major cities of the U.S. second and third generation of immigrants are advancing educationally, economically and job security. A minimum wage lifestyle in Los Angeles is still better than a middle class life style in most Third world countries.

This is not true in the third world major cities. "The majority of migrants to the mega-cities will move into the *slums* (Bangkok), *squatter areas* (Manila), *shanty towns* (South Africa), *bustees* (India), *bidonvilles* (Morocco), *favelas* (Brazil). *Casbahs* (Algeria), *ranchitos (Venezuela), cuidaid perdidas* (Mexico), and *barriadas* or *pueblos jovenes* (Peru). All are the same starting places for the immigrants. Poverty. "Some of the worst suffering is found among the people who recently arrived in cities. People from the rural peasant classes are seldom prepared for the difficulties they encounter. They lack the skills required for the jobs that are available. They cannot afford to buy properties r pay high rent. They are forced to live in squatter settlements, in shacks built of discarded wood, tin, and tar paper, usually located on the fringes of the city."[13]

The 21st Century church must realize that the migrants in their cities are their responsibility. We need to reach them while they are adjusting to a new world, adapting to a new way of life, and admitting their lostness in the city. As Viv Grigg, who has personally lived in the slums among recent immigrants to Manila, states: "Among the most reachable of people groups are migrants living in community, groups of peasants who have moved to cities and live in squatter areas."[14]

They have left everything that was comfortable and safe to come to the city. They do not know anyone or at best, a few people in a sea of millions of people. They have lost all security, have gained no peace, and are in the survival mod in life. The Church has the hope of the World, the Friend to the hopeless, the Father to the fatherless, and the one who can keep them safe and secure. We have JESUS! We need to share the Gospel with the people when they are vulnerable and open to new options.

3.   POVERTY -

The most common and simplest definition of poverty is that it is the condition of those groups of people we abstractly describe as "the poor." Bryant Myers reminds of another fact that we cannot forget: "But the poor are not abstract. They are human beings with names, made in the image of God, those for whom Jesus died. People who live in poverty are valuable to God – as important to Him, as those who do not live in poverty."14

From a Christian perspective on poverty we need to understand that poverty consists of:

A)   The lack of *things*. Poor people do not have the necessities for a normal life, as we know it. They lack food, clean water, housing and jobs.

B)   The lack of *knowledge* and *skills*. They are not stupid! They lack the education opportunities to improve their lifestyle. They have not had the opportunity to develop job skills.

C)   The lack of *opportunities* to advance to a better way of life. In so many cultures, the caste system and/or the system that controls social interactions have oppressed and downgraded the poor that they are literally stuck in the rut of poverty.

D)   The lack of *self-worth* in the individual. After a person has been degraded and dehumanized so many times--all their life--the person loses their self-worth. With the lack of self-worth comes the feeling of unworthiness. Combine those two feelings together and the "poor" find themselves in a vicious downward cycle of despair.

E)   The lack of being *included*. Poverty involves being excluded. We make people poor when we label them as the other, the outsider, and the outcast. We begin the process of exclusion when we say people are lazy, dirty, uneducated, crazy, or unsafe to be around."15

F) The lack of the knowledge of GOD. The poor can find them down so far in despair that they do not think they can know God. Sadder still, is their feeling that God does not know them!

In the United States, the economic downturn has affected poverty more than any time, except the Great Depression. "The Great recession has brought about failing incomes and increased economic hardship across the country. But income for the typical American household had stalled even before its onset. By 2007, median income in the United States had fallen by almost $1600 since the start of the decade. It fell further in 2008 to $2,241, a real decrease of 4.1 percent. This country also saw a significant increase over the 2000s in the number of individuals living below the poverty line. From 1999 to 2008, the poor population in the United States grew by 5.2 million people, or 15.4 percent – almost twice the growth rate of the population as a whole. By 2008, more than 39.1 million individuals lived in poverty, or 13.2 percent of the nation's population. By and large, poor residents of cities and suburbs resemble one another on key social and demographic characteristics. City residents are just slightly more likely to live in "deep" poverty with incomes half the poverty line.[16]

Poverty and the number of poor have increased drastically in the United States within the past ten years. Ron Thomas, who pastors Set Free Church of Skid Row, a church for the poor in downtown L.A. tells me that the people he ministers to has increased three times. The poor and needy is increasing, especially among the marginal families who are just squeezing by on minimum wage salaries. When they lose those jobs, they become homeless. The new poor are families with children.

Yet, we in middle class America need to remember that the middle class of Calcutta, India is poorer than the poor of Los Angeles. There are staggering numbers of poor all over the world.

Viv Grigg explains to us that: "We may talk of three major international categories of urban poor – inner-city slumps, squatters, and specialized groups."

He goes on to explain the differences in the different areas:

Inner-city slums are decaying tenements and houses in what were good middle class and upper-class residents. They may be described as *slums of despair* where those who have lost the will to try and those who cannot cope live. Yet here too are the recent immigrants, living near employment opportunities.

Squatter areas tend to be *slums of hope.* Here, people have found a foothold into the city, some vacant land, jobs and some communal relationships similar to the *barrio* back home.

Specialized groups tend to be clustered around an addiction that drags them down to despair and hopelessness. The traditional model of the homeless is the alcoholic sleeping on the streets. Now included in that stereotype is the drug addict that gets stuck in poverty because of his addiction.[17]

As we look at reaching the major cities of the World for Christ, we cannot forget the urban poor! As Viv Grigg writes, "Missions today must reach the last tribes and fulfill prior commitments to the rural poor. But new mission strategies must focus on the crucial point of spiritual warfare for the mega-cities. Within these broad objectives, mission to the urban poor becomes a central target, as they are the ultimate victims of the oppression and evil of the mega-cities and nation States. They loom large in the heart of God. They are the key to the elite and the heart of the city."[18]

4. HOMELESSNESS. "Homelessness and poverty are inextricably linked, poor people are frequently unable to pay for housing, food, childcare, health care, and education. Difficult choices must be made when limited resources cover only some of these necessities. Often it is housing, which absorbs a high proportion of income that must be dropped. Being poor means: an illness, an accident, or a paycheck away from living on the streets."[19]

People are homeless for a variety of reasons in the United States:

A. The *JOB MARKET* has declined drastically. In 2009, the job market was losing 741,000 jobs a month. By January 2010, it is only 20,000 a month. But that affects the poor and those who were just squeezing by on low-income wages. No job equals homelessness. Low-wage workers have been particularly hard hit by wage trends and have been left behind as disparity between rich and poor has mushroomed. To compound the problem, the real value of the minimum wage in 2004 was 26 percent less than in 1979 (The Economic Policy Institute, 2005). [20]

B. The HOUSING MARKET has been struggling through the 2000s. Because of the economy, houses have stopped being built. Thus, there is less housing available, Because of the economy people are out of work, cannot pay their rent or mortgages and losing their homes. The greatest growth in homelessness is among families with children. This is tragic to see children without the security of a home.

C. The DECLINE IN PUBLIC ASSISTANCE has caused many people to be homeless. Presently, most states have not replaced the old welfare system Homeless individuals obtain above-poverty employment and to sustain themselves when work is not available or possible.

D. The DECLINE OF AFFORDABLE HEALTH CARE has caused a multiple of repercussion: sickness and mental health issues affect the homeless on the streets. Probably 60 percent of the homeless people on the streets could live a normal life if they had medication. Individually they cannot afford to pay for their medication with a sad debilitating affect on their lives.

E. The rise of DOMESTIC VIOLENCE has sent many women and women with children onto the streets of our major cities – homeless. Battered women who live in poverty are often forced to choose between abusive relationships and homelessness. "In a study of 777 homeless parents (the majority of whom were mothers) in ten U.S. cities, 22 percent said they had left their last place of residence because of domestic violence (Home for the Homeless, 1998). In addition, 50 percent of the cities surveyed by the U.S. Conference of Mayors identified domestic violence as a primary cause of homelessness (U.S. Conference of Mayors, 2005). Studying the entire country reveals that the problem is even more serious. Nationally, approximately half of all women and children experiencing homelessness are fleeing domestic violence. (Zorza, 1991; National Coalition Against Domestic Violence, 2001) [21]

Homelessness in the United Sates is on the increase. We can put our head in the sand and hope they all go away. The cities of the U.S do not want them. Tougher and meaner rules against the homeless are on the increase. The heartlessness of our cities can be seen by the fact that there is even a list of the ten worst places to be homeless. Arthur Delaney reports in an article that he wrote May 21, 2010, entitled, " The 10 Worst Places to be Homeless," that "municipal meanness is increasing nationwide, Tulin Ozdeger of the NLCHP, citied a 7 percent increase in laws prohibiting "camping", an 11 percent increase in laws prohibiting loitering. A 6 percent increase in laws prohibiting begging and 5 percent increase in laws prohibiting aggressive panhandling in the 224 cities surveyed. There is even a list of the 10 worst places to be homeless. Here is the 2008 list:

1. Los Angeles
2. St, Petersburg, FL.
3. Orlando, FL.
4. Atlanta
5. Gainesville, FL.
6. Kalamazoo, MI.
7. San Francisco
8. Honolulu
9. Bradenton, FL.
10. Berkeley [22]

Across the world, homelessness is totally out of control. Millions are sleeping on the streets nightly in the world. In Calcutta, more than half of the 3.5 million living within the metro core are slum dwellers. There is a level of poverty still lower than that experienced by beggar, street-dweller, or bustee-dweller – the poverty of those approaching death. The dying are the faces along the streets. Bodies of those who died during the night will be picked up by the government workers and cast aside in an unmarked grave. Homeless, helpless and, sadly, hopeless.[23]

5. CRIME. The increase in crime and violence over the years in the United States, as well as the rest of the world is frightening. One good example is in the rise of murder in the United States. In 1960 there were 9,110 murders, in 2008 there 16,272 murders. An unbelievable increase in robberies has occurred in the past forty-eight years. There were 107,840 robberies in 1960 compared to 447,403 robberies in

2008. An inner city resident would probably also say that that crime is on the rise in America.

"From a sociologist perspective crime in America, and the rest of the world, could be seen on the rise because of an increase in underlying problems in the lives of individuals and in the community. These problems are typically economic, social, and/or psychological in nature. While there are certainly genetic and biological factors involved in the development of an individual's propensity towards committing crimes, environment also plays a role in this arena. People from problematic backgrounds or especially difficult circumstances are not only more likely to participate in criminal activities, but are also more likely to continue their destructive activities to the point at which serious run-in with the law develops."[24]

The United States has witnessed a tremendous growth in the size of its urban underclass each year. The percentage of the population persistently poor is large and rapidly increasing, meaning that more and more teenagers are joining gangs, and that the need for welfare is exploding in most cities. Statistics repeatedly show that violence and crime are on the increase, young people are dropping out of school in record numbers, and higher percentages of the population are withdrawing from the labor force.[25]

The ten worst cities for murder in the United States in 2002 were:

CITIES	Per 100,000
1. WASHINGTON, D.C.	45.8
2. DETROIT	42.0
3. BALTIMORE	38.3
4. MEMPHIS	24.7
5. CHICAGO	22.2
6. PHILADELPHIA	19.0
7. COLUMBUS	18.1
8. MILWAUKEE	18.0
9. LOS ANGELES	17.5
10. DALLAS	15.8

The ten worst countries for murder were: (Late 1990s statistics)

COUNTRY	Per 100,000
1. Columbia	84.4
2. El Salvador	50.2
3. Puerto Rico	41.8
4. Brazil	32.5
5. Albania	28.2
6. Venezuela	25.0
7. Russian Federation	18.0
8. Ecuador	15.9
9. Mexico	15.3
10. Panama	14.4 [26]

Crime is on the increase all over the world. It can be seen, especially, in countries and cities where poverty and hunger controls the majority of the population.

Looking at just the murder rates, the first thing that stands out is that, in every city and country listed all have the same major issues: unemployment, poverty, homelessness, drugs and crime. Add to that list the drug problem that engulfs millions of people in our world cities. The addiction to drugs just multiplies and magnifies the issues the people of the inner city face everyday.

John Dawson sums up the situation in our cities by writing: "How has all this impacted humankind socially? The city is supposedly developed for our benefits. The city is a giant architectural machine commissioned to shelter, transport, empower and enrich its inhabitants; yet individual men and women increasingly feel like victims of their own creation." Dawson has put together a list of twelve factors that contribute to the disorientation of modern city dwellers:

1. Authority is distant and impersonal, *they feel powerless.*

2. The great majority of people are total strangers to the individual. *They feel alone.*

3. Culture, race and language are so diverse that these factors are no longer basis for security or identity. *They feel vulnerable.*

4. Superimposed on the diversity is a universal commercial culture of identical chain restaurants, businesses, malls, theaters and architecture, producing a nationwide urban uniformity that dwarfs regional culture. *They feel lost.*

5. Urban people have their senses continually bombarded by powerful media. *They feel controlled.*

6. Functional specialization is to the point where family members lead completely different lives in different environments with different schedules. *They feel rejected.*

7. So many options are available in life-styles, products and entertainments that the promise of happiness through affluence has been swallowed up in anxiety over decisions making. *They feel bewildered.*

8. An information overload has dulled the appetite for true understanding. *They feel foolish.*

9. The rapid pace of change in vocations and housing has undermined all forms of covenantal relationships. Nearly all friendships are short-term. *They feel insecure.*

10. They are surrounded by relentless activities day and night, suggesting that others are busy achieving wealth and success. It is difficult to rest. *They feel stress and anxiety.*

11. The marketplace values them only for their skills and their labor; if they fail, they are rejected like cast-off machinery. *They feel used.*

12. Public values are reduced to the promotion of production and consumption. All other values are considered private. *They feel void of meaning.*[27]

After looking at all the issues that face the major cities of our world, what is the <u>real</u> issue?

WHY ARE THE CITIES SO WICKED?

When we read about 20-30 killings a weekend in Los Angeles, when we hear of child prostitute in Bangkok, when we hear of human trafficking in Mexico City, when we hear of 25,000 babies left to die on the streets of the major cities in the U.S.A.. When we hear of gang membership at over 100,000 in New York City, when we hear of drug rings right in the middle of the upper middle class communities. We conclude that there is something drastically wrong. We come to believe that that the real problem is just below the surface.

Robert C. Linthicum states: "What are the roots of a city's evil? There is no more critical question for urban Christians to ask than this one, because we Christians as individuals and the church as the body of Christ are hopelessly naïve about the nature of evil in the city, This is why the church has been essentially ineffective in urban ministry."

Linthicum goes on to say, "Social injustice (especially toward a city's own poor), exploitation, sexual perversity, pride, gluttony, arrogance, complacency are all terrible sins. Combined, they are capable of destroying the soul of a city. Nothing is as evil as idolatry. To worship something other than God as god is to reject the only One who can actually bring salvation. This was Jerusalem's sin, for the city placed national security ahead of God; the city was willing to sacrifice God in order to worship security." [28]

John Dawson agrees, when he writes, "To practice idolatry is to substitute something man-made for God. All three persons of the trinity have their functions imitated by idols:

- The counterfeit of the work of the Holy Spirit is false religion.

- The Son is replaced in the form of human heroes and deliverers.

- The Father is replaced by institutions.

From the Father we receive identity, security, provision, protection and direction. The moment we turn to an institution as the prime object of our faith, we have become an idolater."[29]

In the Bible, Ezekiel 16 tells the people of Israel:

> Now this was the iniquity of your
> sister Sodom: she and her daughters
> had pride, plenty of food, and
> comfortable security, but didn't
> support the poor and needy. They
> were haughty and did detestable
> things before Me, so I removed
> them when I saw this, But Samaria
> did not commit even half your sins.
> You have multiplied your abominations
> beyond theirs and made your sister
> appear righteous by all the abominations
> you have committed. (Verses 49-51)

The bottom line is: <u>SIN</u>.

The soul of the cities has been captured by the enemy - Satan, because of the sin of the people in the cities. Sin is simply man attempting to take God's place. It all goes back to idolatry: The sin of the angel Lucifer is the sin of idolatry. He tried to take God's place in Heaven. There is only One God and that is the Lord God Almighty. Look what Satan had the audacity to say in Isaiah 14:

You said in your heart, I will ascend to heaven; I will raise my throne above the stars of God; I will sit enthroned on the mount of assembly, on the utmost heights of the sacred mountain. I will ascend above the tops of the clouds; I will make myself like the Most High. But you are brought down to the grave, to the depths of the pit. (Vv. 13-15)

The problem of the city today is SIN. Here is the simple truth: The more people there are in the city, the more SIN there will be. Sin soon dominates the life style, mind-set and hearts of the city dwellers. The SIN of the city is the sin of rebellion against God Almighty.

We also need to be aware of and ready to overcome the spiritual strongholds that the enemy has embedded into the cities.

First, lets get a good definition of a spiritual stronghold. Ed Silvoso gives a great definition of a stronghold. He says, "A stronghold is a mind-set impregnated with hopelessness that causes the believer to accept as unchangeable something he or she knows is contrary to the will of God."[30]

The enemy can control nonbelievers with spiritual strongholds because they do not even know that there is "right" and "wrong". Satan has blinded their minds so much that they have come to believe the "liar and father of lies" is telling the truth and Christian morals are wrong.

Cindy Jacobs describes the different kinds of strongholds: personal strongholds, strongholds of the mind, ideological stronghold, social strongholds, strongholds between city and church, sectarian strongholds and strongholds and iniquity. Satan's influence in a city can be weakened by tearing down the strongholds that give him legal right to perpetuate evil in the city (2 Corinthians 2:10-11; Ephesians 4:2-27; Revelations 2: 9,13), and the more we know about the strongholds the more precisely we can target our intercession against them."[31]

The only hope for the wickedness of the city to be turned around is the transforming power of the Gospel! The Church, under the leadership of the Holy Spirit, <u>must</u> take the Gospel back into the City. The Church <u>must</u> believe that the power of the gospel is still able to save, change and transform individuals as well as a whole city.

We must apply what Paul tells us, when he writes. "The weapons of our warfare are not carnal but mighty in God for pulling down strongholds, casting down arguments and every high thing that exalts itself against the knowledge of God., bringing every thought into captivity to the obedience of Christ" (2 Corinthians 10:4-5).

Can any good come out of the city of Cali, Colombia? For years, it had the reputation of being one of the toughest and meanest cities in the world. If God could do something special in such a wicked city, maybe He could do it all over the world in all of the major cities of the world.

John D. Robb, Unreached Peoples Program director for MARC shares a story of what GOD can do even in Cali, Colombia: "Until recently, this

Latin American city was in the grip of the infamous Cali drug cartel. It has been called the largest, richest and best-organized criminal group in history - controlling most forms of government and huge amounts of money and perpetrating the most obscene violence. Anyone who opposed them was simply liquidated. In sheer desperation, the pastors of Cali agreed to meet every week to pray for the city, beginning in January 1995.

In May of that year, the pastor's association hosted an all-night vigil at the civic auditorium, which seats 27,000. They had hoped for a few thousand people would turn out and fill the bottom section. Instead, 30,000 showed up to pray throughout the night! In the words of one organizer, 'The primary purpose of the vigil was to take a stand against the cartels and their unseen spiritual masters. Both have ruling our city and nation for too long. After humbling ourselves to God and one another, we symbolically extended Christ's scepter of authority over Cali- including its bondage over cocaine, violence and corruption'."

The first result of the prayer meeting was that immediately after the prayer meeting the city went one day without murder. This was a newsworthy event in that the average had been multiple homicides per day (There had been fifteen thousand murders during the first six months of 1993 – giving it the highest homicide rate in the world). During the next four months, 900 cartel-linked officers were fired from the police force. Then several intercessors reported dreams in which they saw angels apprehending the leaders of the drug cartel. Within six weeks of these visions, the Colombian government declared all-out war on the drug cartel bosses. By August of that year – only three months after God's revelation to the intercessors – Colombian authorities had captured all seven cartel leaders.

Special prayer meetings continued in the city. Again, dramatic changes followed. Colombian authorities launched an anti-corruption investigation- not only within the government of Cali, but even up to the office of the nation's president.

Since that time, the city of Cali has grown economically with more than 25 percent improvement. Upon seeing the impact of the believers' prayers, the mayor of Cali announced, 'This city needs Jesus Christ to bring peace'."

The churches in Cali have grown tremendously in a 'spiritual explosion'. According to church growth specialist, Peter Wagner, Cali has become a cutting edge city, since its spiritual awakening is spreading to other cities. But a price has been paid in spiritual backlash. In 1996-1997, over 200 pastors in Colombia have been killed by guerillas or paramilitary forces."[32]

GOD did a miracle in Cali, Colombia! If God could do in that wicked city, can He not do in your city? Can He not do something special in every World City?

As John Dawson wrote:

> When I look at my city, the youth
> appear to be as devastated as they
> were in the sixties. This time it
> is crack and gang violence. The
> situation looks hopeless, but God
> is still a God of revival. God still
> comes in mercy to the undeserving
> and the deceived when we intercede
> on their behalf. [33]

QUESTIONS:

1. Are we going to be scared off from the cities because of the symptoms? Ask God to show you which fear you are not trusting him with.

2. Are you going to deal with the REAL ISSUE – SIN? Which one is going laying on your heart?

3. Will you go and share the Cure for Wickedness – JESUS - with the people of the cities?

FOOT NOTES:

1. Roger S. Greenway, "The *Challenge of the Cities*", <u>PERSPECTIVES ON THE WORLD CHRISTIAN MOVEMENT</u>, Ralph D. Winters and Steven C. Hawthorne, editors, Pasadena: William Carey Library, 1999, p. 556.

2. Roger S. Greenway, APOSTLES TO THE CITY: BIBLICAL STRATEGIES FOR URBAN MISSIONS, Grand rapids: Baker Book House, 1978, p. 19.

3. Greenway, Apostles, p. 20.

4. Ray Bakke, <u>A BIBLICAL WORD FOR AN URBAN WORLD</u>, Valley Forge, PA: Board of International Ministries, American Baptist Churches in the U.S.A, 2000, pgs. 2-3.

5. Roger S. Greenway, p. 556.

6. Roger S. Greenway, p. 554.

7. Greenway, p. 555.

8. William M. Frey, *"Population and Immigrants,"* <u>STATE OF METROPOLITAN AMERICA,</u> Washington, D.C.: The Brookings Institute, 2010, p. 66.

9. Brookings, p. 67.

10. Brookings, p. 68.

11. Brookings, p. 65.

12. Greenway, p. 554.

13. Viv Grigg, "The *urban Poor: Who Are They?"* <u>PERSPECTIVIES ON WORLD CHRISTIAN MOVEMENTS</u>, p. 581.

14. Bryant Myers, "What is Poverty?" <u>PERSECTIVES ON WORLD CHRISTIAN MOVEMENT</u>, p. 578.

15. Bryant Myers, p. 579.

16. Elizabeth Kneebone and Emily Garr, "Income and   Poverty," <u>STATE OF METROPOLITN AMERICA</u>, Washington, D.C: The Brooking Institute, 2010, pgs. 132-143.

17. Viv Grigg, p. 584.

18. Viv Grigg, p. 581.

19. "Why Are People Homeless?", National Coalition for the Homeless, June 2006, Washington, D.C., 2006, p. 1.

20. National Coalition for the Homeless, p. 1.

21. National Coalition, p. 5.

22. Arthur Delaney, "*The 10 Worst Places to be Homeless,*" http://www. huffingtonpost.com2009/07/14.

23. Viv Grigg, p. 583.

24. *"Crime in America"* <u>http://www.essortment.com/all/crimeunitedstates rehah</u>.

25. Ibid.

26. Ben Best, *"Death by Murder,"* <u>http://www.benbest.com/lifeext/murder. httl#usa</u>

27. John Dawson, <u>TAKING OUR CITIES FOR GOD: HOWQ TO BREAK SPIRITUAL STRONGHOLDS</u>, Lake May, FL.: Creation House, 1989, p. 49 – 50.

28. Robert C. Linthicum, <u>CITY OF GOD, CITY OF SATAN: A BIBLICAL THEOLOGY OF THE URBAN CHURCH</u>, Grand Rapids: Zondervan Publishing House, 1991, p. 44.

29. Dawson, pgs. 50-51.

30. Peter Wagner, <u>CHURCHES THAT PRAY</u>, Ventura: Regal Books, 1993, p. 23.

31. Peter Wagner, p. 211.

32. John D. Robb, *"Strategic Prayer,"* in <u>PERSPECTIVES</u>, pgs. 149-150.

33. Dawson, p. 54.

CHAPTER FIVE

SO, WHAT MUST THE CHURCH DO?

"The Church faces huge city populations growing still more enormous. Her task is to disciple, baptize, and teach these urban multitudes. It was the urban multitudes that the Lord would have gathered as a hen gathers her brood under her wings; and His Church, indwelt by Him, longs to do the same." Donald McGavran[1]

"Then the word of the Lord came to Jonah, a second time: 'Get up! Go to the great city of Nineveh and preach the message that I tell you.' So Jonah got up and went to Nineveh according to the Lord's command." JONAH 3:1-3

In 1998, I got a phone call from a lady that I had met at a church. She told me that she had a young lady at her home, who needed help. I went to her home. The young lady, Sheri, and her two-year-old daughter, were homeless. She was afraid that Child Protective Services would take the little girl away from her. I suggested going to the Set Free Church's Women's Discipleship Ranch. She agreed. On the way out to the Ranch, I asked her if she had a personal relationship with the Lord Jesus Christ?

She told me a beautiful story. One night she was alone in a motel room. Scared, tired and worn-out she opened the nightstand drawer and pulled out the Gideon Bible. She started reading the book of John. After reading for awhile, she bowed her head and said a prayer asking God to forgive her of all her sins and to come into her life. That was a great testimony and I praised the Lord!

Then she went on to tell the rest of the story. She has been a prostitute, working a corner in the innercity of Pomona. She also said, that she worked the streets right across from a church (When she said that, I was hoping that it was not the church I had pastored in the same city. It was not, but I knew the street she had worked).

She then asked me a haunting question "I have worked that same corner for the past seven years. Why didn't those church people come across the street and tell me about Jesus?"

I did not have a good answer for her. Do you?

Sheri stayed in Set Free Church's discipleship program for eight months and got strong in the Lord. She and her daughter left to start a new and better life for themselves.

GOD told Jonah to go to the "great city" of Nineveh and preach the message of repentance, before it was too late! After going through a whole lot of stuff: trying to go the opposite direction, going through a terrible storm, being thrown overboard into a raging sea, ending up in the belly of a big fish – Jonah finally obeyed.

A quick side bar: Are you as slow about obedience as Jonah? Do you have to, or have you gone through enough stuff yet – to finally obey?

Finally, Jonah did get up and go to Nineveh according to the LORD'S COMMAND (I capitalized those last two words to get our attention.)

According to the *LORD'S COMMAND*: He has called us to *GO*!

Today, GOD is calling His Church to go across the street, around the block, across the country, and around the world to tell people about Jesus before it is too late for hundreds of thousands of people!

The Great Commission is still the marching orders of the 21st Century Church just as well as it was for the First Century Church! Jesus told his disciples:

> Then Jesus came near and said to
> them, 'All authority has been given
> to Me in heaven and earth. Go, there-
> fore, and make disciples of all
> nations, baptizing them in the name
> of the Father and of the Son and
> of the Holy Spirit, teaching them to
> observe everything I have commanded
> you. And remember, I am with you
> always, to the end of the age.
> (Matthew 28: 18-20)

Will you go? It's His *COMMAND*. Or, do you have a good excuse? Will you go to the cities where the populations of the world are clustering together as never before? God has clustered the multitudes into our cities, so that there can one more great ingathering before the Lord comes again. Who will help harvest the great harvest in the World cities?
Will you be one of those who will go you the city?

God's marching orders are before us, "As you are going, make disciples" (Matthew 28:19). The power of the Resurrected Christ is upon us, "But you will receive power when the Holy Spirit has come upon you, and you will be My witnesses in Jerusalem, in all Judea and Samaria, and to the ends of the earth." (Acts 1:8), and God Almighty will be with you always, "And remember, I am with you always, to the end of the ages" (Matthew 28:20).

The masses have come to the major cities of the world and are still coming in great numbers daily. Will we, as God's people, go to the cities and share the love of God with them?

Napoleon was a great military general. He led his French armies to conqueror most of Europe, quickly and effectively. One day the battle was not going well. The army was losing. Napoleon turned to his young trumpet boy and told him to play retreat. The young boy was bewildered and had to admit to the General that he did not know how to blow retreat. He has never had to play retreat before. Napoleon turned to the young boy and said, "Play what you know". The only thing he knew was "charge". So, he played it. The soldiers, hearing the trumpeter play "charge," rallied and won the battle!

I want to be that little trumpet boy, and with all my heart tell you that we must "charge" the spiritual fortresses of our cities. We must "charge" forward as God's Church to "take back" our cities for Christ. We need to claim the promise that Jesus had given His disciples and charge ahead against the gates of Hell: "And I say to you that you are Peter, and upon this rock, I will build my Church; and the gates of Hades will not overpower it" (Matthew 16:18). The Church has allowed the enemy to have his way in the cities of the world for too long.

We must bring the "light" of the World – JESUS - into the City. The Light of the World must be brought back into the "dark corners" of the cities. We must go to the least of the people of the world that get lost in the crowded streets of the cities. We must get the attention of those, who do not even have GOD on their agenda, let alone the church. That is a big job, an almost impossible task – just like it was in the day of the early Church. Did the impossibility of the task overwhelm the early church? Did it make them quit when it got hard? NO!

Samuel Zwemer, pioneer missionary to the Arabs, said it this way: "We have our 'marching orders.' As the Iron Duke (Arthur Wesley, Duke of Wellington) said, and because our Commander-in-Chief is not absent, but with us, the impossible becomes not only practical, but imperative"2

The disciples obeyed Jesus and went to the cities of the World. When they were told to shut up and be quiet about the Good News of Jesus Christ death and resurrection, they could not be quiet: "But, Peter and John answered them, 'Whether it's right in the sight of God, you decide; for we are unable to stop speaking about what we have seen and heard." (Acts 4: 19-20) When they were knocked down, they got up praising the Lord: "After they called in the apostles and had them flogged, they ordered them not to speak in the name of Jesus and released them. Then they went out rejoicing that they were counted worthy to be dishonored on behalf of the name. Every day in the Temple complex, and in various homes, they continued teaching and proclaiming the Good News that the Messiah is Jesus" (Acts 5:40-42). When the Holy Spirit gave them marching orders that didn't make sense, they still obeyed: "An angel of the Lord spoke to Philip: 'Get up and go south to the road that goes down from Jerusalem to Gaza.' So he got up and went." He left a great movement of God in Samaria to go to a deserted road. But, God knew best.

"There was an Ethiopian man" reading the book of Isaiah in his chariot. Philip got up in the chariot and shared, "and Philip proceeded to tell him the Good News about Jesus beginning from that scripture." When they came to water the Ethiopian Eunuch asked him why he should not be baptized. Then Philip told him, "if you believe with all your heart you may.' And he replied, 'I believe that Jesus Christ is the Son of God.' Then Philip baptized him right then and there. After that, the Word of God tells us "when they came out of the water, the Spirit of the Lord carried Philip away, and the eunuch did not see him again." (Acts 6:26-40) When they were chased out of Jerusalem, they saw it as an opportunity to share the Good News in the next city: "Those who had been scattered as a result of the persecution that started because of Stephen made their way as far as Phoenicia, Cyprus, and Antioch speaking the message to no one but Jews. But there were some of them, Cypriot and Cyrenian men, who came to Antioch, speaking the message to the Hellenists, proclaiming the Good News about the Lord Jesus. The Lord's hand was with them, and a large number who believed and turned to the Lord" (Acts 11:19-21).

The Good News changed the World, as the First Century Christians obeyed the command: "As you are going, make disciples."

Will the 21ˢᵗ Century Christian be obedient to the command – "to go" – to go to the Cities of the World and share Jesus? Or, will we continue to make excuses?

Will the church continue to use the same excuses she has used for the past two thousand years? Excuses such as: It is not as easy today, as it was then. We live in a much too sophisticated world for people to listen to the simple Gospel. There are just too many people in too many places for us to get the job done. But wait a minute, we serve the same God as they did right? Hebrews 13: 8 tell us: "Jesus Christ is the same yesterday, today, and forever."

In Acts 2, the Resurrected Christ, who came in power and glory and used 120 discouraged and defeated disciples on the day of Pentecost: "When the day of Pentecost had arrived, they were all together in one place. Suddenly a sound like that of a violent rushing wind came from Heaven, and it filled the whole house where they were staying," and God did something special that day, so that all the people groups of the known world could hear the

Gospel, all in one place. "When this sound occurred, the multitude came together and was confused because each one heard them speaking in his own language" (verses 1, 6). Look at how God had gathered the ethane: " Parthians, Medes, Elamites; those who live in Mesopotamia, in Judea and Cappadocia, Pontus and Asia, Phrygia and Pamphylia, Egypt and the parts of Libya near Cyrene; visitors from Rome, both Jews and proselytes, Cretans and Arabs – we heard them speaking in our own languages, the magnificent acts of God" (verses 8-11). The end result on that powerful day was a great harvest of souls: "So those who accepted his message were baptized, and that day about 3,000 people were added to them" (2:41), and the New Testament Church was started in Jerusalem with all the people of the World, being a part of it. Can He who is King of Kings and Lord of Lords do the same in our time?

In God's providence, He has gathered the nations to the major cities of the world. Can He not use His Church today to bring in a great Harvest before the Lord comes again? YES, HE can! My philosophy of ministry: I am just running to catch up to where God is working. It is time for His people to run to catch up to God working in the cities.

It is time for the Christians to become *STRATEGIC,* as we attempt to *IMPACT* the cities of the World for Christ:

As Jonah, we need to obey God's commands. God has told us to go and "make disciples" (Matthew 28:19). As we go, we must be willing to *pour* our lives into the city where God has called us!

1. INCARNATIONAL LIVING. We <u>must</u> go to the cities and pour our lives into the people lives. As Jude Tiersma writes, "It is significant because the Gospel does not lie in a vacuum but must be incarnated, 'fleshed out' anew in each context. We know that when God had a message, he sent a messenger, his own son. Likewise, we are privileged and honored to be God's messengers. God's ambassadors."[3]

As we become neighbors in a neighborhood and began to share our lives, we discover the joys and treasures of life hidden in neighborhoods forgotten by most of the world. We can see the joy of the little child that gets a new pair of shoes, a teenage girl as she gets some makeup, and parents who have enough food on the table – for the first time in a long time. But, as we get immersed in life and open our hearts, we also see the tremendous suffering, inhumanity, and evil that seems to surround us on all sides. We watch as the police take away that delinquent teenager, who got caught stealing from the local store again. We watch as HIV destroys a young girl's health. We attend one more funeral of an innocent child killed by another gang drive-by. We feel so helpless. We can feel so overwhelmed, and the despair around us begins to take over within us.

If we are not careful in the urban world, we can allow the despair of multiple situations control us more than the Resurrected Christ living in us. That is when we go back to the word of God. John 5:19 reads: "I tell you the truth, the Son can do nothing by himself; he can only do what he sees the Father doing, because whatever the Father does the Son also does." Jude Tiersma says, "The same is true of us urban workers; we must also participate in what God is doing. We do not bring God into the city. God is already there. He invites us to join him in his activity. In humility, we must realize that we will never have all the answers. We cannot meet all the needs. We are not the answer. The ministry belongs to God, not to us." [4]

Viv Grigg shares his own experience as he spent the first night in the slums of Manila: "As I prayed into the dark hours of the first night in Tatalon, I wondered what the next steps would be. *How do you bring a whole city to the light? How can you rescue three million squatters and slum dwellers?*"

He then went on to say, "Within the inner recesses of my spirit God seemed to be speaking – directly, personally:

> Carry my cross. It is an instrument
> of death. You must die to yourself
> in order to be a servant of this people.
>
> For unless a grain of wheat falls into
> the ground and dies, it cannot bear
> fruit. If it dies, it bears much
> fruit. This cross commands
> absolute authority over all people,
> all history, and all cultures.

105

> Preach the Cross! In it is the salvation
> of this people: from drunkenness
> and despair, from broken families
> and oppression, from poverty
> and desolation. In it alone is their
> hope.
>
> Remember, it is a rugged cross.
> Do not return to a tinsel cross.
> Take up my cross. Take up my
> cross and follow in my footsteps,
> for I too choose poverty.[5]

We must love people like Jesus did – laying down His life for us. Loving us so much that: "But God proves His own love for us in that while we were still sinners Christ died for us. Much more then, since we have now been declared righteous by his blood, we will be saved through Him from wrath. For if, while we were enemies, we were reconciled to God through the death of His Son, then how much more, having been reconciled, will we be saved by His life!"(Romans 5: 8-10)

A simple definition and challenge for incarnational living is "To follow Jesus in his compassion and love. This involves the being of the person involved in ministry, not just the doing of Missional tasks."[6]

Let's be honest – great advertising campaigns on television, or great newspaper ads, or great Billboard advertisements scattered throughout the city will not impact our cities for Christ. Impersonal, uncaring methodology will never impact the cities for Christ. People are scattered throughout the major cities of the world that are lonely, forgotten and in great need of someone who cares about them as a human being. They do not need to be depersonalized by a program or methodology that does not care about them as human beings.

E.M. Bounds hits the nail on the head when he writes, "What the Church needs today is not more machinery or better, new organizations or more and novel methods, but men whom the Holy Ghost can use. Men of prayer, men mighty in prayer. The Holy Ghost does not flow through methods, but through men. He does not come on machinery, but on men. He does not anoint plans, but men – men of prayer."[7]

Today, GOD is calling us to the cities to LOVE people just like He loved us. Jesus set the example for us when He gave up heaven and came to earth just to show us God's love. Jesus told the crowds, "If you have seen me, you have seen the Father", and "The Father and I are One." Therefore, Jesus showed God's great love by coming to earth and walking among mankind, healing and performing miracles as no one had ever done. He taught as no one had ever taught. He loved and cared for the hurting and broken people of this world. That is why the religious people critized him, because, "He was a friend of sinners and tax collectors." That is why they called him a "wine bibber," because he loved those who were living in sin.

Thomas and Elizabeth Brewster, wrote, "The missionary's task thus parallels the model established by Jesus who left heaven, where he belonged, and became a belonger with humankind in order to draw people into a belonging relationship with God." They went on to say, " A missionary is one who goes into the world to give people an opportunity to belong to God's family. The missionary goes because he or she is a belonger in the most meaningful of relationships. His or her life should proclaim, ' I belong to Jesus who has given me a new kind of life. By my becoming a belonger here with you, God is inviting you through me to belong to him'."[8]

If the church is going to impact the cities, the Christians must plant their lives and ministry in the cities. We must plant our lives among the hurting and broken and love them just like they are and just where they are – so we can point them to JESUS. William Pannell wrote, "The challenge to empower the poor begins with presence."[9] And as John Perkins said, "The importance of our physical presence in these communities cannot be overstated, whether it means moving to them for the first time, coming back, or just staying put."[10]

Eighteen years ago, God, in His grace, called me out of a traditional pastorate to go minister to the multi-housing complexes in Pomona, an inner city suburb of Los Angeles. In His grace, He led me to the toughest apartment complex in the city (I did not know that at the time). I started with prayer walks, then we moved to children clubs and then to Bible studies. Every week we knocked on every apartment's door to tell them that God loves them and to see how we could help them. Many times little kids would run up to me and ask me if I was going to be their daddy this week, as their mothers would have a string of different men come through their lives. I trained a young man and he took the ministry to further levels of ministry. Gang members and drug dealers threatened him many times because they were "losing" money as people were coming to Christ. The police told him: "some thing was different. There use to be a shooting a week in the complex. Now it is a safer place to live." It was the presence of Jesus in people who just took time to live among them and love them, just like Jesus would do!

People are watching and waiting for God's people to show them that Christianity really works in everyday living. They want to know that you really live what you believe – that your walk and talk is real.

Are you living an incarnational life, the life of Jesus in you among the people of your city?

Jeremiah told the people, who were in Exile in Babylon:

> Seek the welfare of the city
> I have deported you to. Pray
> to the Lord on its behalf, for
> when it has prosperity, you will
> prosper. (29:7-9).

They were asked to seek *peace* not for Jerusalem, the "city of God," but Babylon, "the city of Satan."

This was extremely hard for the Israelites because Babylon represented total evil. In the Israelite culture, Babylon was a virtual synonym for depravity. GOD asked them to "pray" for the city of wickedness. In Genesis 11:1-9 the Tower of Babel (the Hebrew form of the name Babylon) is he symbol of the place of the "confusion of the language," where the unity of the world is shattered. It is also a place where the people demonstrate total rebellion. *Throughout* Scripture Babylon is pictured as evil (2 Kings 20:12-19; 24:10-25; 24:10 -25:30; Isaiah 13-14; 47-48; Jeremiah 25:8-14; Acts 7:43). It was so hard for the Jews to pray for Babylon. But God placed them there – and one of their tasks was to pray.

It was so hard for Jonah to pray for the city of Nineveh, because it represented evil to him. They performed evil all over the world. Why should he go to Nineveh and pray over it, and share God's love with them? The same reason God told the Jews to pray for the *peace* of Babylon. Because God loves them!

Today – the same struggle is found in most churches. Why should we pray for the cities? All we see is wickedness and depravity and sin. All we see is people who are in rebellion to God. Why should we? Because GOD told us to PRAY!

"According to His *COMMAND:* " PRAY without ceasing." (I Thessalonians 5:17)

2.   PRAYER <u>MUST</u> be our TOP PRIORITY.

PRAYER is where we meet with God, hear His heartbeat, and get totally in tune with His Spirit. Prayer is where we come to a place of *obedience.* Prayer is a place of *surrender.* Prayer is a place that we need to learn to *rest* in. As L.R. Scarborough wrote, "Prayer is the Christian's most glorious privilege, most enlarging opportunity, and most essential obligation; for it opens the door to communication with God, makes easier his access to men, and is the surest way to bring God and men together in saving and keeping relationship. The prayer of Abraham, Jacob, Moses, Nehemiah, and Daniel, marked turning points in the history of nations. The kingdom of heaven swings on the pivot of Christ's and Paul's prayers. Jesus, the Son of God, and Paul his greatest apostle, had well developed prayer habits. They allowed no intrusions into their prayer life and no substitutions for their supplications. Prayer as essential to their spiritual ongoing as well food to their spiritual ongoing as was food to their physical wellbeing."[12]

Victory is won in prayer! We need to understand that the battle is not against people, places, governments or organizations. The battle is in Heavenly places. Paul challenged the Christians at Ephesus when he wrote,

> For our struggle is not against
> flesh and blood, but against rulers,
> against the authorities, against the
> powers of this dark world and against
> the spiritual forces of evil in he
> heavenly realms. (Ephesians 6:12)

PRAYER does not change God, it changes us. When we get serious about prayer, we have to get in tune with God. He tells us: " This is the confidence that have in approaching God: that if we ask anything according to his will, he hears us- whatever we ask – we know that we have what we asked of him." (I John 5:15) Thus our main responsibility in prayer is to catch up with God and to "Delight yourself in the Lord and he will give you the desires of your heart." (Psalm 37:6) As we delight ourselves in the Lord our desires change to be like his desires, and we do not pray selfishly, but according to his perfect will. Thus, victory is won in prayer – over discouragements, doubts, fears, and the devil. What a joy to seek his face and fellowship with our Heavenly Father, knowing that He cares for the hurting, lonely people of our cities! LET US PRAY!

When we engulf our lives in the city – observing, caring and loving people we can become overwhelmed. The hurts of the "soul" of the city can bring much pain to those who passionately care about the people of the city. Many times, as I pray over the city of Los Angeles I am overwhelmed with the *lostness* of the people. As I drive through street after street, the words of the Lord Jesus comes to my heart:

> Jesus went through all the
> towns and villages, teaching
> in the synagogues, preaching
> the good news of the kingdom and
> healing every disease and sickness.
> When he saw the crowds, he had
> compassion on them because they
> were harassed and helpless like
> sheep without a shepherd. Then
> He said to his disciples, 'The
> harvest is plentiful but the
> workers are few. Ask the Lord of
> the harvest therefore, to send
> out workers into the harvest field.
> (Matthew 9: 35-37)

As the Church of God looks at the major cities of the World with the same eyes as Jesus, may the Church PRAY! The praying that I am talking about is not "now I lay me down to sleep" kind of praying. It is not "here are all my needs Lord, go get them for me". The kind of prayer that I am talking about is STRATEGIC PRAYING!

Strategic praying must consist of:

A. PRAYING FOR THE "SOUL" OF THE CITY.

GOD has a Divine purpose for each city of the World – and it is not just to house a bunch of people. Sin and rebellion has destroyed or limited the purpose for many of the cities of the world. The Church needs to pray for God's purpose for our city to be fulfilled. A good example is the tragic circumstances of Jerusalem. Mount Zion is ordained by God to be a city of peace and praise. Instead, it has become a place of conflict where God's character is continuously misrepresented through religious controversy. Psalm 48 embodies the appreciate of God's people for Jerusalem and shows what care God takes in locating our cities:

> Great is the Lord, and greatly to be praised.
> In the city of our God,
> In His holy mountain.
> Beautiful in elevation,
> The joy of the whole earth,
> In Mount Zion on the sides of the north,
> The city of the great King (Psalm 48:1-2).

The Lord has a plan for each of our cities. Sin of the people has messed that plan up. The Sovereign Lord wants to use his Church to fulfill that eternal plan!

As I look at Los Angeles, the city I live in, I can see that there is a wonderful Master Plan for it. John Dawson writes about it, "When I look at my own city, Los Angeles, I have to hold two truths in tension. On one hand, it is the technological tower of Babel, polluting the world with is communications and entertainment industry. On the other hand, it is a city with the gift of communications. Los Angeles is a city blessed by God with certain resources that can either be perverted or converted.

Even the name of the city speaks of its destiny. Los Angeles is Spanish for the "The Angeles". *Angelos* in Greek means "Messenger." God wants LA to be a messenger, communicating the good news in the midst of an end time harvest.

Indeed, this plan of God has already enjoyed success several times in history: in 1906 through the Azusa Street revival; in 1949 through the evangelistic renewal leading to the birth of such groups as Campus Crusade for Christ and the launching of the Billy Graham crusades as a national ministry; in 1972 with the beginning of the Jesus movement.

Today the city is torn by violence, and it pumps pornography into the minds of millions. However, L.A. is also filled with dynamic Christian ministries reaching the whole world. The church is not asleep. We are expecting God to demonstrate His mighty power in our city." Dawson closes with this statement, "God is always up to something. What is He planning for your city?"[12]

The enemy attempts to influence the "soul" of the cities through the institutions within the cities. We need to understand that the city is a cluster of overlapping institutions. All institutions have a servant function. The army, the school, the hospital, the national and city government are all there for good reasons – to serve and assist the people living in the city. The enemy has stolen the purpose of the institutions and is so doing corrupting the "soul" of the city. John Dawson says, " Satan seeks to rule by influencing these institutions, especially through the church, arts and entertainment, and commerce. He seeks not only to demonize the atmosphere of these institutions but to mark them with his own characteristics, to make them into an extension of his kingdom."[13]

The Church needs to pray for the "soul" of our cities to be revived and a great break through come in our cities. In so many places and societies the "soul" of the city has been crushed by sin, decay and corruption. Prayer is the only hope for our cities.

B.   PRAY FOR THE SOULS OF THE PEOPLE.

The church needs to get serious about praying specifically and intentionally for the precious souls of the people. God wants to answer our prayers for the salvation of precious souls.

When I was a little boy, I didn't like to eat peas. My mother always tried to guilt me into eating them, by saying, "Remember all the starving children in China. They would love to eat those peas." I always wanted to say, "Give me one name of a hungry Chinese kid and I will send him my peas." If I had said that aloud I know I would have been punished, so I kept my mouth shut, but I was thinking it. Yes, we can pray, "Save all the lost people of China', but it is more effective if we pray for people by name.

The last great revival that swept across all of America was the Prayer revival of 1857-1858. It was a movement of prayer. There was no preaching involved, no personalities to control or programs to promote. They just prayed – prayed for the souls of their friends, relatives and neighbors. And God heard their prayers and sent a real spiritual awaking. Nate Krupp gives us an overview of this prayer movement:

"The Dutch Reform Church was considering closing their eighty-year-old church at Fulton and William Street in downtown New York City, since most of their original families had moved away, and the neighborhood was now mostly made up of transient immigrants and laborers. They decided to make one last effort. They hired Jeremiah C. Lamphier, a 49-year-old merchant with no experience in church work, at $1,000 a year, to knock on doors in the neighborhood and see what he could do. He knocked on doors for three months. A few families came, but it was slow wearying, discouraging work. Then he got the idea of opening a room in the church building once a week, at noontime, for those businessmen who might like to spend a few minutes in prayer. The small sign he put outside read, 'Prayer meeting from 12 to 1 o'clock, Stop for 5, 10, 20 minutes or the whole hour as your time permits.' On the first Wednesday noon, September 23, 1857, only Lamphier was there to 12:30. But before the hour was over, there were six. On the next Wednesday there were twenty. During the third week, a financial crisis and panic began at Wall Street - banks failed, business closed, the railroads went into bankruptcy. Man's extremity was God's opportunity! There were forty at the Wednesday noon prayer meeting that week, and they decided to start meeting daily in a larger room. In a short time there were 3,000 attending, and they were using the entire building. Within six months 10,000 businessmen (out of a population of 800,000) were gathering daily in many places throughout New York City for prayer.

From Maine to California, Christians gathered to pray for revival. In many towns, church bells summoned the people to prayer meeting morning, noon and night. In Chicago (a city of 100,000) two thousand men met at noon for prayer. In Albany, New York, the state legislators started their own early morning prayer meeting.

Christians prayed for revival, and revival came! A mighty outpouring of God's Spirit swept the nation. Every major denomination was awakened. Over one million people were converted to Christ out of a national population of thirty million. There were several New England towns where not a single unconverted adult could be found. The revival was born in prayer, was interdenominational, and was essentially a layman's movement. The Awakening occurred mainly during the two years of 1858 and 1859, but the effects were still being felt in the 1860's. By the end of the Civil War (1861-1865), one-third of the Confederate Army was confessing Christians."[14]

Could this happen in New York City again? YES! Could it happen in every major city in the world? YES! Could God bring a sweeping victory in ALL of the cities of the World? YES!

So, we need to get serious about prayer. Tom Eliff touches us where we are weak and vulnerable - in our prayer life - when he writes these words; "Why has a practice so passionately pursued by Jesus become so ignored by those who call Him Lord? Where are the believers who have our Lord's passion for praying? Of all the disciplines of the Christian life, it is perhaps the most neglected."[15]

The Church needs to get serious about praying – praying for precious souls. We need to remember God's heart is to "save" the cities and the souls of precious souls.

James 5:16-18 challenges to get serious about praying:

> Therefore confess your sins to
> each other and pray for each
> other so that you may be healed.
> The prayer of a righteous man is
> powerful and effective. Elijah
> was a man just like us. He prayed
> earnestly that it would not rain
> and it did not rain for three and
> half years. Again he prayed, and
> the heavens gave rain, and the
> Earth produced it crops.

CAUTION: As you, as an individual or as a Church starts praying over a geographical area or a certain people group, GOD will lay a burden for their souls upon your heart. God will give a burden that you cannot get away from and must do something about it.

C. STRATEGIC PRAYING FOR THE CITIES.

God's COMMAND is "Therefore, pray to the Lord of the harvest."(Matthew 9:35-38. Therefore, we need to get serious about praying to the Lord of the Harvest. We need to get serious by:

1. PRAYING FOR PEOPLE GROUPS and GEOGRAPHIC AREAS.

When you look at a city of 5 to 20 million people how do you start to pray? How do you get a handle on the vast *lostness* of the city? When you look at the multitudes, the large number of various people groups, the multiple language groups, vast number of religions and worldviews, how do you pray?

The old saying, "How do you eat an elephant? One bite at a time," fits real well. We need to break down our cities into a *strategic* plan or grid to put prayer into practice. As the Los Angeles Southern Baptist Association, under the leadership of Dr. Mark Hammond, looked at the vastness of the people in the city they made a plan to break it into geographic zones. As the leaders looked at the city, there were some natural and/or man-made barriers, that helped break up the city into geographical zones. They developed seven geographical zones so that they could get a "handle" on the *lostness* of Los Angeles.

Each of the city missionaries need to look at the maps of their designated geographic areas and answer these questions:

a. Are there some true natural barriers in our city? These would consist of rivers, hills, lakes, and parks, etc. Do these natural barriers divide a section of the city off to itself?

b. Are there man-made barriers in our city? These would be historical sites such as parks, cemeteries, and museums. There would also be freeways, airports, major train depots, and business areas verses commercial.

And, of course, there would be city limits of the various communities that are engulfed by the major city.

c. Are there some unwritten" barriers? These are barriers that are not so much physical as they are psychological. For example, the young professionals do not live in the "old downtown." The up and outers live in a certain part of the city, while the blue-collar workers live in another part of the city. Today, many of those psychological type barriers have been broken down. But they are still very much real and alive in many cities where caste is still a reality.

Another reality in the large Mega-cities is, even if you break then down into zones or districts, we are still talking about millions of people. So the struggle point is, "How small a bite do we need to break the city down into?"

This brings us to a reality check. John Dawson wrote in 1989, "When I look at the cities in the United States, I see the Christians as a group of bewildered survivors going about their daily business with little sense of unifying purpose."[16] And the condition of the Church world has not changed much up to today. We need to become more united in PRAYER for the Cities!

Once the city has been broken down into some kind of functional system, the churches within each zone must get involved.

They need to get involved in PRAYER through Concerts of Prayer. There is a three-fold purpose for this combined prayer services.

(1) The first one is that the churches will combine together as God's people in prayer. There must be a *Unity in prayer.* "How can two walk together unless they agree" (Amos 3:3). In today's church-world, there will never be a total agreement on all theological issues, but we can agree on the importance of prayer and that our God answers the prayers of His people. And, we can PRAY together in love for the Lord and for the Lost of our cities.

(2) A true Concert of Prayer is for the Church. As we humble ourselves together in prayer at the foot of the Cross - we are putting ourselves in a

place where God can do a deeper work in us. The first work that He must do is a deep cleansing. We, as a church, needs to repent of neglect, of disobedience, and of selfish living when it comes to the Great Commission. Then God can call out those who need to go to the cities of the World. Isn't that how the early missionary movement was started? " In the local church at Antioch there were prophets and teachers: Barnabas, Simeon who was called Niger, Lucius the Cyrenian, Manaen, a close friend of Herod the tetrarch, and Saul. As they were ministering to the Lord and fasting, the Holy Spirit said, 'Set apart for Me Barnabas and Saul for the work that I have called them to. Then, after they had fasted, prayed, and laid hand on them, they sent them off" (Acts 13:1-3).

(3) In prayer, we can pray for the salvation of our cities, our neighbors, our friends and relatives, asking God to fulfill His promise when He says in 2 Peter 3:9, " The Lord does not delay His promise, as some understand delay, bur is patient with you, not willing to wanting any to perish, but all to come to repentance."

Getting a little closer to the *lostness* in the cities, there must be a strategy of PRAYER WALKS. The church needs to get outside the walls of the church buildings and out on the streets in order to be able to pray for the lost of their community.

PRAYER WALKING as defined by Steve Hawthorne is, "Praying on site with insight…praying in the very places in which you expect your prayers to be answered." Peter Wagner writes, "The idea of praying on site brings the prayer-ers into the community. It helps complement 'Every place that the sole of your foot will tread upon, I have given you' (Joshua 1:3). The idea of walking brings us into the closest contact with those in the community for whom we are praying."[17]

PRAYER WALKING is simply: taking a section of the community – I suggest four city blocks and walk and pray. Prayer walking is learning to be sensitive to the leading of the Spirit of God, and praying for God to break down "strong-hold' of unbelief, doubt, pride and indifference in the homes in that four block section of the city. Prayer walking can be done as an individual, as a family, as a group from the church. We need to go and pray, expecting God to do something special in the community.

About ten years ago, Rick Curtis, who is now the Director of the High Desert Baptist Association, was planting a church in a new housing development in Palmdale, CA. As I met with them I encouraged them to do prayer walking first before they did anything else. He and his wife and two small children started praying over the four blocks closest to their house. After two weeks of doing the prayer walks they then knocked on the doors and asked people how they could pray for them. Well, as they did that they found a family two doors down from them that were interested in ministry. The husband said that, "God had told me to move to Palmdale a year ago, because I was going to help start a church." He became Rick's assistant pastor. After conducting home Bible studies, they started Sunday services in a local school. Things were slow at the beginning. Then about one month after they started, all of a sudden, about 8 to 10 families started attending the church. Some of the families said that they were driving by the school and they felt compelled to drive into the parking lot and come to church. When I asked Rick, where did all the people come from, he realized that they were all living within that four city block radius that he and his family had prayed over in the beginning.

We need to realize that GOD *initiated* prayer, *hears* our prayers, and *answers* our prayers. We need to remember that God commanded us to PRAY! " Pray without ceasing!"(I Thessalonians 5:17). Let us obey Him!

2. EVAGELISM <u>must</u> be our HEARTBEAT as we go to the cities.

> "But you will receive power when
> the Holy Spirit comes upon you,
> and you will be My witness in
> Jerusalem, in all Judea and
> Samaria, and to the ends of
> the earth (Acts 1:8).

David Garrison writes, "We have yet to see a Church planting movement emerge where evangelism is rare or absent. Every church planting movement is accompanied by abundant sowing of the Gospel. The law of the harvest applies well: 'If you sow abundantly you will also reap abundantly.' In Church planting movements, hundred and even thousands of individuals are hearing the claims of Jesus Christ has on their lives."[18]

In the cities of the world, this is what must be done! Evangelism <u>must</u> be at the heartbeat of all that we do as Christians.

Michael Green give us a crisp definition of evangelism when he writes, " Evangelism in the strict sense is proclaiming the good news of Christ to men and women with a view to their conversion to Christ and incorporation into His church."[19]

The final declaration of the 1966 World Congress on Evangelism in Berlin declares, "Evangelism is the proclamation of the Gospel of the crucified and risen Christ, the only Redeemer of men, according to Scriptures, with the purpose of persuading condemned and lost sinners to put their trust in God by receiving and accepting Christ as Savior through the power of the Holy Spirit, and to serve Christ as Lord in looking toward the day of his coming glory."[20]

This is exactly what our Lord Jesus Christ wants us to do! GOD told Jonah to go to that great city Nineveh and preach against it! He did and the people repented and turned to God. He wants the same thing to happen today in every city in the World!

The early Church got the commission, as Peter Wagner writes, "The main purpose of the incarnation was summarized by our Lord when He said, 'For the Son of Man is come to seek and to save that which is lost' (Luke 19:10). He purposes to find the lost and provide salvation for them. In order to accomplish this, in His grace, He has elected to use His people, Christian men and women. Before He left the earth, Jesus made sure His follower had clear instructions as to what His will was for them."[21]

These instructions were, "Go into all the world and preach the gospel to all creation" (Mark 16:15). Peter Wagner writes, "The Great Commission commands Christians of 'all nations.' This clearly implies every believer or (born-again) Christians of 'all nations.' This clearly implies that it is God's will that multitudes of men and women become true disciples of His Son."[22]

In obedience to the Heavenly Father, that is exactly what the early Church did! They started on the day of Pentecost! We read in Acts 2 of Peter standing up before the crowd in the Temple and declaring, "Be saved from this perverse generation! So that those who received his word was baptized and that day there were added about three thousand souls." Later we read, "Day by day continuing with one mind in the Temple, and breaking bread from house to house, they were taking their meals together with gladness and sincerity of heart, praising God and having favor with all the people. And the Lord was adding to their number day by day those who were being saved." (2:40-1; 46-47)

When the disciples were threatened and even beaten for preaching the Good News, they did not quit. They prayed, and something special happened. In Acts 4 and 5, we read, "And when they had prayed, the place where they gathered was shaken, and they were all filled with the Holy Spirit and began to speak the word of God with boldness." The result was that, "And all the more believers in the Lord, multitudes of men and women, were constantly added to their number." (4:31; 5:14)

The *saturation* of Jerusalem with the Gospel was a constant thing. "The word of the Lord kept on spreading; and the number of the disciples continued to increase greatly in Jerusalem, and a great many of the priests became obedient to the faith." (Acts 6:7)

As persecution chased the believers out of Jerusalem, the believers did not stop sharing the gospel. It just meant that wherever they went they continued to *saturate* that community with the Good News. "So then those who were scattered because of the persecution that occurred in connection with Stephen made their way to Phoenicia and Cypress and Antioch, speaking the word to no one except to Jews alone. But there were some of them, men of Cyprus and Cyrene, who came to Antioch and began speaking to the Greeks also, preaching the Lord Jesus. And the hand of the Lord was with them, and a large number who believed turned to the Lord. The news about them reached the ears of the church in Jerusalem, and they sent Barnabas off to Antioch. Then when he arrived and witnessed the grace of God, he rejoiced and began to encourage them all with resolute heart to remain true to the Lord; for he was a good man, and full of the Holy Spirit and of faith. And considerable numbers were brought to the Lord. And he left for Tarsus to look for Saul; and when he found him, he brought him to Antioch. And for an entire year they met with the church and taught considerable numbers; and the disciples were first called Christians in Antioch." (Acts11:19-26)

I can imagine that those early Christians, as they went about their daily lives, would put their arm around anyone who would listen and say, "Let me tell you about the greatest thing that ever happened to me," or "Let me tell you about the greatest man who ever lived, His name is JESUS!" The town of Antioch was *saturated* with the Good news of Jesus Christ!

Paul continued this practice in his three missionary trips. After Paul spent two years in Ephesus, it could be said of his efforts there, "This took place for two years, so that all who lived in Asia heard the word of the Lord, both Jews and Gentiles" (Acts 19:10). Paul summed up the end results of his missionary efforts when he wrote to the Roman Christians these words: "For I will not presume to speak of anything except what Christ has accomplished through me, resulting in the obedience of the Gentiles by word and deed, in the power of signs and wonders, in the power of the Spirit; so that from Jerusalem and round about as far as Illyricum. I have fully preached the gospel of Christ." But, that was not enough for him, as he goes on to write, "And thus I aspired to preach the Gospel, not where Christ was already named, so that I would not build on another man's foundation." (Romans 15:18-20)

How did the early Church impact the World of their day? They went to the cities and *saturated* the cities with the Good News of Jesus Christ. They told everyone that Jesus loves them and then they showed them by their actions!

Why was the early Christians so driven? Why was Paul so driven? Because they understood the call of God on their lives. As L.R. Scarborough so pointedly writes, "Every Christian is called in the hour of salvation to witness for Jesus Christ. Nothing in heaven or earth can excuse him from it. God gives no furloughs from this heaven-born obligation. Not ignorance, or poverty, or environment, or difficulties of any kind – nothing can exempt or excuse any child of God from its pressing daily importance." He goes on to write, "The appeal comes from above. God calls with a Fatherly love, Christ pleads with a redeemer's compassion, and the Holy Spirit urges with a constant intercessory insistence. The Bible repeatedly presses this universal duty upon us. To refuse to witness of a saving gospel to a lost world day by day is nothing short of high treason, spiritual rebellion, and inexcusable disobedience to God's holy commands."[22]

Today, the same Command and Commission - to go to the World, to go to the Cities are before God's Church. How are we going to *impact* the Cities? I believe that we must go back to New Testament methods of evangelism – *saturation evangelism!*

We need to understand the concept of *SATURATION* EVANGELSIM:

The AIM of *saturation* evangelism is to present the Gospel in spoken and written form to every people of the land, to every stratum of society, to every home and individual, overlooking no area and no community. We should attempt to share the Good News to everyone in every place as we fulfill the command of Christ that He declares in Mark 16:15 "Go into all the world and preach the Gospel to all creation."

The MEANS is for every Christian to be used of God to share the Good News any time, wherever they are, and with whoever is present. As George Peters writes, "The church is not to be thought of as the only place for evangelism. The time for evangelism is not only when the church holds an evangelistic campaign. Saturation evangelism seeks to mobilize and train every believer available to become an active and effective evangelizer for Christ."[23]

The TIMING of *saturation* evangelism lies in the coordination of all evangelistic efforts, methods and opportunities so that the maximum effect can be achieved among a "people group" and/or geographical section of the city.

The SCOPE is as large as we will let it be. George Peters explains it, "The scope of *saturation* evangelism includes as many churches, missions, and denominations as will cooperate in an evangelical and evangelistic program in order to express the unity of the body of Christ, strengthen the cause of evangelism, involve and train as many believers as make themselves available, and create the greatest possible impact upon the churches and communities."[24]

In 1996, I started working with Set Free Church of Yucaipa, CA. where Willie Dalgity was pastor. Pastor Willie had grown up in church, walked away from Church as a teenager, and at 32 years of age, God got a hold of his heart. God set his heart on fire. As a deacon at the local church, God called him to minister to the poor, homeless, drug addicts, ex-cons, and bikers. He started ministering to them and soon there was a church of hard core Christians. After eighteen years, the church now averages about 400 in attendance, runs four Discipleship ranches for people coming off the streets and out of addictions, does outreaches in the cities every week and has trained up and sent out Church planters all over America. I helped them with their first church start in San Bernardino, CA, an inner city suburb of Los Angeles. They have seen 15,000 to 20,000 conversions to Christ! They are willing to go to the tough parts of the cities in Southern California. I have walked along side them as they have planted churches. They have developed a New Testament process of starting churches:

A. SATURATE an area with PRAYER:

Six months before Set Free starts to do evangelism in a city, they have some people who PRAY for that area. Their prayer process is:

(1) They will gather a prayer team and start praying weekly for the city that God has lain upon their hearts.

(2) They will start doing PRAYER WALKS throughout a distinct part of the city – block by block.

(3) They will then start knocking on doors of the community and ask, "How can I pray for you and your family?"

PRAYER will break down the "strong holds" of unbelief and indifference in the inner cities.

B. SATURATE an area with OUTREACH events.

As they have the prayer ministry working, they will start having weekly "outreach" projects in the area where they are praying. They will send out a "flyer crew" into the area before the outreach. At the outreach they will set up the band, play loud music, gather a crowd, give out hot dogs and soft drinks, and share testimonies and give a short Gospel message and people will get saved. Now, when the homeless person gets saved, they do not leave them there. They take them "home" with them. They take them to the Discipleship ranch, so they can get dried out, discipled and strengthened in the Lord.

This process will operate every Friday or Saturday for six months as they *saturate* the area with the Good News.

Notice, I did not say that they did a publicity blitz or an advertising campaign. In the inner city of our world, personal and outreach evangelism is needed!

C. SATURATE an area with SERVANT MINISTRY.

This is what I call a "ministry based" Church start. They will have "contact points" where they can give food away every week and sometimes everyday. They will give clothes away and do counseling of the homeless, the abused and battered everyday. If someone needs a place to say at 2:00 AM because the husband came home drunk and beat the wife and kids, they will have a place for them. Whatever the "felt need", they will be there to meet it. Simply put, they will *saturate* a community with LOVE. They are there to meet their "felt needs," so that they can tell them about their greatest need – JESUS!

D. *SATURATION EVANGELSIM* is a COOPERATIVE EFFORT.

When one of the Set Free Churches are ready to launch out into another community all the Set Free churches will combine their efforts into the task of *saturating* that area and starting a Church.

The Set Free Churches in Southern California have successfully applied these principles to *saturating* an area for Christ. They have planted over sixty churches in California and in ten other States.

SATURATION EVANGELSIM is the best way to reach a new city or part of a city for Christ. We need to think strategically where the "ripe" harvest of souls are and then saturate with prayer, ministry and evangelism!

3. CHURCH PLANTING <u>MUST</u> be a "natural" result of our *saturation* activities.

Missiologist have declared Matthew 28:18-20 as the *Church planting* Commission. As you GO and reach people for Christ, as you disciple them and baptize them – what do you have? A New Testament church!

If the church is going to *impact* the great cities of the World the Church needs to start churches. As I have ministered in church planting all these years and as I have watched how the world around has drastically changed – physically, morally, and spiritually I <u>must</u> challenge the Church to do MORE than it has dome or is doing.

I have come to conclude that ADDITION is good, but MULTIPLICATION is better! If we continue to just start one church at a time, we will never reach our world for Christ. For example, just in Los Angeles County with 15 Million people we need 10,000 more churches right now – just to get a handle on the *lostness* of the Los Angeles basin. Tomorrow, we will need more!

The other reality in the major cities is that in some of the largest cities in the world the name of JESUS has not even been declared!

Three reasons for the starting of new churches in the cities are:

(a) The City is so LARGE that ONE church cannot minister to the needs of everyone. In hamlets and villages one or two churches are enough to serve the community and everyone knows who is Christian and who is not. In the city, a great many congregations are needed to reach all people.24

(b) The DIVERSITY of modern cities. City churches tend to serve their own kind of people. That is called the *homogeneous* principle. Within a short distance in a city there can be several languages spoken, more than one type of life-style exhibited and even some affinitive groups scattered into the mix. Everyone in the major cities needs to be able to hear the Gospel in their "heart" language. That is why multiple styles and types of churches need to be started. The doctrine will never change, but the methodology must be flexible to minister to everyone in the city.

In downtown Los Angeles there will be a Spanish speaking church in a store front on the corner, a traditional African-American Church with a large facility in the middle of the block, and a Set Free type church on the other corner to minister to the homeless and drug addicts. A Korean speaking church and a Christian school also use the large church facility on Sunday afternoons and during the week. Each of the various churches will preach the Good News of Jesus Christ, but each will do that in a style that relates to the people "just like them." And the kingdom of God will be increased and grow in the city!

(c)   The RAPID GROWTH of the cities is another reason to start more churches. The result is a great neglect of entire areas of the city. "Whole shanty towns and suburbs rise with not a church in them – and the surrounding churches are totally unaware of this." [25]

The Church has a mandate from GOD to "Go and make disciples, baptizing them in the Name of the father, Son and the Holy Spirit. And teaching them everything that I have taught you, and I will be with you even until the end of the ages." (Matthew 38:19 – 20) As we GO to the cities, to do that the best way to fulfill the Great Commission is by starting Churches.

In 1989, Tim Keller started Redeemer Presbyterian Church in New York City, with fifteen Christians meeting weekly for prayer. Tim Keller and his church soon learned the importance of church planting. He told Warren Bird in an interview that, "The only way to increase the number and percentage of Christians in a city is to plant thousands of new churches." He went on to say, "the only way to change the culture in the city is to increase the number of churches engaged in it." [26]

"Redeemer has positioned itself as a church that wants to bless the city and to do good to it – spiritually, socially and culturally. Its mission statement brings out this idea, emphasizing church planting as a way to replicate and extend such influence. Redeemer's stated vision is "to spread the Gospel, first through ourselves and then through the city by word, deed, and community; to bring about personnel changes, social healing, and cultural renewal *through a movement of churches* and ministries that change New York City and through it, the world (emphasis added)." [27]

As the Los Angeles Southern Baptist Association under the direction of Dr. Mark Hammond, examined the Los Angeles Basin, we discovered large geographic areas where there were no or not enough evangelical churches. This also meant that there were large segments of people that were not being touched with the Gospel.

One of those areas was the suburb of Cerritos. The city with a population of 45,000 people was recognized as the most diverse city of its size in the L.A. Basin. We realized that starting just one church would not be good enough. We realized that there was a need to minister to English, Spanish, Korean, Pilipino and Chinese speaking people. We needed to start a church for each of these groups. Not one after another – but ALL at once.

Our strategy developed into *saturation* church planting. In God's grace, we were able to rise up a Spanish-speaking Pastor, a Korean pastor and a Pilipino pastor. We prayed together, did outreach projects together and witnessed together. They became a team! Each one of the churches started in a public school auditorium meeting in separate time frames, one right after the other. God has blessed them – each one of the churches are growing and reaching people! The Spanish church under the leadership of Victor Solórzano has already planted another church in another community. And they still do evangelistic outreaches together!

If the cities are to be reached for Christ, we must be about multiple church planting. We need to realize that one form of church will <u>not</u> work for everyone in the city. "One thing is clear. There will be no one-form of church that serves as the model for all the others. There will be house churches, storefront, local congregations, and megachurches; ethnic churches and integrated churches; churches that stress high ritual order and those that emphasize informality. No one of them can serve the spiritual needs of all people."[28]

The cities of the World need to be *saturated* by prayer, with aggressive evangelistic efforts, which will result in a large number of Churches being started and reproducing themselves throughout the city.

The traditional model of only using "professional" church starters must be broken. Need trends must be developed and applied to the major cities of the World:

A. INDIGENEOUS leadership must be developed and released.

GOD has a call upon every one of His children, on each one of the believers. He has saved them and kept them and inspired them for an eternal reason!

That reason is TO SEEK and to SAVE THOSE WHO ARE LOST!

Not all believers are called to preach, teach or pastor a church. But ALL are called to "be MY witness" (Acts 1:8) The responsibility of the Church is to raise up people from the Harvest field of the cities, train them and release them to be leaders. The people who have been raised and lived in the city all their life know how to relate, love and share with the people in their indigenous people group or circle of influence. They can *impact* their part of the city better than anyone else. God saved them and placed there in the city to do their part in changing the World through the Cities.

B. INDIGENOUS   CHURCHES   <u>NEED</u>   TO   REPRODUCE THEMSELVES.

GOD in His grace will raise up people from the harvest field and God will have a call upon them to go back to the people group or geographical area that they love and know the best.

Hector Cedillo had migrated from Mexico as a young man. He fell in love with Los Angeles – the fast life, the freedom of the drug scene and he stayed and engrained himself into the drug culture of Macarthur Park in downtown Los Angeles. He soon made a mess of his life through a heavy drug addiction. Though his life was a mess, his wife stayed with him. She got saved and started praying for his salvation. After having one overdose experience after another, and abusing his body repeatedly, Hector came to the end of his rope. He had been on a drug binge for days – ending up unconscious and almost dead! His wife brought him home and started praying for him. As he came back to life, he knew that he needed help. His wife brought him to her pastor in West Los Angeles. Hector soon gave his life to JESUS. God started to do a deep work in his life. Soon he was teaching Bible studies and preaching wherever he could. God soon called Hector back to Macarthur Park to preach in the park.

Macarthur Park is one of the most beautiful, old historical parks in downtown L.A. The park had been a great place for family picnics and Sunday afternoon walks. But, starting in the 1970's drug and crime started taking over the park. Now, it is one of the most dangerous places. That is exactly where Jesus would be! That is exactly where Hector needed to be every Sunday afternoon preaching the Gospel.

Why? Because he knows the "culture" there better than any denominationally sent missionary. He knows the mindset of the drug addicts and of the homeless. In the past ten years, he has seen hundreds of desperate people come to a saving knowledge of Jesus Christ. There have been seven men raised up out of that ministry to go and plant churches in Mexico and in Southern California. These men are going back to the people group that they know best, and introducing Jesus to them! That is how the cities are to be reached for Christ in the 21ˢᵗ Century!

C. *SATURATION* CHURCH PLANTING <u>MUST</u> be the MAJOR STRATGEY to reach the cities of the World.

One church at a time may be a good strategy if we only needed to start one church a year. But that strategy will NOT make even a dent in the *lostness* of our cities.

That means ALL kinds of churches in ALL kinds of places and locations, reaching ALL kind s of people and neglecting NO ONE!

We <u>must</u> make it HARD to GO to HELL from our cities! We need to plant as many churches that can reach the people of the city as fast as we can.

4. We <u>MUST</u> minister to everyone in the cities.

When Jesus spoke in his home synagogue in Nazareth, he stood up and read from Isaiah 61:

> He came to Nazareth, where He
> had been brought up. As usual,
> He entered the synagogue on
> the Sabbath day and stood up
> to read. The scroll of the
> prophet Isaiah was given
> to him, and unrolling the scroll,
> He found the place where it was
> written: The spirit of the Lord
> is on me, because He has anointed
> Me to preach good news to the poor.

> He has sent Me to proclaim freedom
> to the captives and recovering of
> sight to the blind, to set
> free the oppressed, to proclaim
> the year of the Lord's favor."
> He then rolled up the scroll,
> gave it back to the attendant,
> and sat down, And the eyes of
> everyone in the synagogue were
> fixed on Him. He began by saying,
> 'Today as you listen this
> Scripture has been fulfilled.' (16-21)

As we go to the cities and see where God is working and join Him there, we need to remember that one of the main strategies is that God has used through the centuries is to go first to the POOR.

In Isaiah 57:6-11, we see God's strategy:

> Is this not the fast which I
> choose, to loose the bonds of
> wickedness, to undo the bonds of
> the yoke, and to let the oppressed
> to go free and break every yoke?
> Is it not to divide your bread
> with the hungry? And bring the
> homeless poor into the house; when
> you see the naked, to cover him;
> and not to hide yourself from
> your own flesh? Then your light
> shall break out like the dawn,
> and your recovery will speedily
> spring forth; and your righteousness
> will go before you; the glory of the
> Lord will be your rear guard,
> Then you will call, and the Lord
> will answer, you will cry and He
> will say, 'Here I am.' If you remove
> the yoke from your midst, the pointing

of the finger and speaking wickedness,
and lf you give yourself to the hungry
and satisfy the desire of the afflicted.
Then your light shall rise in darkness
and your gloom will become like midday.
And he Lord will continually guide
you, and satisfy your desire in
scorched places, and give strength
to your bones; and you will be
like a watered garden, and like a
spring of water whose water do not fail.

JESUS has always gone after the needy, the broken and battered people in life. He first went – not to Rome or even Jerusalem, but to the poor village of Bethlehem and the hill country of Nazareth. He was first announced not to the royal family in Jerusalem but to the shepherds as they tended their sheep by night. Even though he confounded the educated scholars in the Temple at the age of twelve, he chooses to go to the uneducated fisherman of Galilee instead. He was touched by the emptiness of the despised women at the well in Samaria. Through her, He was able to touch a whole Samaritan village. He was willing to reach out and touch the "untouchable" lepers of the day. He was willing to make the blind beggar to see again. He was willing to make the crippled man at the Pool of Bethesda to walk after 32 years of being bed ridden. Why? Because His heart is broken over the needy, the hungry and the poor, and so should our heart.

It has been proven down through history that if we were willing to humble ourselves and go after the down and out, the poor and the needy, God would honor that effort. We need to go back to the basics. We need to start where Jesus always started – with the poor and broken in spirit.

"Since the industrial revolution, almost every major city has had its share of squatters and slum dwellers. Earlier this century, when European cities were growing, nations were able to cope with the problem through the increased exploitation of the Two-Third World resources, the creation do a welfare state, emigration, and industrialization. But the post-war phenomenon in Asia, Africa and Latin America mega-cities is an irresolvable conflict between over-urbanization, due to too rapid a move of millions to the capital cities, and a slow industrialization providing too few jobs. Migrants swell the ranks of the under-employed and unemployed. New urbanites adjust to their environment by creating permanent slums, which are now far beyond the control of any planning or administrative body. In most of these mega-cities the slum population will grow faster than the rest of the population, increasing from present rates of 30% up to 75% in some cities."[29]

Today, with the worldwide economy failing there is more than ever an "air" of despair that has engulfed our cities. The immigration from nation to nation, from the countryside to the city has increased with a sense of urgency. With slums growing faster than any other part of the world-class cities, people are being crammed into terrible living environments. People have become more miserable, more irritable and more apt to crime and drugs.

So, given all the misery and heartache, all the pain of hunger and homelessness and hopelessness in the Mega-cities of the World, where would JESUS be today? Where would JESUS be on any given Sunday morning?

Jesus would be down in the shantytown that sets on the city dumb, outside of Rio de Janeiro with His arms wrapped around the lonely mother and five children that are gathered around her. He would be whispering in the ear of their hearts that He loves them very much. Jesus would be in that "crack house" in South Central Los Angeles holding a dear soul in His loving arms, as he is hurting from the pain of drug addiction. He would be in that little broken down walk-up apartment in Brooklyn, New York, holding the hand of the sweet widow lady who has not had a visitor since her husband of 65 years passed away three years ago. He would be in the cheap motel that the migrant family from Mexico has rented one more time in downtown Chicago showing the parents of three little ones that he will be there for them. He will be in the back bedroom that a newly married couple is renting from another family, encouraging them to trust Him for the next meal, the next rent money, the next job. He would be by the side of the mother who is weeping over the dead body of her five-year old son, who was killed in a drive by shooting in Compton, an inner-city suburb of Lo Angeles. And Jesus would be, and is, in a million other places of pain and sorrow right now – because "He has come to seek and to save those who are lost," and He has come to love and care for the broken in spirit.

Now, the question that I have to ask myself and ask you – where will you be? Will you be in the classy cathedrals? Will you be in the "self-serve" mega-church, in the "warm, comfortable, feel good" family chapel? Or, will you be out with the hurting and broken where JESUS will be?

The young popular musical group Leeland sings a challenging song, which should be our theme songs:

> *And I will follow you into the homes of the broken*
> *Follow you into the World.*
> *Meet the needs of the poor and needy, God*
> *Follow you into the World.*[30]

As God's servants in the cites of the world, we need to go to those who are hurting and broken and love them, as Jesus first loved us. We can do that in many ways and in various ways. We should be willing to go and do whatever we need to do to show people that we really do love them! In Matthew 25 JESUS gives us His requirements for His missionaries to the city:

"Then the King will say to those on his right hand, ' Come you who are blessed by your Father, take your inheritance, the kingdom prepared for you since the creation of the world. For I was hungry and you gave me something to eat, I was thirsty and you gave me something to drink, I was a stranger and you invited me in, I needed clothes and you clothed me, I was sick and you looked after me, I was in prison and you came to visit me."(Vs. 35-36)

When the "righteous ones" asked when did we do that for you? Jesus answered, "I tell you the truth, whatever you did for one of these brothers of mine, you did for me." (v. 40)

If, God's church performs the ACTS OF KINDNESS listed in Matthew 25: 31-46, we can touch and change thousands of lives. They are:

(1) FEEDING THE HUNGRY:

As you meet their need for hunger and thirst, the people in need will learn to trust you – for someone who cares about them. They will see that you care for them as individuals because you feed them.

n 1996, Set Free Church in Yucaipa, CA. was doing an outreach in a very poor and needy area of San Bernardino. CA. They usually give away hot dogs and soft drinks to gather a crowd, preach the Gospel, and take people home with them. Marty Souter had been living on the streets for seven years. He was doing drugs and ruining life. That Friday night he wore a pair of shorts and a shirt with one button and no shoes. He had a broken arm because of a bad drug deal, which had just gone wrong. Some friends came by him and asked him if he wanted to go get a free hot dog and a soft drink? He had not eaten all day and was hungry. So he went with his friends. At the outreach in the Park, Marty got a free hot dog – but he also stayed around to hear testimonies and the Gospel preached. That night he got saved, went to the Set Free Discipleship Ranch and grew in the Lord. Now, he is the mission pastor of Set Free and has helped start churches all over Southern California. GOD used *feeding* the *hungry* to touch and transform a life and to use that man to touch and minister to hundreds of lives.

But, let us not just *feed* them. In downtown Los Angeles, the Skid Row area is where most of the homeless hang out. Pastor Ron Thomas of Set Free Church on Skid Row was asked by a Buddhist service organization if they could use his facilities to feed the homeless on Saturday afternoons. Pastor Ron said, "Yes, but you need to let me share the Christian Gospel with the people," The leaders agreed with that requirement. For the past six-year they come faithfully, bring all the supplies and cook for and feed over 400 people. They are there every Saturday. But, as Pastor Ron has shared the Gospel with the crowds people have accepted Christ, and 12 of the Buddhist have become believers. The Buddhist director of the program has watched, as his whole family has become Christians, through hearing the Gospel weekly. He has asked Pastor Ron, "Are you going to make all of my family Christian?" Pastor Ron's answer was – YES! We need to feed the body with bread and their souls with the *BREAD OF LIFE* – JESUS! *Lets go feed the hungry!*

(2) Provide DRINK for the THIRSTY:

As we minister to the poor and needy, we need to realize that just the littlest "act of kindness," may produce everlasting results.

I was a missionary on the island of St. Vincent in the Caribbean from 1976 to 1980. One day a section of Kingstown, the capital city, was without water. The majority of the people had to walk to the closest faucet to get water for their family. The faucet was not working. Somehow I heard about it. I filled up some containers full of water and took them to that part of the community. I shared the water with the needy people.

One of the boys watched me do it – without any charge or strings attached. Eleven- year -old, Cecil Richards decided that if a white man would do that for his community, he should go to his church to see what he had to say. He and his older sister and three younger brothers came to church. Soon they were coming every Sunday. They all accepted Christ and I had the privilege of baptizing them. Now, 32 years later, Cecil Richards has been the pastor of Kingstown Baptist Church in St. Vincent for eighteen years; his three brothers all play musical instruments and lead a great praise team for the church. His older sister is a leader in the church also. The church is one of the strongest churches on the island. GOD used the giving of a "cup of cold water" in His name to make an eternal impact on a young man, a family and now an island-nation. JESUS is the only one who can quench the *thirst* of a *thirsting soul! Lets go and give a cup of cold water in the name of Jesus!*

(3) Provide HOUSING FOR THE HOMELESS.

One of the most hopeless feelings a person can have is to not know where they are going to live and sleep. In the shantytowns and the sections of every major city where you can find the homeless desperate for a place where they can feel safe and rest. The Church needs to be that place. WE need to be willing to invite them home with us.

One night Set Free Church of San Bernardino was doing an outreach in a park. It was in the park where most of the homeless people hung out in and stayed at night. The Gospel was preached and an invitation for those who wanted to receive Christ to come to the front of the stage was extended to the crowd. One young man came forward. I talked to him and he prayed with me to accept Jesus as Lord and Savior. I then invited him to come with us and go to the Discipleship Ranch. He said he would like that. Then all of a sudden he ran off to the other ends of the park. One of the young men ran after him. They soon came back. I asked him, "Why did you run away?" He answered. "I had to go someplace and throw away the statch of marijuana I was hiding in my sock." He went with us and God changed his life through the Discipleship Ranch and he is still walking with the Lord! Jesus is the only One who can give shelter to the homeless and hope to the hopeless! *Let us go out and find the homeless and bring them home with us!*

(4) Provide CLOTHING for those who need clothes.

Unless you have been in a similar situation you will never understand how a homeless person feels when they can get a free set of *clean* clothes instead of wearing the wet and dirty clothes they have been wearing for weeks. It is a feeling of self-worth and value. Just to be able to get a clean pair of socks to wear after a cold rainy night on the streets can really make a difference in a person's life.

One Christmas, our church in Pomona, an inner city suburb of Los Angeles, was having a lunch for the homeless and needy in the area. It was to be held right after our Sunday morning worship service. One couple came early for the lunch and ended up in the worship service. After hearing the Gospel story, they accepted Christ. One of the young couples, who had recently accepted Christ themselves, took them home with them. They allowed them to shower and clean themselves up again. They also allowed them to select clean clothes out of their personal closet. They came back to thank the Church for our kindness. They looked like new people. When I asked them to stay and let us help them, they told me that they had been "burned" by Churches in the past and just didn't trust Church people. On that Christmas day, Mary and Joseph walked away new people in Christ. *Lets go out there and provide clothes for those in need!*

(5) Minister to the SICK.

Everyone in every major city of the World is busy! Every hour of the day is filled up to the maximum. But, one of the most blessed moments a Christian can have is to (1) visit the sick in the hospitals, (2) visit the convalescent homes and take time with the shut-ins, (3) visit the AIDS patients, and (4) love the sick of mind that are wandering the streets of all the major cities – all for one reason – to love them as Jesus would love them. We need to love them as Jesus has first loved us!

There is a growing tragedy that is spreading throughout every major city of the world. It is estimated that 40 to 50 percent of the homeless and dangerous people living on the streets could function at a semi-normal rate if they had their prescribed medication and someone made sure they took the meds at the right time. However, because of the calloused or defeated hearts of the churches and governments of the cities and nations, the *sick* are walking the streets hurting and broken and in a state of bewilderment. Are the *sick that are walking the* streets loved by Jesus? YES! Do we love them like Jesus?

Jesus was not afraid to "touch and heal" the lepers, those who were "unclean." In Mark 1: 40-42, we read,

> And a leper came to Jesus,
> beseeching Him and falling
> on his knees before Him, and
> saying,' If you are willing,
> you can make me clean.'
> Moved with compassion, Jesus
> stretched out His hand and
> touched him, and said to
> him, 'I am willing;
> be cleansed.' Immediately the
> leprosy left him and he was
> cleansed.

Will we go to the AIDS clinics in the cities and touch someone for Jesus sake? Will we go to the mentally ill and touch them for Jesus sake? Who and where are the lepers in your city?

Bill and Cozette Gibson were called into the ministry later in life. While in their fifties they went back to seminary to be trained for the ministry. After praying through where God was calling them, they felt led to "go" to the Senior citizen group homes. These homes are refurbished residential homes which can house from five to seven senior adults. They live there, at different levels of health, until they pass away. Every Sunday they minister seven different homes.

Bill and Cozette have a worship service in each home for the residents and the caregivers. They serve communion to the receptive ones. They go by the bedside of those who cannot get out of their room and pray for them.

Why do they do it? It is not a glorious ministry; they will never get their names in the paper for doing it. Because God told them to minister to those who are forgotten and forsaken, and share Jesus with them – maybe one more time, so that they can be ready for eternity. Several of the residents have accepted Christ. Several of the Jewish residents have even prayed to receive Christ just before passing on into eternity. That is why they go!

The Great Physician has told us to visit the sick. *Let us go to the sick and wrap our arms around them and tell them that Jesus loves them* – just like *Jesus* did when we were *sick* in SIN.

(6) Visit those in PRISON

TODAY, there is over a million men and women incarcerated in prison in the United States alone. The USA has more prisoners than any other country.

We need to realize that the prisons in third World countries make prisons in the Unites States look like Hilton Hotels. Suffering and misery accompanies the prisoners to jail. There is no mercy given. But, there is story after story of how God is sweeping through the prison houses in the Third world countries and the prisons are becoming Houses of praise because so many of the prisoners are surrendering to Jesus! Let it continue, Lord Jesus, let it continue. The Great Liberator has commanded us to go to those in prisons and help *set the captives Free!*

As we started the Baptist work on the island St. Vincent in the Caribbean, we found that there was segment of the population that was not being ministered to by any of the established churches.

No one was going to the prison to minister to the prisoners. We started going there. The theme of our church was "The Whole Gospel for the Whole Man," so we applied Matthew 25 to the prison ministry. We brought dentist and doctors to minister to them. We had reading and educational classes to help the prisoners. We had weekly Bible studies. God did something special in that prison- 75 percent of the prison became born-again Christians. As the men were being released, we provided housing, job training and Bible studies for them.

One Monday morning after a great Sunday service, Sister McDonald, one of the pillars of the church, asked me if I had noticed that there were five ex-murderers setting on the back row of the church yesterday. I said I had noticed that. She went on to say, "Pastor, my friends tell me that if there were <u>not</u> so many prisoners attending our church, they would attend. And we would not be critized so much by the other churches." I told her, "You know what we have to do not to be critized and to be the popular church to attend?" NOTHING! OH Yeah, that is exactly what the enemy would like for God's church to do – nothing. If these men are keeping them away, then they don't belong."

GOD is calling us to minister to those in prison. *Let the church go to the prisons and set the captives FREE!*

(7) Provide for the STRANGERS:

There are millions of people that are being dislodged from their homeland, home countries and moving from the country to the cities. When they come to the major cities of the World, they are scared, bewildered and helpless. Many times they do not speak the language, have a place to stay, or have a way to earn a living to provide for their families. It is a great time in their lives to share the love of Jesus with them. There is an "open window" of opportunity to show them love by simple acts of kindness – providing food, clothing, furniture, transportation, language skills and job training. All in the name of Jesus!

Henry Blackaby shares his experience in reaching out to the immigrants that were moving to Vancouver, British Columbia, Canada, when he was Director of the Baptist Association. He writes, "I was told that 65 percent of the people did not have English as their mother tongue. These 1.5

million people were from every ethnic and culture group in the world. We asked our Lord, 'Every person?' He replied with a command, 'Every person! Follow me, and I will take you to them!' We began to 'go with Him' and it took us immediately to the main ethnic groups. We began to share Christ with them, and one by one they were accepting Him as Savior.' Blackaby goes on to share a phenomenon that he observed, "… we noticed an 'unusual' happening' in the lives of these refugees who had often been in danger of their lives in their former countries. They realized they had been saved physically, but now they were saved spiritually as well by the continuing love of God. They were so overwhelmed with this truth, they felt they owed God the rest of their lives, and about 80 percent of the young men were called into the ministry – ready to be trained to reach out to their fellow countrymen." The results of their ministry to the immigrants were, "All new Christians became catalyst for God's Kingdom – reaching their people, where they were, across the nation and to the ends of the earth."[33]

That is a good enough reason to go and share the love story of Jesus with the "strangers in our land." *Let us go to the strangers in our land and tell them "Welcome Home." Welcome home to the loving arms of Jesus!*

Where would Jesus be? He would be among the *least of these my brothers."* Will it also be said of you and me? *Let's go to the least of these and tell them that Jesus loves them! Let's go now!*

Randy White shares a great quote from Martin Luther King, Jr. He says: "Martin Luther King, Jr. in his own echo of Jesus, said it best; 'Anyone can be great because everyone can serve. You don't need a college degree to serve. You don't need to make your subject and verb agree to serve. You only need a heart full of grace, and a soul generated by love.' This is for me. I can do this. So can everyone."[34]

As we finish this chapter, let us go back to Jeremiah 29: 4-7.

WHAT is the CHURCH to do in the CITY?

In God's Master plan of the Ages, He has placed you and me in a major city of the world at this time in our lives, and as God's servants to the city, we must OBEY Him. We are to work and pray for the *shalom* of the city in which GOD has placed us.

Robert Linthicum gives us insight when he writes, "A city is an entire metropolitan area that is interwoven economically, by transit (both public and private), by public communication and by identification. Thus, Los Angeles doesn't simply consist of the political entity named Los Angeles. It is 124 "cities" tied together by economics, expressways, rail lines, four international airports, common television and radio stations and a common identity as "Los Angeles." It consists of the entirety of one county and portions of four other counties covering a geographical area wider than the state of Indiana. It consists of very wealthy areas (Beverly Hills, San Marino, Santa Monica) and very poor areas (East Los Angeles, Compton, Pomona). Fifty-two of its 124 member cities contain inner cities, slums and even squatter settlements. It has over twenty downtowns. A similar litany can be recited on any major city in the United States today. It is very easy for the church to say, 'We are not inner-city and therefore we are not city.' That is simply not true, and to make that claim severely limits the effectiveness of the church in seeking the welfare of the city. As the body of Christ and as Christians, we are responsible to bring *shalom* both to our neighborhood, and to our entire metropolis. So, whatever 'Babylon' may be to you, God calls you to seek its welfare – whether it is an inner-city neighborhood, a wealthy suburb, a small town or a university campus." He goes on to write, "It means that nothing is outside the purview, concern or commitment of the church, whether it is political, economic, religious, social, cultural, environment or spiritual, whether it is in the public domain or in the private. The essential task of the church is to work for its society's *shalom* – to work for the full and total transformation of all people, forces and structures with the love of God."[35]

Presence, prayer, practice, proclamation – these are the shalom-building ministries of the church in society. They are <u>not</u> optional. We must OBEY the Lord's commands.

So, what MUST the 21st Century Church do to reach the "great" cities of the World?

We <u>must</u> OBEY GOD by:

GOING to the Cities

POURING our lives into the CITIES

PRAYING over the Cities

SHARING JESUS in the Cities

And

STARTING Churches for EVERYONE in the CITIES

That will MINISTER to EVERYONE

Rich and poor

And

Everyone in between

In the HEART language of EVERY PERSON

And we <u>must</u> do it NOW!

QUESTIONS:

1. Will you and your church get serious about going to the city?

2. ARE YOU WILLING TO BE INCARNATIONAL? Living and loving the city?

3. WHAT has GOD called you to do to reach the cities of the world for Christ?

FOOT NOTES:

1. Donald McGavran, <u>UNDERSTANDING CHURCH GROWTH</u>, Grand Rapids: William B. Eerdmans Publishing Co., 1970, pgs. 279-280.

2. Samuel Zwemer, <u>THE UNOCCUPIED MISSION FIELDS OF AFRICA AND ASIA</u>, London: SVN Publications, 1911, p. 216.

3. Charles Van Engen and Jude Tiersman, editors, <u>GOD SO LOVED THE CITY: SEEKING A THEOLOGY FOR URBAN MISSION</u>, Monrovia: MARC, 1996, pgs. 10-11.

4. Tiersman, p. 15.

5. Viv Grigg, <u>COMPANION TO THE POOR</u>, Monrovia: MARC, 1997, p. 6.

6. Tierrsma, p. 16.

7. E.M. Bounds, <u>POWER THROUGH PRAYER</u>, Grand Rapids: Zondervan Press, 1962, p. 28

8. E. Thomas and Elizabeth S. Brewster, *"The Difference Bonding Makes,"* from <u>PERSEPECTIVES ON THE WORLD CHRISTIANMOVEMENT</u>, Pasadena: William Carey Library, 1999, 3rd edition, p. 445.

9. William Pannell, <u>EVANGELSIM FROM THE BOTTOM UP: WHAT IS THE MEANING OF SALVATION IN THE WORLD GONE URBAN?</u>, Grand Rapids: Zondervan, 1992, p. 50.

10. John Perkins, *"A Seek and Touch Gospel"*, RESTORER, FALL, 1993.

11. L.R. Scarborough, <u>WITH CHRIST AFTER THE LOST</u>, Nashville: Broadman Press, 1983, pgs. 23-24.

12. John Dawson, <u>TAKING OUR CITIES FOR GOD: HOW TO BREAK SPIRITUAL STRONGHOLDS</u>, Lake May, FL: Creation Press, 1989, pgs. 42-45.

13. John Dawson, p. 51.

14. Nate Krupp, <u>THE CHURCH TRIUMPHANT AT THE END OF THE AGE</u>, Shippenburg, PA: Destiny Image Publishes, 1988, pgs. 16-17.

15. Tom Eliff, <u>A PASSION FOR PRAYER</u>, Wheaton: Crossway Books, 1998, p. 11.

16. John Dawson, p.136.

17. Peter Wagner, <u>CHURCHES PRAYING</u>, p. 170.

18. David Garrison, <u>CHURCH PLANTING MOVEMENTS</u>, Richmond, VA: International Mission Board, SBC, 2000, p. 33.

19. Michael Green, <u>EVANGELISM IN THE EARLY CHURCH</u>, Grand Rapids: William B. Eerdmans, 1970, p. 7.

20. Peter Wagner, <u>FRONTIERS IN MISSION STRATEGY</u> , Chicago: Moody Press, 1971, p.133.

21. Wagner, p. 20.

22. Wagner, p. 25.

23. L.R. Scarborough, <u>WITH CHRIST AFTER THE LOST</u>, Nashville: Broadman Press, 1952, p. 3.

24. Wagner, p. 135.

25. Wagner. p. 135.

26. Ed Stetzler and Warren Bird, <u>VIRAL CHURCHES: HELPING CHURCH PLANTERS BECOME MOVEMENT MAKERS</u>, San Francisco: Jossey-Bass, 2010, p. 68.

27. Stetzler and Bird, p. 68.

28. Paul G. Hiebert and Eloise Hiebert Meneses, <u>INCARNATIONAL MINISTRY: PLANTING CHURCHES IN BAND, TRIBAL, PEASANT AND URBAN SOCIETIES</u>, Grand Rapids: Baker Book House, 1995, p. 341.

29. Paul G. Hiebert, p. 341.

30. Paul G. Hiebert, p. 328.

31. Viv Grigg, <u>COMPANION TO THE POOR</u>, p. 11.

32. "Follow You," @ 2009 Meaux Mercy (BMI)/Meaux Jeaux Music(SESAC)

33. Henry Blackaby, *"No* Waiting *is Required to Reach the World," ON MISSION Magazine,* March-April, 2001, p. 14.

34. Randy White, <u>JOURNEY TO THE CENTER OF THE CITY: MAKING A DIFFERENCE IN AN URBAN NEIGHBORHHOD</u>, Downers Grove: InterVarsiy Press, 1996, p. 52.

35. Robert Linthicum, <u>TRANSFORMING POWER: BIBLCAL STRATEGIES FOR MAKING A DIFFERENCE IN YOUR COMMMUNITY</u>, Downers Grove: InterVarsity Press, 2003, pgs. 74-75; 77-78.

CHAPTER SIX

WHO WILL GO TO THE GREAT CITY?

The city is an amazing place of beauty,
blessing, and fulfillment for those who have
ready eyes to see it that way. It is also a place
that draws and forms those who are
willing to explore what it means to be
broken before God. Brad Smith[1]

"Then the word of the Lord came to Jonah, a second time 'Get up! Go to the great city'." JONAH 3:1.

He had grown up in a Christian home. He grew up with his grandfather, who was a preacher. He had worked hard as a professional cook all his life. However, because of a crack cocaine addiction Ron Thomas found himself jumping in and out of dumpsters gathering cans and bottles. That was the way he sustained his addiction. He slept in a box in an alley not too far from Staples Center in downtown Los Angeles. He wandered the streets trying to find something to satisfy the pain in his heart. One Christmas Day, as he walked the streets, he was shot by a drive-by shooter.

One day in 2001, he was pushing his shopping cart across Macarthur Park in downtown L.A. looking through the trash cans and desperate for something more than doing this day in and day out. As he was standing by a trashcan, he noticed a husband and wife and their little daughter having a picnic. The little girl got up and came over to the trashcan. Ron thought she was going to throw trash away.

She stopped in front of him and said, "Mister, GOD loves you," and then went back to her family.

Those words broke his heart. The hard shell that he had put over his heart, so that he could feel no pain, fell off and he cried out to God for help. About an hour later a flyer crew from Set Free Church in Yucaipa, CA, were passing out flyers about an outreach that they were conducting the next day. Chewy, who gave him the flyer, told Ron that he could go to a Discipleship Ranch about one hundred miles away from Los Angeles. The "far away" element touched his heart. He knew he needed to get away from the drug scene and get strong in the Lord. He knew it was the right thing to do – so much so that he did not go back to his box to sleep because he would be tempted to do drugs. He slept under a bush in the park all night.

The next day at the outreach, he was the first one to come forward to give his life to Christ. He was also the first one to get on the bus to go to the Discipleship Ranch. GOD changed his life. His testimony is, "I knew all about God, but I did not know GOD. Now, I do. I have a personal relationship with God through Jesus Christ. He is real and alive in me!"

Ron felt called into the ministry, went through the Set Free Pastor school training program, and started preaching wherever he could. Soon, GOD called him back to the streets of downtown Los Angeles. He is now pastor of Set Free Church of Skid Row, downtown Los Angeles. They help 10-15 people a week get saved and sent to the Discipleship Ranch. He has helped start five other churches. He is sold out for Jesus and committed to the great city of Los Angeles!

Can GOD use a man like Ron? Can GOD take a drug addict and use him to preach the Gospel to hundreds of people every week? YES! What about all his mistakes and failures? That is not a problem, for "God causes all things to work together for good to those who love God, to those who are called according to His purpose." (Romans 8:28) Through it ALL God was getting Ron ready to go to the poor and needy in downtown Los Angeles!

GOD called Jonah to go to the great city of Nineveh. Yet, he rebelled and tried to run the opposite direction. He was reluctant to obey – God had to go to extreme measures to get Jonah to obey. When he did obey, the great city was brought to its knees in repentance and God showed His mercy to them.

Who started the church in Antioch, which became the Missionary sending church of the New Testament? Was it a fully funded professional staff of disciples from Jerusalem? Who was the lead church planter? Was it a church planter who had gone through all the professional assessment materials, went to all the boot camps for potential church planters? NO, it was just a bunch of believers who were chased out of Jerusalem by persecution. "But there were some of them, men of Cyprus and Cyrene, who came to Antioch and began speaking to the Greeks also, preaching the Lord Jesus. And the hand of the Lord was with them, and a large number who believed turned to the Lord." And, again the way God was working with them, it was also recorded: "And for an entire year they met with the Church and taught considerable numbers; and the disciples wee first called Christians in Antioch" (Acts 11: 20-21; 26).

So, maybe even average God-loving followers can reach a city for Christ?

What about a murderer? Saul had been an active enemy of the early Christian church. He had arrested and punished hundreds of Christians in Jerusalem. But, God had a better plan for him. On the way to Damascus, God knocked him off his donkey and he saw the Resurrected Christ in Heaven. "And he fell to the ground and heard a voice saying to him, 'Saul. Saul why are you persecuting Me?' And he said, 'Who are you Lord?' And he said, 'I am JESUS whom you are persecuting, but get up and enter the city, and it will be told you what you must do.'" Then the Lord came to Ananias to tell him to go to Saul and tell him what God's purpose is for Saul's life. "But the Lord said to him, 'Go for he is a chosen instrument of Mine, to bear My name before the Gentiles and the kings and the sons of Israel" (Acts 9:4-6:15). YES, God can use the worst of sinners, as Paul called himself –"chief of sinners". God in His grace and mercy used Paul to share the Good News throughout the known world of his time. God was again, "working ALL things together for good."

So, it looks like GOD is able to use anyone and everyone to reach the cities for Christ. Will we allow Him to use even us?

The urgent question is: WHO CAN GOD USE TO REACH THE CITIES FOR CHRIST?

Our ministry to the city will be driven and controlled by our *heart passions* that God plants in our hearts, our *character* that God shapes and prepares through our life experiences and our *abilities* that can be shaped and used in our daily service. Let's see how all these work together to make a person God can use to reach the cities of the World for Christ.

First, Our *HEART COMPASSIONS:*

In the Bible, God used a rebellious prophet, a bunch of average everyday Christians, and even a murderer. Why and how could He use them?

Because they all had ONE thing in common – they had been BROKEN! Broken by circumstance, situations, mistakes and messes in their own individual lives. However it happened, God broke them.

Jonah is a great example. God had a plan for his life. Yes, he was called to be a prophet in Israel, but God had a greater plan for Jonah. God was calling Jonah to go to the "great" city of Nineveh – to go outside Israel to a lost and dying world and tell them of God's love one more time before judgment came upon Nineveh.

And, to get Jonah to do God's perfect will for him and the kingdom, God had to break him! "I called to the Lord in my distress, and he answered me. I cried for help in the belly of Sheol; You heard my voice." (Jonah 2:2) Jonah was broken – at the bottom of the ocean, in the bottom of the big fish belly. He had to get all the way to the bottom of Sheol before he looked up and cried out to God. He should have been dead – the moment he was thrown overboard. He should have been destroyed in the waves and rush of the ocean. He should have been dead in the belly of a big fish! But, God in his mercy provided the belly of the big fish as a place of mercy and grace. "But, you raised my life from the Pit, Lord my God!" (Jonah 2:6) This is the turning point. "Here is an expression of praise, a recognition of God's sovereign power. Jonah was referring to God's miraculous intervention by way of the great fish. Jonah was acknowledging that he had been brought back from the depths of the sea. This is one of the many 'but God' verses in the Bible (e.g. Genesis 8:1; 45:7; 50:20; Joshua 14:12, Psalm 37:13, 17, 33; 49:15; John 1:18; Acts 2:24; 3:15; 10:40; 13:30; Romans 5:8; I Corinthians 1:27; 2 Corinthians 7:6; Ephesians 2:4; Philippians 2:27). Jonah had been retrieved by God from a hopeless situation. The God from whom Jonah thought he was banished had reached down and pulled him out of death and despair; showing that he was still 'Yahweh my God'. Jonah was overcome with praise for his God, who had shown him such compassionate grace."[2]

Isn't that so GOD - grapping us, who were in total rebellion and picking us up out of the Pit – actually "Sheol" means a place of separation from God", a place of death to God and His way and will. But the God of a second and third and one hundredth chance is there in the pit – to pick us up, wrap his loving arms around us and put us back in the place of obedience.

Now, let's go to the New Testament. God had a great plan for Saul who was changed and transformed into Paul, the missionary. Saul had his own plans. He was running hard and fast to fulfill his own plans and dreams of success. He also had to be broken so that God could use him. Paul's testimony of that is:

> If anyone else
> thinks he has grounds for
> confidence in the flesh,
> I have more: circumcised
> the eighth day; of the nation
> of Israel, of the tribe of Benjamin,
> a Hebrew born of Hebrews; as to
> the law, a Pharisee; as to
> zeal, persecuting the church;
> as to the righteousness that is
> in the law, blameless.
> But everything that was a gain
> to me, I have considered to be
> a loss because of Christ. More
> than that, I also consider
> everything to be a loss in
> view of the surpassing value
> of knowing Christ Jesus my Lord.
> Because of Him I have suffered
> The loss of all things and consider
> them filth, so that I may gain
> Christ.(Philippians 3:4-8)

Proud, self-righteous and arrogant Saul had to be knocked off his donkey, so that he could look up into Heavenly places and see the Resurrected Christ. As he saw the Risen Lord in all His glory, God got hold of his heart. He was humbled and broken.

He was broken, but he was also sold out! He knew and understood "Amazing Grace" better than anyone. He had met the One who loved Him so much that He gave His life for Him, that loved him so much that He rose again from the grave for him, and loved him so much that he chased him down – knocked him off his "high horse" of pride and religious arrogance and broke him. That is the Jesus Christ who Paul made the Lord of his life and he served all the rest of his life.

Has not the God of amazing grace done the same thing for you? Hasn't God done the same thing for the 15 million people living in one of the major cities of the world? Isn't it only right for those 15 million people to hear about the amazing grace of God? As Paul says it so beautifully in Romans:

> But how can they call on Him in
> whom they have not believed? And
> how can they believe without hearing
> about Him? And how can they hear
> without a preacher? And how
> can they preach unless they
> are sent? (10:14-15)

Today, as God is calling us to the World cities we must go as broken vessels willing to be used as God sees fit. If we go in a spirit of pride – the pain and agony of the millions in utter poverty will break us, the utter *lostness* of the cities will overwhelmed us. Our pride will be discouraged, defeated and disappointed because the *vastness* of the cities, the *pain* of the cities, and the *hopelessness* of the cities will overwhelm our prideful hearts.

As I was writing about the city, I had to take a break from writing, so that I could go into Los Angeles to remind myself of the *lost feeling* surrounding and covering a Metropolis. (You see this is not a theoretical book, it is something I live and feel everyday for the past forty years.)

My heart was touched as I drove through the streets of Chinatown, in downtown Los Angeles, as I looked into the eyes of the older Chinese gentlemen walking the streets and wondering – have they ever heard the love story of Jesus? As I stopped at the Jonah Project Ministry Center located in the Skid Row area of downtown L.A. and watched the homeless men hanging out there – wondering what had gone wrong in each of their broken lives and hurting inside for their brokenness. Before I left downtown L.A. I had to stop in front of a set of new high-rise condos, where the young, up and coming professionals live – in a gated community. They are living and working in downtown L.A. but in reality living isolated from the hurts of the city. And I wondered – how could the church somehow get past the security gates to tell each one of those young adults that Jesus died and rose again for each one of them. Then my heart ached for all those little kids playing in the streets as I drove through East Los Angeles – wondering would they ever have a chance to hear the truth – that Jesus loves them very much!

In each one of those situations, I had to stop and pray, because the pain of watching *lostness* engulfing people would have overwhelmed my heart.

To be used of God in the cities of the world, we need to be humbled under the Mighty Hand of God: "You younger men, likewise, be subject to your elders; and all of you, clothe yourselves with humility toward one another, for God is opposed to the proud, but gives grace to the humble. Therefore humble yourselves under the mighty hand of God, that He might exalt you at the proper time." (I Peter 5:5-6)

We need to realize, it is only by the Grace of God that He allows us to do anything in His Kingdom. It is not because we had more abilities, talents or giftedness than anybody else that God called us to be servants of the city. It is because of the grace of God that we have the privilege to serve the cities of the World. We need to keep the same attitude that Paul had, "To me, the very least of all saints, this grace was given, to preach to the Gentiles the unfathomable riches of Christ." (Ephesians 6:14)

Here is the sweet thing about brokenness: as you serve the Lord, you are <u>not</u> worrying about who gets the credit, praise, or attention. It will be easier to put your arm around a homeless man, who has not showered for six months and stinks to high heaven, and tell him that God loves him. It is easier to go the second and third mile to help that drug addicted young man who keeps failing over and over again. It is easier to go to the young professional who wants to argue world-views and just love him through all his doubts. It is easier to go to the rich businessman and tell them that God loves him. Why, because God is in charge of the situations. It becomes easier to work through the needed red tape to rent a storefront downtown to reach out to the homeless, to deal with finding blankets, and clean clothes for the homeless after a cold rainy night. It is easier to trust God to provide food to feed 400 people, because God is faithful! As we are broken – it is <u>not</u> about us, but all about Him, who never fails.

Brokenness is the starting place and the place where you must "camp out" at for all the rest of your ministry. The key question: *Have you HUMBLED YOURSLEF UNDER THE MIGHTY HAND OF GOD* yet?

Jack Taylor challenges us, "Go ahead and admit it! You are your greatest problem. Of all the four letter words, SELF is the worst. If you can just face it and acknowledge it, you will be one step closer to victory." There is but one cure for self and pride. . . DEATH! Taylor continues to write, "Death is the only means of deliverance from the self-life. We cannot kill ourselves nor does God intend it. He does intend that we accept the full implications of the death of Jesus. If He died for us, then we died. If we died, we are no longer alive. We are then to 'reckon' ourselves to be dead to sin and alive to God through Christ Jesus."[3]

Paul said it this way: "I am crucified with Christ: nevertheless I live; yet not I, but Christ lives in me." (Galatians 2:20)

As God calls us to the Mega cities of the world, He is also calling us back to the Cross! The only way we can be used of God in the city is to stay close to the Cross, because that is where we find victory in Jesus.

Listen to Baker James Cauthen's heart as he shares from his life experience as a missionary in China during World War II:

> If you are like me, you will have to return very frequently and stand by the cross, to be made aware of the majesty of the love that has laid hold of you. No matter how little you may understand your circumstances, or how bitter your experience,

you are always in the grip of the mighty love that is seen at the cross. You will need to stand there frequently, realizing that the grace available for you is greater than your blunders, failures, and sins. Standing at Calvary, we are caught into what God himself is. We turn our eyes upon him and say, 'Thank you Lord,' for whatever comes. Return to the cross to renew your own sense of calling."[4]

Another *passion* of your heart that you <u>must</u> have to be able to *impact* the cities of the world is:

A *GOD given LOVE for the city!*

This *love* is not a love for the beauty of the architectural structures of the city. It is not a love for the pace and flow of the city. It is not a love for the diversity of the multitudes. It is a deep-set *heart compassion* and *passion for the multitudes of people in the city.*

Dr. Francis DuBose, professor of Missions for over thirty years at Golden Gate Baptist Seminary in Mill Valley, just north of San Francisco, was a lover of the city who wrote a poem that explains what I am trying to say

> To love the city is to
> love her people,
> To befriend the forgotten,
> To feel the feverish
> forms of the forsaken,
> To stoop to touch the
> twisted torsos of the tormented.[5]

A side note, DuBose loved the city so much that after he retired from teaching at GGBTS, he and his wife moved to the city. The last time I saw him, he was teaching a Bible study at Page Street Center in the Haigt-Ashbury district at the age of 83. He passed away in 2009.

The Lord Jesus Christ, who wept over the city of Jerusalem, can only give this love of the city to you:

> O Jerusalem, Jerusalem! The city
> that kills the prophets and stones
> those who are sent to her. How
> often I wanted to gather your
> children together, as a hen
> gathers her chicks under her
> wings, yet your were not willing.
> (Matthew 23:37)

Will you allow the Lord to break you of any and every prejudice against the Metropolis of the World? Will you allow the Holy Spirit to convict you of any fear or mistrust of the city and the people of the city that God so loves?

Then – will you allow Him to fill you up with His love for the precious souls found in the major cities of the World?

So the question is still – WHO will go, and whom shall I send? (Isaiah 6:8)

So, WHO can go to the World-class Cities of the World?

Through forty-five years of urban church planting, I have struggled with the separation between *action-orientated, project driven* people and the more *mystical spiritual* people.

Brad Smith puts it this way, "People who are drawn to city ministry are usually action-orientated. They like to see a problem and fix it. They often like to start doing something and figure they will learn by trial and error along the way."

"People who are drawn naturally to spiritual formation tend to be reflection-orientated. They like to read great devotional writings of the past centuries. They can sit for long period of time in prayer and meditation. They realize as they explore the depths of their own motives, they find new areas of their soul that they can surrender to God."[6]

Both types are important and necessary in order to be able to reach the city. I am persuaded that it is not – either or, but both/and. For a church planter to stay faithful in the city he must be spiritual and very action driven.

I have learned over the years that as I go out to do ministry, the more I realize that I need God's help to be able to do what God has called me to do. I run back to God, and spend time with my ABBA.

To make it in the Major World-class Cities, one must be a mystical evangelist. To be an evangelists, an urban church planter must have a *passion* for the people of the city. He must be *going* and *sharing* the love of Jesus with everyone and anyone that he can. If you attempt to do that in the flesh, it will wear you out and people will know that you are not *real*.

John Wesley said that the three most miserable years in his many years of service was when he went to Georgia as a missionary. Why? Because he went there and tried to serve in the flesh. It just does not work! Then he went home to England. One Wednesday evening at Aldersgate Chapel while a deacon read a Commentary on the book of Romans, God touched John Wesley's heart and soul. He felt "warmly touched" then and there, and dates his true conversion to that moment. Then in the power of the resurrected Christ, Wesley could go out and share the Gospel. He truly was a mystical evangelist!

For the Christian worker in the major cities of the World to make a solid long-range *impact* on a city or a people group he must spend time with JESUS. Power and peace in our hearts in the inner cities of the world comes only from the time a person spends with Jesus. I love that passage in Acts, where the religious leaders finally "saw" what made the Apostles different: "Now as they observed the confidence of Peter and John and understood that they were uneducated and untrained men, they were amazed, and began to recognize as having been with JESUS." (Acts 4:13) That is what I mean by being *mystical evangelist.*

I said all that so that I could simply challenge every Christian to develop the balance between inward spirituality and action-driven ministry.

Let's look at some of the *KEY CHARACTERISTICS* that Church planters need to exhibit in their lives, in order to be able to reach the cities of the World for Christ. They are:

1. Men and women of GREAT FAITH.

It is scary to go to a city where you know no one and attempt to *impact* that city for Christ. It is scary to go to just a section or a people group of a large Mega-city and attempt to *reach* that section or people group for Christ. But that is exactly what GOD is calling us to do in the Mega-cities of the World. And we must do it! The eternal consequences for millions of people in the cities depend on the Church going and telling them of the love story of Jesus. And do it NOW!

That is where and when FAITH must be applied!

As young men come to me and tell me that God has called them to start a church, I love it when they say, "But I am scarred!" I tell them that that is good because it will teach them to apply faith in the Almighty God, who has called them to the task to do it and fulfill the call. It makes us *depend* on GOD by FAITH. That is what it is all about.

But, everyone who comes to God has faith. Even if it is just faith as small as a mustard seed, they still have faith to trust in the Lord Jesus to forgive them of their sins and be their Lord and Savior. "For by grace you are saved through faith, and this is not from yourselves; it is God's gift – not from works, so that no one can boast" (Ephesians 2:8-9).

Yes, that is true and God is going to continue to stretch and grow that "mustard seed" faith until every born-again Christian can walk by faith. I thank God for His continuing stretching of our faith – even when it pulls us out of our "comfort zones." I am thankful that is a lifetime process of growing in faith!

As a Church planter, I am talking about GREAT FAITH. Two times, Jesus uses that phrase to explain some people's faith. When Jesus came to Capernaum one day, a Roman centurion asked Jesus to come heal his servant. Jesus said he would do it. Listen to the centurion's reply:

"'Lord,' the centurion replied, 'I am not worthy to have You come under my roof. But only say the word. And my servant will be cured. For I too am a man under authority, having soldiers under my command, I say to this one, 'Go!' and he goes; and to another, 'Come!' and he comes; and to my slave, 'Do this!' and he does it.' Hearing this, Jesus was amazed and said to those following Him, ' I assure you; I have not found anyone in Israel with so great a faith!" (Matthew 8: 8-10)

The other time, a Canaanite woman came to Jesus asking him to heal her daughter. He answered her, "It isn't right to take the children's bread and throw it to their dogs, 'Yes, Lord', she said, 'yet even the dogs eat the crumbs that fall from the masters table!' Then Jesus replied to her, 'Women, your faith is great. Let it be done for you as you want.' And from that moment her daughter was cured." (Matthew 15; 26-28)

GREAT FAITH is:

A. Simply KNOWING and TRUSTING the GOD who has called you to "GO" to the city!

It is deep-rooted TRUST in the Lord of the Universe and the Lord of your very soul. It is a faith that says, "I know for sure whom I believe in and can trust Him to fulfill the Call to the City - that He has given you. This is the foundation stone on which you can continually come back to when: the people you are attempting to reach ignore you and reject you; when you cannot see how you can ever make an *impact* on the deep *lostness* and deep *darkness* that engulfs the place that God has called you to go and reach for Jesus.

When those days of discouragement and despair come, and they will, because we are human and the enemy will sow those seeds of doubt into your heart and mind, you <u>must</u> go back to that place of "calling" – where you met with The Lord, and He spoke to you and He told you to "go." Baker James Cauthen, who was President of the International Board, SBC for over 25 years says it this way, "Have faith that he can use you because when he called you, he knew what he was doing. He was under no illusion but knew all about you. Have faith that his word will not come back empty. Have faith that the step you are taking is right because he has shown the way. In this faith stand fast and you will see what God can do." [7]

We were at the International Missions Board, SBC missionary candidate conference in Richmond, Virginia when God very distinctly and powerfully called us to go to the Caribbean and to the English speaking Windward Islands. It was the last day of the conference; we were supposed to tell them what country we felt called to go to. The night before we had gotten on our knees and asked God to show us exactly where He wanted us to go. The Board wanted us to go to Panama. That would have been a great mission field, but I did not have peace about it. The last day came and while we were talking with other missionaries in the lobby, God spoke to me loud and clear, "Go to the Windward islands." We went back upstairs to the office of Charles Bryant, director of mission work in the Caribbean and Middle America. We told him, that God had called us to the Windward Islands. Six months later, we were in St. Vincent, one of the Windward Islands in the Caribbean.

I never really understood why Joshua would tell the priests to take twelve rocks out of the Jordan river and place them as a monument once they got on the other side (Joshua 4:1-7), until I hit some of those days – where everything in my human logic and reasoning, and every fiber of my body was crying out "Just go home!" Joshua told the Israelites to make a memorial, so that when their children asked: Why are these rocks here? They could tell their children, GOD delivered us through the Jordon River, so that we could come into the "promised land."

Going to a country where you knew no one, going to a country where you were the minority for the first time in your life, going to a country where you were not known or cared about can be overwhelming. So where did I go? I went back many times to that place of "calling." I stayed there until by *faith* I could say – GOD has called me to this island/country to take it for Christ, and no matter what goes on around me, or even in me, I will obey King Jesus!

B. Being able to look ahead, with GREAT FAITH, and see and believe what the final product will look like. GOD has called you to go to one of the great cities of the world! He has called you to not just exist until Jesus comes again. He has called you to *impact* the whole City for Christ! He has called you to start a movement of God that will touch and transform hundreds and thousands of people in that GREAT CITY. It may not sound logical and definitely does not feel possible, but GOD has shown you through faith that that is exactly what is going to happen.

This *VISION* will keep you going, when all of your friends and relatives think you are crazy. When all the key church members tell you – "We cannot do that," the *VISION* will keep you going. Because of the GREAT FAITH that God has given you, you can keep pressing on to Victory. We have learned just like Paul learned, as he wrote, "For we walk by faith, not by sight" (2 Corinthians 5:7).

When times get hard and progress is not being made as fast as you thought it should, you need to go back to the foundation of GREAT FAITH. We need to remember how we came to Christ and apply that to our daily walk with God: "Therefore as you have received Christ Jesus the Lord, so walk in Him." (Colossians 2:6)

How did you accept Christ? By FAITH. How much faith did it take? It only took a faith as little and small as a "mustard seed". How do you live out the Christian life? You live it out by FAITH. As God works in your life and then calls you to go to the Great Cities of the World, you <u>must</u> also live by FAITH!

Listen to what Paul could say, as he grew in faith, as he served the Lord. He said, "For I am not ashamed of the Gospel, for it is the power of God for salvation to everyone who believes, to the Jew first and also to the Greek. For in it the righteousness of God is revealed from faith to faith; as it is written, 'But the righteous man shall live by faith." (Romans 1:16-17)

C. Exhibiting GREAT FAITH is *trusting* a GREAT BIG GOD to do much more than we can ever expect or see ahead of time.

On May 30, 1792, William Carey stood before the Ministers and Messengers at the local Baptist Churches quarterly meeting. He preached from Isaiah 54:2-23, his famous sermon of "Expect great things (from God). Attempt great things (for God)." It was after he preached that powerful life-changing, world-changing sermon that John Ryland, one of the leaders of the pastors, said, "Mr. Carey, sit down and be quiet. If God wants to save the heathen, He does not need your help, nor ours."

But Carey could not set down and be quiet. The next day, as all the business of the Baptist convention was completed, it looked like again, one more time, that nothing was going to be done about going to the whole world. It was then that Carey turned to William Fuller and said, "'is there nothing again going to be done, sir? This was a creative moment in the history of Christ's Kingdom. Deep called to deep. Fuller trembled an instant under that importunity, gesture, and heartbreak, and then his soul was stabbed awake, and the Holy Ghost flooded his spirit. He also heard 'God's sigh in the heart of the world.' Often he had sympathized with Carey's propaganda, though too timorous for committal. Now he became convert and comrade, the first of Carey's captives, the first of Christ's new 'expectant attempters'. He crossed his Rubicon. He put both hands to the plough, not ever thence looked back. He stood from that instant as Caleb with Joshua."[8]

Soon a motion was presented and passed to start a Baptist Society for "propagating the Gospel among the Heathens." On June 12, 1793, William Carey and his family started the modern day missionary movement by sailing to a forty-year mission to India. He truly believed what he preached, "Expect great things from God. Attempt great things for God."

I love what Dr. F.W. Gotch wrote about that sermon. "I call that sermon of Carey's wonderful, because there has, perhaps been no sermon preached in modern days, which has had so distinct and traceable an effect on Protestant Christianity throughout the world."[9]

In his day, William Carey set the pace for the rest of Christendom, as he practiced what he preached – by going, and staying and living and dying among the people of India.

Today, it is time for us Christians to step up and go, and stay and live and die among the precious people of the major cities of the world! It is time to exercise GREAT FAITH! It is time to believe that GOD died for the whole world – including those in the cities, that GOD so loved the world – including the precious souls in the cities, that he does not want any one of them to perish – and it is time for us to GO!

J.D. Payne writes, "Has God called you to the great cities of this world to see disciples. Leaders, and churches multiplied for the kingdom? Though all missionaries must respond to God with a reckless abandonment and a total dependence on him, the cities of the world amplify the need to make certain that a God dependency is at the heart of everything the church planter does. A daily dying to self and being filled with the Spirit absolute musts (Ephesians 5:18)."[10]

Applying a great faith that God has filled your heart with let us go and expect GREAT things from a GREAT BIG GOD and attempt GREAT THINGS for Him and in Him – to reach a city that desperately needs JESUS!

2.   Men and Women who are PRAYER WARRIORS.

"For *you to be effective in church planting, prayer must precede your arrival on the field, saturate every step of the church-planting strategy, and continue for the new believers and churches after your team departs to plant other churches"* writes J.D. Payne. He goes on to write, "The permeation of prayer throughout the ministry is of paramount importance to *everything* the church-planting team does. Church planters must be people of prayer."[11] (Italics his)

There is a BATTLE over the cities of the World. We all know that the enemy thinks he owns the cities. Because of the darkness found in our cities – because of crime, drugs, gang activities and sinful life styles, too many Christians have given up on the major cities of the World! The Church of the Lord Jesus Christ has almost surrendered the "rights" to the city to the enemy. That is <u>not</u> right!

Randy White says, "We need to understand the city is not inherently evil in itself. It is an environment that provides greater opportunities for human sinfulness to manifest itself – and therefore greater opportunities for the gospel to show its empowering and healing relevance."

"We need to see Jesus weeping over Jerusalem (Luke 19:41-420 – Yahweh expressing His concern over Nineveh (Jonah 4:11), crying out over Moab (Isaiah 15:5), weeping over Simbah, Heshbon, and Elealeh, even 'drenching with tears' (Isaiah 16:9). We must pay attention to God's instructions to Israel to settle down and invest in Babylon, the 'evil' city of its captors, and to seek its welfare and prosperity (Jeremiah 29:7). We need to grasp God's vision for the poor rebuilding their cities (Isaiah 61:4) and for the city being transformed into a place of righteousness (Isaiah 62:1-12)."

"And we need to expose the church to the biblical call to take no rest and give God no rest – that is, to commit ourselves to pray for the city until God fully establishes and heals it (Isaiah 62:6-7). Believing that God is already at work in the city, we listen to God in prayer and through his word. We listen to find out how he is calling us to respond to him as Lord, as we become his hands and feet in serving the city."[12]

We need men and women who will take PRAYER seriously, for the battle over the cities is constantly being fought in Heavenly places, not just in Chicago, New York, Bombay or Calcutta.

Paul challenged the Ephesian church with these words: "Finally be strong in the Lord and in the strength of His might. Put on the full armor of God, so that you will be able to stand firm against the schemes of the devil. For our struggle is not against flesh and blood but against the rulers, against the powers, against the world forces of this darkness, against the spiritual forces of wickedness in the heavenly places." (6: 10-12)

For the church of Jesus Christ to touch and transform the cities of the World we need PRAYER WARRIORS! Men and women who are serious about the battle that is going on in our cites and know that main weapon we have at our disposal is PRAYER.

Oh, if we can only grasp the significance of prayer, we could understand what John Wesley meant when he wrote, " Give me one hundred preachers who fear nothing but sin and desire nothing but God, and I care not a straw whether they be clergymen or laymen; such alone will shake the gates of hell and Set up the kingdom of heaven on earth. God does nothing but in answer to prayer."[13]

The kind of praying I am talking is:

1. INTENSE PRAYER – People must be serious about praying. This kind of intense prayer can be seen in the early morning Korean meetings and in the all night prayer meetings in many churches in Brazil.

2. MILITANT PRAYER – The praying Christians expect the enemies' forces to yield in power encounters, leading to significant movements to Christ in former resistant people groups.

3. Expressed in a VARIETY of ways – The movement of prayer that must sweep through a city will vary in style. I am talking about prayer

walking, marches for Jesus, hands raised to heaven, lying prostrate before the Lord. There is not just one-way to pray – we must apply all energy to prayer as possible.

PRAYER is two-fold in importance. It affects the individual prayer warrior, but it also affects the cities we are praying over!

A. COMMUNION in prayer with the Father is critical for growth and for daily strength for the Prayer Warrior!

As God's servants called out to reach the cities pray and learn to abide in Jesus, they will experience a peace and a victory. Peter Wagner writes, "Equally important is that when we abide in Jesus we know the Father's will. When we pray, we then pray according to the will of the father. The only prayers that can be answered are prayers according to the will of God. Intimacy with the Father is not only the key to effective prayer, it is the essence of prayer."[14]

When we pray according to the Lord's will, we will pray for God to break lose His power in the cities and we will pray that God will transform the lives of thousands in the cities!

We need to follow the example of our Lord Jesus. As William O. Carver wrote about Jesus, "Jesus was the Supreme Man of Prayer. Nothing is more characteristic of Him. He lived by prayer. He lived by prayer. He met all his crisis in prayer." He goes on to write, "He was nailed to the Cross in prayer, in prayer he marked the stages of his dying and in prayer breathed out his spirit into the father's security. His life of prayer has brought his followers into such relationship to him that they can return from Olivet 'to Jerusalem with great joy; and were continually in the temple blessing God.'"[15]

"The apostles knew the necessity and worth of prayer in their ministry. They knew that their high commission as apostles, instead of relieving them of the necessity of prayer, committed them to it by a more urgent need; so that they were exceedingly jealous else other important work should exhaust their time and prevent them from praying as they ought; so they appointed laymen to look after the delegate and engrossing duties of ministering to the poor, that they (the apostles) might unhindered,

'give themselves constantly to prayer and to the ministry of the word.'
Prayer is put first, and their relationship to prayer is more strongly – 'give
themselves to it,' making a business of it, surrendering to praying, putting
fervor, urgency, perseverance, and time to it." He goes on to write, " How
holy apostolic men devoted themselves to the divine work of prayer! ' Night
and day praying exceedingly,' says Paul, 'we will give ourselves continually
to prayer is the consensus of apostolic development." [16]

Time in prayer is the most important thing an urban church planter can
spend doing. J.D. Payne explains it this way, "In the New Testament prayer
was not a magical incantation that mystics wielded over God to manipulate
him to accomplish their desires. Instead, prayer can be compared to
breathing. Just as we naturally breathe as long as life is present, the disciples
naturally communed with their Father. The apostles knew that the mission
of the gospel is God's mission to be accomplished by his means. The battle
is intense; therefore, an upright life that includes speaking and listening to
the Commanding General is necessary for the multiplication of disciples,
leaders, and churches throughout the world."[17]

In prayer, our relationship with the Lord of the Harvest is knitted together
– heart to heart. Prayer is where, we as His servants, catch up with His
heart an fall in tune with it, and walk in it – simply, trustingly, and
victoriously.

B. Praying to the LORD of the HARVEST. This is a two-fold task. First,
    we must pray to the Lord to overcome the enemy in spiritual warfare
    (Ephesians 6: 10-20). Secondly, that we pray to the Lord of the Harvest
    for workers in the Harvest field (Matthew 9:36-38). Let's look at these
    two critical aspects of prayer in more detail:

1. SPIRITUAL WARFARE Praying.

We need to understand that church planting is: (a) going into enemy
territory. The enemy thinks he owns the cities of the world. Through
deception, lies and false religions, the enemy controls the minds, souls
and the very lives of millions of people in the major cities of the world.
The enemy is not going to let go of the souls of the oppressed and hurting
people of the city. The enemy will not go down without a fight! Fred
Herron hit it on the head, when he wrote: " Church planting is actually

strategic warfare and is similar to attempting to establish a beachhead in enemy territory."[18]

That is why we <u>must</u> put on the "full armor of God, so that you will be able to stand firm against the schemes of the devil." (Ephesians 6:11)

From personal experience and working with church planters for 45 years, I can tell you that the enemy, the liar and father of lies will first try to destroy you and your family. If he can defeat you, he already has the people around you wrapped up in sin and headed to Hell! So he will work extra hard on defeating you. Again, as I have struggled through and observed over the years the battle can be categorized into three areas:

a.   FAMILY – If the enemy can get your family discouraged, defeated or even depressed he has you tied up in knots already. I always say, "You can kick my dog (which I do not have), call me all kinds of names, but don't mess with my family." That is where I am the most vulnerable, because I love my wife and children. It is hard to stand by and watch your loved ones go through the battle, watch them struggle with the "call" to the city, struggle with their place in the ministry, struggle with sickness or depression. I have seen this happen in so many church planters lives. Today more than ever I have watched he battle over the marriages of the young church planters. It is hard and it is difficult to go into the city - to take back the souls of men from the enemy to bring light into darkness, and not be attacked. We need to guard the family as more than ever. We need to PRAYER!

b.   FINANCES – Another area where urban church planters are vulnerable is in the area of finances. The enemy will battle urban church planters in various ways in relations to finances. Concerns over how much they gave up to come to the city, or how much it costs to live in the city or what conveniences they have or do not have will be constantly attacking the mind and souls of our families. I have had to go back to Philippians 4:19, where Paul writes so powerfully that, "And my God shall supply all your needs according to His riches in glory in Christ Jesus", over and over again and apply to our own family and personal finances. GOD has proved Himself faithful to supply all of our needs over and over again – right at the right time. So, lets *trust* Him and *pray* to the Lord of the Harvest who knows all of our needs before we even ask – and will provide for us all our *needs* not always all our wants!

c. HEALTH - The enemy will attempt to knock you down or even knock you out through health issues. He will hit you hard with health issues that will drag you down, drain your energy level, and disrupt your family structure.

In his booklet, <u>Church Planting Movements</u>, David Garrison writes, "Students of Church planting movements suggest that the affliction may be related to a higher spiritual price required for rolling back the darkness (Revelations 12:10-12). Whatever the cause, the disproportionate degree of suffering by the Missionaries intent on the course of action are well-advised to be on their guard, to watch, fight and pray."[19]

I personally know that from experience. Since 1996, my liver has failed and I had to have a liver transplant. I had colon cancer plus three operations to straighten out the "plumbing problems" caused by the cancer. I had kidney cancer removed and several skin cancer operations. But, through all those battles with my health, the Lord has been there in a very special way.

The Lord has also taken me back to 2 Corinthians 12: 8-10; "Concerning this I implored the Lord three times that it might leave me. And He has said to me, 'My grace is sufficient for you, for power is perfected in weakness.' Most gladly, therefore, I will rather boast about my weaknesses, so that so the power of Christ may dwell in me. Therefore I am well content with weaknesses, with insults, with distresses, with persecutions, with difficulties for Christ's sake; for when I am weak, then I am strong."

I can honestly thank the Lord for allowing me to go through those trials because He has been there with me and made me stronger through them. I Thessalonians tells us: "In everything give thanks for this is the will of God's will for you in Christ Jesus."(5:18), and as I have learned to apply it to my situations, the Lord truly has been there to make me stronger!

The other thing that I have learned through it all is truly that when I am weak, He is strong! And He has shown His power through moving and working in church planting in the Los Angeles Basin. Since 1996, I have had the privilege to see over 300 churches started – of various styles, reaching multiple people groups and life styles. It has been a blessing to see over 15,000 people come to Christ in the inner cities of the Los Angeles Basin. Lives, families and communities changed and transformed through the power of the Resurrected Christ, who still chooses to use weak vessels – so that He is the only One who gets the glory! For He is worthy of all glory and praise and honor!

Dr. Rodney Harrison, a church planter who now teaches at Midwestern Baptist Theological Seminary, tells of going years of without medical insurance as a church planter in Minnesota and the Dakotas. During that time, his family was never ill, had no dental issues and no emergencies. Once he moved to a position that provided insurance, he or someone in his family was in the clinic each month. Do we trust God for our health, or some insurance company?

The battle is on! If Satan can defeat our families and us then he can take the multitudes of the cities with him to Hell. We can either give up or not try, or we can do something about it! Let me suggest that we take the initiative by developing a series of PRAYER SHIELDS. A prayer shield is simply a network of people praying over you – daily, weekly or as often as possible –to ward off the spiritual attack that the enemy will throw at you. We need to incorporate prayer shields:

1. Over your INDIVIDUAL life. The enemy will throw his whole arsenal of demons against you when you attempt to *impact* and *transform* a city for Christ. Look at the long list of demons that Satan will throw at you: "For our struggle is not against the rulers, against the powers, against the world forces of this darkness, against the spiritual forces of wickedness in the heavenly places" (Ephesians 6:12). We need to cover the enemy's attacks through a "covering" or "shield" of prayer by the saints for you. I usually ask each church planter to enlist at least 50-100 PRAYER WARRIORS who will faithfully and consistently pray for him or her.

The prayer warriors that you are looking for are; (a) people who you know care about you and KNOW how to pray; (b) Prayer warriors that are faithful in PRAYER – which you can call upon at any time and for any situation. And you know they will pray right then and there! And, (c) People who are burdened for the *lostness* of your city and loves you – so they will PRAY!

Your personal prayer warriors need to pray over your spiritual safety – that you will " be strong in the Lord and in the strength of his might." (Ephesians 6: 10) They need to pray for your spiritual discernment – that the Lord in all matters will lead you. They need to pray for your spiritual protection against the temptations and trials of everyday living in the city!

2. Over your FAMILY. Again, as we all know: if the enemy can defeat your family through emotional, physical, social and/or interactive issues, he can defeat you. Our families are more vulnerable than we are – because so many of our children are young and innocent. Our mates are vulnerable because they are under extreme pressure to help you in the ministry, to help the children and to have a family life, as well as adjust themselves to the major city of the world where God has placed them. They carry a heavy load! That is why Paul tells the Ephesians to "Put on the full armor of God, so that you will be able to stand firm against the schemes of the devil" (6:11). I think of the devil setting at his computer with your picture on the screen and he knows which button to push to hit you, your mates or your family – to get you all upset, bothered and disturbed – and eventually defeated! That is why we need people – real PRAYER WARRIORS protecting you and your family in PRAYER against the devil and his demons attack.

3. Over your MINISTRY. The city where GOD has placed you is critical in the kingdom work for all eternity. There are precious souls there that need to be touched with the Gospel NOW, for their souls salvation, and for precious souls all around them right NOW! But also for the impact they can have on the city in the future generations.

Thus, we need to have a PRAYER TEAM praying over the city and the geographical area where you are planning to plant your life and your ministry/church. You need to enlist a team of prayer warriors to: (1) PRAY over your city – all the city in a general way, (2) PRAY over the geographical area where you will be planting – location/people group/ and spiritual stronghold is needed to be prayed for and prayed over – everyday!

(3) PRAY on location/ on site of the ministry place. This might be a group of people praying in front of the school, or around the storefront, or walking the neighborhood and praying for God's spirit to do His deeper work in the city. (4) EMERGENCY PRAYER, whether at 2 AM or at 12

noon, you know that you can call this team and they will get busy praying against the enemy's attacks.

NOTE: Some of the best PRAYER WARRIORS are our senior citizens. They may not be able to do a prayer walk – but you can give them a map of the area, and/or a picture of the people. They will pray for you and your ministry and they will be faithful.

To reach the cities of the World, we need PRAYER! We need concentrated prayer to the Lord, and prayer that overcomes the enemy!

4. PRAY to the Lord of the Harvest for workers for the Harvest field. Mathew shares with us the heart of Jesus when he writes:

> Seeing the people, He felt compassion
> for them, because they were distressed
> and dispirited like sheep without
> a shepherd, Then He said to His disciples,
> 'The harvest is plentiful, but
> the workers are few. There beseech
> the Lord of the Harvest to send
> our workers into the harvest.
> (9:36-38).

I do not have a fancy, sophisticated plan to recruit and raise up church planters. All I know to do is to:

A. PRAY to the LORD of the Harvest. He is in charge of the harvest. It is His heart's desire that no one should go to hell. Peter tells us:

> But do not let this one fact escape
> your notice, beloved, that with the
> Lord one day is like a thousand years,
> and a thousand years like one day.
> The Lord is not slow about His promise,
> as some count slowness, but is
> patient toward you, not wishing for
> any to perish but all to
> come to repentance. (2 Peter 3:8-9).

We need to remember that it is God's desire that "none should perish". It is God's desire that <u>everyone</u> on earth come to have a love relationship with Jesus Christ. And, yes, it is God's desire that <u>everyone</u> in the major cities of the World come to Christ! It is His desire more than it is ours!

So, the first thing we need to do is PRAY – not so we can change God's mind, or get him to agree with our great plan, but so we can get in tune with his heart. Prayer does not change God – it changes us. As we pray and surrender to Him the desires of our hearts, we can then pray in agreement with His purposes. Remember, when Jesus saw the crowds of people His heart ached for them, as should our hearts, as we pray and agree with His desires. Then we can ask the Lord of the Harvest for his will to be done.

As God has called you to the city, as you have spent time in the city, as you have seen the *lostness* and the spiritual *darkness* in the city – you <u>must</u> PRAY! JESUS told his disciples to PRAY!

J.D. Payne writes, "Paul recognized this connection between prayer and the rapid dissemination of the gospel when he wrote to the newly planted church in Thessalonica, 'Finally, brothers, pray for us, that the word of the Lord may speed ahead and be honored, as happened among you." (2 Thessalonians 3:10) Payne goes on to say, "There has always been a connection between rapid kingdom advancement and intentional fervent prayer."[20]

B. Then, I GO out into the Harvest fields of Los Angeles County and PRAY over the cities and/or geographic areas where there is no evangelical work, let alone Baptist (I am Baptist) churches. I PRAY to the Lord of the harvest – to raise up church planters for that area and/or city.

We must pray to the LORD of the Harvest. He is in charge of the Harvest. He is going to do the reaping of the precious souls from the Harvest field. He already knows which workers (church planters) need to work in which field. We must pray and surrender the harvest field to Him.

That means we can quit trying to squeeze the wrong person into the wrong field of service. We need to quit trying to put a square peg in a round hole. The *key* issue in this kind of praying is *TRUST*. Can we really *trust* God to provide the workers? Yes, we can!

Then why do we keep trying to help God out, by trying to put a good man and/ or team where God has not called them to be planting?

We need to PRAY for:

(1) PERSONS OF PEACE – When Jesus sent out the seventy in pairs to go before him to every city and to the places where he would be going and he gave them some marching orders, " The harvest is plentiful, but the laborers are few; therefore beseech the Lord of the harvest to send laborers into His harvest. Go; behold I send you out as lambs in the midst of wolfs. Carry no money belt, no bag, no shoes; and greet no one on the way. Whatever house you enter, first say, 'Peace be to this house. If a man of peace is there, your peace will rest on him; but if not, it will rest on you." (Luke 10:2-6)

As you go to the cities and pray over the cities, you need to break it down a little bit closer to the grassroots. As you do prayer walks through the area where GOD has called you to start a church you need to pray to the Lord of the Harvest, that He would raise up "persons of peace."

In New Testament times, as a stranger would enter one of the walled cities there would be a group of town leaders setting at the main gate. One of them would stand up and invite the stranger to be a guest in their home as long as the stranger was in their town. As the stranger entered the home, he would pronounce *shalom* (peace) on the family and the home.

In today's world, the *person of peace* you are looking for are people who are believers or even those who are "seekers", but they know everybody in the community and every place. They can be the person who can help connect you with everyone in the community. There are people out there in each people group/ geographical area that are *seeking* for God, and when they get God, they will be able to help you *impact* that part of the city!

In the Gospel of John, Jesus <u>had</u> to go through Samaria, because there was a whole town to be reached. The person He chose to use to reach that community was a messed up lay – the women at the well. She had an encounter with Jesus. He changed her. Then: "So the women left her waterpot, and went into the city and said to the men, 'Come see a man who told me all the things I have done; this is not the Christ is it?' They came out of the city and were coming to him." After he spent two more days with them, the people could say: "Many more believed because of His word, and then they were saying to the woman, 'It is no longer because of what you said that we believe, for we have heard of ourselves and know that this One is indeed the savior of the world." (John 4:28-30, 41-42)

Isn't that the way it should be in our live? We must go to the city that God has called you to, and share the Good News of Jesus with as many people that we can. In the process God will raise up the person of peace, that will be able o *impact* even more through their changed life and living testimony!

I learned this principle in my first little pastorate in the countryside outside of Bakersfield, CA. At one of the first Wednesday night prayer meetings, I asked the church people, who was the toughest guy in the community. They all said *as one, "Thomas". Then they told me that he* was one of the foremen on one of the biggest ranches in the area. He hated God and the church. He would never allow his children to come to church. We started praying for him. About a month later, one of his relatives asked for prayer for Thomas. He was going into the hospital to see if he had cancer or not. We prayed. The next day, I went to his hospital room. I tried to share God's love story with him. He wouldn't even talk to me. He just stared at me. After a while I had to leave. The next day when the doctors opened him up, he was eaten up on the inside with cancer. All they could do was sew him up and send him home. A few days later, I was praying and the Lord impressed upon my heart to go see Thomas. I went to his house and asked to see him. His wife pointed me to the bedroom. I set down by the bed and simply asked, "Are you ready now?" He said, "Yes," and we prayed the sinner's prayer together. Thomas was changed by the power of the resurrected Christ. He lived two more years. In those two years, he led most of his relatives to the Lord and many people came to church because of his living testimony. He told me over and over again that, "I wished I had done this a long time ago, this has been the happiest time in my life!"

When you reach out to that key person, that "shot caller" in the gang world, or more spiritually speaking, that "person of peace" God can use that person to reach a whole community, people group for Christ!

Let us PRAY for the *persons* of *peace* for your city – believing that God has already got them there in place to catalyze a real movement of god in your city!

(2) We need to pray for CHURCH PLANTERS – Jesus challenged us to "pray to the Lord of the Harvest to send out workers into the harvest."

I agree with Tim Keeler when he said, "The vigorous, continual planting of new congregations is the single most crucial strategy for the numerical growth of the Body of Christ in any city, and for the continual corporate renewal and revival of the existing churches in the city." He goes on to say, "New church planting is the only way that we can be sure we are going to increase the number of believers in a city and one of he best ways to renew the whole Body of Christ,"[21]

To make an *impact* on the cities of the world we <u>must</u> start more churches!

Now, if we believe that it is God's Church that needs to be started and multiplied then we need to get in tune with His spirit and ask Him to send out the church planters for the right places and right people groups. HE will do it!

As I have observed over the years He will:

(a) RAISE then UP – out of the Body of Christ. He is still a God who calls out the called. We see first happening in Antioch: "Now there was at Antioch, in the church that was thee, prophets and teachers: Barnabas, and Simeon, who was called Niger, and Lucius of Cyrene, and Manaen who had been brought up with Herod the tetrarch, and Saul. While they were ministering to the Lord and fasting, the Holy Spirit said, 'Set apart for Me Barnabas and Saul for the work to which I have called them.' Then, when they had fasted and prayed and laid hand on them, they sent them away."

There are people in every congregation that has a call upon their lives, we need to PRAY for them, then PRAY over them, then SEND them out and continue to PRAY for them!

T.J. O'Donnell grew up in a tough environment. After running a tattoo shop for seven years, he found himself in jail for a shooting incident. While in jail, he came to know Christ as Lord and Savior. He came out and became involved in ministry at Sandals Church in Riverside; CA. Pastor Matt Brown saw the potential in him and gave him leadership roles. Four years ago, he felt called to plant a new church called 777 Church in Riverside, CA. The Sandals Church sent him out – out of their body. That is the way it should be done. God calls them out, and the church sends them out.

T.J. caught the principle early on. When the church was two years old, he told me,
"We are two years old, it is time to start another church. They did. Now they have raised up three teams from their body and have sent them out to plant new churches. Now, each one of those churches are preparing teams to be sent out – to start more churches.

There are people in every church that can and will start churches/home churches/ outreach ministries – if we will just allow them! It is time for God's church to get serious about multiplication.

(b) RAISE them up – out of the HARVEST FIELD. When we go out into the Harvest field, we go to bring people out of *darkness* into *light,* out of *death* into *LIFE!* But, GOD is not done there – He has a call upon people's lives even before they were saved. As they are raised up out of the streets, disciple, trained, and then called out by God to preach the Gospel. It is so exciting to see sinners transformed and changed by the power of God, trained and NOW called out to preach the Good News!

That is how GOD will work – as we seek His face and humble ourselves under His Mighty Hand, we will see GOD raise up a new Army of Gospel warriors to go out into the Harvest filed from which they came! "As those involved in starting new churches, we will do well to pray and pray and pray!"[22]

5.   We need people who have an APOSTOLIC CALLING on their lives. A calling that comes from the Lord and is imbedded deep into your very soul! Characteristics of that Apostolic calling are:

A. The APOSTOLIC CALL HAS CAPTURED THEIR HEARTS.

Before we go any further lets get a definition of an apostolic calling. I am not saying that the office of Apostle that the twelve had is applicable here. Nor am I saying that the Apostolic gift is the highest position in the order of gifts in the church, as we find them in Ephesians 4:11, "and he gave some as apostles, and some as prophets, and some as evangelists, an some as pastors and teachers." Some Christians has tried to make these gifts as a hierarchical list of offices in the church. Where I believe that is sequential in nature. The apostle/missionary goes first into new territory and reaches people for Christ, and then the rest of the gifts can function in the church that the apostle has started.

R. Pierce Beaver states, "The words apostle, apostolic, and apostolate come from the Greek root having the idea of the sending of a messenger with a special task or message sent by the sender. Apostle in the New Testament denotes a man sent directly with the full authority of Christ or as a commissioned representative of a congregation of believers." *Apostello* means to be sent with a particular purpose or with a specific commission from the one doing the sending. When this is done, "the envoy has full powers and is the personal representative of one sending him."[23]

David Cannistraci defines the word "apostle" as "one who is called and sent by Christ to have spiritual authority, character, gifts and abilities to successfully teach and establish people in kingdom truth and order, especially through founding and overseeing local churches."[24]

Robert Garrett, Professor of Missions at Southwestern Baptist Seminary adds to those thoughts when he writes, "The term *apostlolos*, or 'apostle' has suffered much abuse in the history of the Church. It has been associated in many minds with arguments about forms of church government. However, behind the rhetoric there is a primitive usage important for any student of the New Testament. The noun *apostolos* is derived from a verb *apostello*, 'to send' thus making an *apostolos* 'a sent one'. Another noun, feminine in form, apostle, refers to the act of being sent, a 'sending away', or a 'mission'. As we have seen in John 20:21, Jesus refers to himself as apostolic in the phrase, 'as the Father has sent me.' Furthermore, it is there his disciples are apostolic because they join in the role of one 'being sent'."[25]

Let us go a step further. The difference between the word apostle and the word missionary needs to be cleared up. J. Herbert Kane states that, "The missionary comes from the Latin *motto,* which means 'to send'. It is the equivalent of the Greek word, which means 'to send'. The root meaning of the two words is identical."[26] A.T. Pierson adds to this thought, "For what is an apostle, or missionary, but one who is sent! Apostle is missionary spelt Greek-wise, and missionary is apostle spelt Latin-wise. But both words mean one thing: God-sent."[27]

From New Testament times to now, God has always called out and raised up people with an apostolic calling – to go to the *unreached* people of the world. God does not want any to perish, so He sends out people to share the Good News with them. It is a passion, a burden a calling that those with the CALLING cannot get away from. They <u>must</u> obey the CALL!

A.T. Pierson writes of the life of William Carey, "Holy zeal consumed him. For ten years with increasing ardor and fervor, he urged in private and public prompt and united effort for a world's evangelization. Whether mending a shoe, reading a read, or teaching a boy, he was 'absent-minded' for his thoughts wandered to the ends of the earth; he saw a thousand millions of lost souls without a Bible, or preacher, or knowledge of Christ."[28]

This Holy Zeal has always been the driving force for those who are called to be apostles--one's sent out by God to people and places that have yet to hear the Love Story of Jesus.

God is still placing that burning desire into Christians across the world today. He is calling out His people to go to the world! God is calling out His people to go to the Great cities of the World – has He got a call upon your life? Are you obeying that call to go to the cities of the World?

Paul writes of his calling as a COMMAND from the Lord! He writes, "Paul, an apostle of Christ Jesus according to the command of God our Savior, and of Christ Jesus, who is our hope." (I Timothy 1:1) When we accepted Christ as our Lord and Savior, we enrolled in the army of the Lord. He has marching orders for each of us. Are you obeying that calling to the cities?

B.   His HEARTBEAT is EVANGELISM.

God the Father sent JESUS, the first apostle/missionary into the world to "seek and to save those who are lost." That call is still real for His followers today: "So Jesus said to them, again, 'Peace be with you; as the Father has sent Me, I also send you'" (John 20:21).

The world is still a great mission field of lost souls without Christ. The cities are still the greatest mission field. God is still calling us to 'go" and to evangelize the cities. Evangelism must be the heartbeat of everything we do!

With all the million of things that the average Christian, let alone the called out missionary has to do, evangelism can get "lost" in the shuffle of everyday living. So how do we keep our focus on the main thing? Here is how it works: As His followers who are commissioned to the city sees the vastness and the impossibility of the task they <u>must</u> run to the Lord and hold on to Him for strength for the task. Then, because the apostle/ missionary has developed a close, intimate relationship with the Heavenly Father, who "so loved the World that He gave His only begotten Son that whosoever believes in Him should not perish but have everlasting life" (John 3:16), his heart starts to beat with the same passion that the Father has for people. That passion for precious souls soon overflows into sharing the Good News with anyone and everyone that he can get hold of and share Jesus with. That is evangelism.

I am persuaded that there are millions of people in the cities of the world that are wanting to hear the Good News and will be amazed the first time they hear they hear the story of God's love for them. There are millions of people in the cities that feel empty and are looking for something to fill that empty spot. As one University student wrote a missionary in a Muslim country, "I'm a student. I feel empty on the inside. I've tried everything, but I haven't found anything that satisfies. Please give me a New Testament." There are millions of people like the prisoner, who also wrote the same missionary, "I want to know about Jesus. Who knows? Maybe in Christianity I will be accepted."

That is why evangelism must be the heart and soul of our lives. As Robert Coleman writes, "Evangelism is not an optional accessory to our life. It is the heartbeat of all that we are called to be and do. It is the commission of the church which gives meaning to all else that is undertaken in the Name of Christ."[29]

Evangelism is the heartbeat of GOD, it is the heartbeat of Christianity, and it is the heartbeat of going to the whole world with the Good News of Christ! Is it the heartbeat of your life?

C. MENTORING is a WAY of LIFE.

JESUS set the pace for us when He called out his disciples and told them to "Follow Me". His disciples walked with Him for the three years of His earthly ministry – learning from firsthand experience to trust Him, to obey Him, and to share Him with others.

Whom did Jesus choose to come with Him? "He called unto Himself his disciples: and of them He chose twelve, of whom He also he named apostles," (Luke6:13). Why did He choose the twelve? He had a two-fold purpose: One, to share His life with them, and the second is He wanted to share His ministry with them. He understood from the beginning that Christianity is caught more than it is caught.

That is also the desire and passion of the apostolic missionary. He is raising up men so that they can walk along with him – so that he can pour Jesus into them and share the what ministry is all about. That is the best way to rise up and train leaders from the Harvest field. Your goal should be to lead them to experience Jesus as Lord of ALL their lives.

As Frank Damazio writes, "mentoring may be the greatest multiplying ministry strategy you will ever employ." A mentor, according to Fred Smith, "is not a person who can do the job better than his followers; he is a person who can get his followers to do the work better than he can."[30] Great teachers are known for the people who have surpassed them.

John Maxwell makes a good point that we cannot over look. He writes, "You've nurtured, equipped, and developed them. You have built a great team and learned to coach them. At this point you may think your job is done. It's not. There is one more critical element, and it is the true test of success for leaders who develop other leaders. The leaders you have developed must carry on the tradition of development and produce a third generation. If they don't the building process stops with them. True success comes only when every generation continues to develop the next generation, teaching them the values and the method of developing the next group of leaders."[31]

The multiplication principle of 2 Timothy 2:2 must kick into your ministry – if God's church is going to *impact* the cities. Paul tells us, "The things which you have heard from me in the presence of many witnesses, entrust these to faithful men who will be able to teach others."

I know there are hundreds of thousands of people in the cities of the world who are waiting you be taught the truths of God, who are willing to grab a hold of those truths and will pour out their lives to share these truths with the ones they love and that God has called them to reach in their home cities. We must go, and tell, and share, and pour ourselves into others to make it happen among the multitudes in the cities. Will you go and give and share the Love of Jesus do that the next generation and the next generation can keep sharing JESUS until He comes again?

D. People Who are Willing to Become ALL THINGS TO ALL PEOPLE that HE MIGHT WIN SOME.

The City is full of the diversity of nationalities, life-styles and worldviews. You can find anything and everything as well as anybody and any life style.

GOD has called us to reach the cities. Now that means that we go to where they are, build relationships within that part of the world and sharing JESUS with them.

QUESTIONS:

1. How is your PRAYER LIFE?

2. Can you TRUST God by FAITH?

3. Who are you sharing your faith with right now?

4. Who are you mentoring?

FOOTNOTES:

1. Brad Smith, <u>CITY SIGNALS: PRINICIPALS AND PRACTICES FOR MINISTERING IN TODAY'S GLOBAL COMMUNITIES</u>, Birmingham, ALA: New Hope Publishers, 2008, p. 13.

2. Billy K. Smith and Frank S. Page, <u>THE NEW AMERICAN COMMENTARY: AMOS, OBADIAH, JONAH</u>, Nashville: Broadman & Holman, 1995, pgs. 249-250.

3. Jack Taylor, <u>THE KEY TO TRIUMPHANT LIVING</u>, Nashville: Broadman Press, 1972, pgs. 32-33.

4. Francis M. DuBose, <u>MYSTIC ON MAIN STREET: REFLRCTIONS OF A CITY SHEPHERD IN VERSE, MOSTLY FREE</u>, Chapel Hill, NC: Professional Press, pgs. 76-77.

5. Baker James Cauthen, <u>BEYOND CALL</u>, Nashville: Broadman Press, 1973, p. 49.

6. Brad Smith, p. 14.

7. Cauthen, p.37.

8. S. Pearce Carey, <u>WILLIAM CAREY</u>, London: Hodder and Stoughton, 1924, pgs. 84-85.

9. Carey, p. 78.

10. J.D. Payne, <u>DISCOVERING CHURCH PLANTING: AN INTRODUCTION TO THE WHATS, WHYS, AND HOWS OF GLOBAL CHURCH PLANTING</u>, Colorado Springs: Paternoster, 2009, p. 74.

11. J.D. Payne, p. 353.

12. Brad Smith, pgs. 46-47.

13. Peter Wagner, <u>FRONTIERS IN MISSION STRATEGY</u>, Chicago: Moody Press, 1971, p. 135.

14. Wagner, p. 20.

15. William O. Carver, <u>THOU WHEN THOU PRAYEST</u>, Nashville: Broadman Press, 1962, p. 28.

16. L.R. Scarborough, <u>WITH CHRIST AFTER THE LOST</u>, Nashville: Broadman Press, 1952, p. 3.

17. J.D. Payne, p. 76.

18. Fred Herron, <u>EXPANDING GOD' KINGDOM THROUGH CHURCH PLANTING</u>, New York: Writer's Showcase, 2003. p. 223.

19. David Garrison, <u>CHURCH PLANTING MOVEMENTS</u>, Richmond: Office of Overseas Operations, SBC, 2000, p. 40.

20. J.D. Payne, p. 84.

21. Ed Stetzler and Warren Bird, p. 72.

22. Tom Nebel and Gary Rohrmeter, <u>CHUCH PLANTING LANDMINES: MISTAKES IN YEARS 2 THROUGH 10</u>, St. Charles, IL: ChurchSmart Resources, 2006, p. 106.

23. R. Pierce Beaver, <u>MISSIONARY BETWEEN THE TIMES</u>, Garden City: Doubleday, 1968, p. 2.

24. David Cannistraci, <u>THE GIFT OF APOSTLE</u>, Ventura: Regal Books, 1996, p. 18.

25. Robert Garrett, "The Gospel and Acts: Jesus the Missionary and His Missionary Followers," <u>MISSIOLOGY</u>, Nashville: Broadman and Holman, 1998, p. 65.

26. J. Herbert Kane, <u>UNDERSTANDING CHRISTIAN MISSIONS</u>, Grand Rapids: Baker Book House, 1986, p.27.

27. A.T. Pierson, <u>THE NEW ACTS OF THE APOSTLES</u>, London: James Niesbet & Co., 1895, p. 56.

28. A.T. Pierson, p. 97.

29. Phillip Keller, <u>A SHEPHER LOOKS AT PSALM 23</u>. London: Pickering and Ingis, 1970, p. 26.

30. Frank Damazio, <u>THE VANGUARD LEADER</u>, Portland: Bible Temple Publishing, 1994, p. 19.

31. John Maxwell, <u>DEVELOPING THE LEADERS AROUND YOU</u>, Nashville: Thomas Nelson Publishers, 1995, p. 198.

CHAPTER SEVEN

WILL GOD BLESS THE CITY ONE MORE TIME?

"We learn in this book that God loves cities. Not only did He love Nineveh that He called Jonah to, but He loves the Ninevehs of our world. He loves Liverpool and London, He loves Lagos and Bangkok, He loves San Francisco and Washington, D.C. The question we must ask is this: Do we love cities the way God does?" Floyd McClung[1]

"Should I not be concerned about the great city?"
JONAH 4:11b

Next, God spoke to Jonah a second time: 'Up on your feet and on your way to the big city of Nineveh! Preach to them. They are in a bad way and I can't ignore it any longer.'

This time Jonah started off straight for Nineveh, obeying God's orders to the letter.

Nineveh was a big city, very big – it took three days to walk across it.

Jonah entered the city, went one day's walk and preached,
'In forty days Nineveh will be smashed.'

The people of Nineveh listened, and trusted God. They proclaimed a citywide fast and dressed in burlap to show their repentance. Everyone did it – rich and poor, famous and obscure, leaders and followers.

When the message reached the king of Nineveh, he got up off his throne, threw down his royal robes, dressed in burlap, and sat down in the dirt. Then he issued a public proclamation throughout Nineveh, authorized by him and his leaders: 'Not one drop of water, not one bite of food for man, woman, or animal, including your herds and flocks! Dress them all, both people and animals, in burlap, and send up a cry for help to God. Everyone must turn back from an evil life and the violent ways that stain their hands. Who knows? God will turn around and change His mind about us, quit being angry with us and let us live!'

God saw what they had done, that they had turned away from their evil lives. He did change His mind about them. What He said He would do to them He didn't do." JONAH 3:1-10 [2]

JONAH had been rebellious against GOD. He had heard God's command –to go to Nineveh, but he tried to run away from obeying that call. He went the opposite direction as fast as he could. As hard as he tried to ignore God's call upon his life it did not work. He could not outrun God. He could not go so far down into the bottom of the boat to hide from God. He could not even sleep through the whole ordeal. He ended up in the bottom of a dangerously storming sea, wrapped up tight in a pile of seaweed in the belly of a big fish, which God in His grace made to grab Jonah out of the depths!

Running and hiding does not seem the best way to handle God's call upon our lives! Have you tried it? How did that work out for you? Probably ended up in the bottom of a pit wrapped up in a big pile of mess! The next question: Are you still trying to run? Staying busy with a lot of good stuff, but not jumping into the middle of God's perfect will for you? How is that working for you?

The Church of the Risen Lord has proclaimed the marching orders for the Lord's Army for 2000 years: "Therefore, go and make disciples of all nations, baptizing them in the name of the Father and of the Son and of the Holy Spirit, and teaching them to obey everything I have commanded you. And surely I am with you always, to the very end of the age." (Mathew 28:19-20,NIV).

But, the church has not been obedient to that calling! We have played the part of JONAH in our time! You see, our ACTIONS speak LOUDER than our WORDS! Great sermons have come from our pulpits on the Great Commission. Churches have made the Great Commission a part of their purpose and mission statement. It has been posted and painted and even chiseled into more church building walls than can be counted. But, we are NOT going to the GREAT CITIES of the World to fulfill the GREAT COMMISSSION!

Instead of obeying the call of God to go to the cities of the world, we have gotten stuck in the busyness of local church life. And the result of that approach is: there are more Churches and even larger churches in America, yet there are less people attending church in America than there was twenty years ago. We have more programs, more activities; more worship service opportunities – yet the world is more LOST than ever! Lost without a Savior. Lost without a hope in this world. Lost with no security for the future! There are more people on the road to eternal damnation than ever!

That should not be, that cannot continue to happen! We must take serious the CALL to the GREAT CITIES of the world!

The Apostle Paul challenged the Roman church to wake up in his day, and that message still rings true today! He wrote to them:

> Besides this knowing the time, it is
> already the hour for you to wake up
> from sleep, for now our salvation
> is nearer than when we first believed.
> The night is nearly over and daylight
> is near, so let us discard the deeds
> of darkness and put on the armor of light.
> (Romans 13: 11-12)

These verses <u>must</u> also be a challenge to the 21st Century Church! We need to WAKE UP to reality and see that the World is lost without Christ. We need to WAKE UP to see that God in His grace has brought the World to the Major cities! We need to WAKE UP to the Call of God to the GO and Reach the cities for Christ – before it is too late!

Floyd McClung reminds us, "The prophets called those who failed to fulfill God's purpose in the city to account for their betrayal of God's glory (see Isaiah 47; Jeremiah 50; Habakkuk 1; Amos 1-3). The writer of the book of Revelation warns of impending doom to Babylon the great city for her harlotries: 'Alas! Alas! thou great city, thou mighty city, Babylon!' (Revelation 18:10,16,19)."

McClung goes on to write, "The cities of our world often look like war zones. There is physical destruction and spiritual despair. Decades of welfare programs have not turned the tide, nor has the recent bent toward conservative economic policies. Because cities have a spiritual dimension, they will be changed only by those who perceive the spiritual nature of the battle and exercise true spiritual authority."[3]

Now, let us see what we can learn from the encounter that Jonah had with the people of Nineveh to see what we can apply to what GOD is wanting to do among us in connection with the cities of the world today.

1. GOD has <u>NOT</u> given up on the CITY, nor has He given up on His people to be the messengers of God's message to the cities.

Then the word of the Lord came to Jonah a second time, Get up! Go to the great city of Nineveh and preach the message I tell you" (3:1-3).

God's call upon Jonah's life was to go to Nineveh. No matter how hard he tried to ignore it, run from it, no matter how far down in the deep he had to go, God's will was to be done! Guess, where the big fish spit him out? Right where God had called him the first time – Nineveh!

God the Father has given us, his children, one of the greatest privileges in the world – to tell another person about the great love God has for them. God has also given us the blessed privilege of going to the cities and sharing the Good News! God has people that only you can share the Gospel with – it is your divine calling! No matter what you do to ignore that call, run away from that calling, or just flat out been disobedient, God the patient and loving Father will make sure you get that privilege.

It was a really hot July day a few years ago. Set Free Church in Yucaipa was doing an outreach in a public park in Redlands. And, did I mention it was hot! I went there to support them. As I was standing in the shade listening to the bands plays and the Gospel preached a homeless man came up to me. He was dirty, and he smelled bad especially on that hot day! His name was Howard. He wanted to know where he could get some food. The church was serving BBQ hot dogs, chips and a cold soft drink. I hurriedly showed him where the food was located and then got as far away as I could from his smell (Yes, I am still a sinner).

The next day was Sunday and as I drove into the parking lot of the Set Free Church I noticed that Howard was walking up to the church. He had walked over ten miles, in the hot sun, to come to church that morning. Again, to my shame, I hurried into the church and found a seat. The church was packed. Guess what, the only other empty seat in the church was right next to me and that is exactly where Howard ended up being seated. Yes, he still smelled to high heaven!

As the invitation was extended at the end of the sermon, I leaned over, putting my arm around Howard, an asked him if he wanted to go to the front to accept Christ. He said that he would. I went with Howard to the altar and he prayed to accept Christ and he went to the discipleship Ranch to get cleaned up and discipled. The last time I saw him – he was cleaned up and filled up with Jesus and going back home to start his life over again.

The POINT: GOD has some divine appointments for all of His children to fulfill. GOD will <u>NOT</u> allow us to get out of those appointments!

We can run away, as Jonah, or we can obey the first time (I am a slow learner, but I did learn that lesson). Have you learned the lesson? *Trust* and *obey, for there is No other way to be happy in Jesus, than to trust and obey!*

If it is God's call on your life to go to the GREAT CITY that He has called you to – then let's go! Quit arguing with the Lord, quit coming up with excuses and let's start obeying – by GOING to the GREAT CITY of His calling.

One other quick point, Nineveh had reigned for 1,500 years as a ruthless city-state without being defeated by another military power. If there had been a vote on which city to destroy – it would have been a unanimous vote for Nineveh! But God still loved them, every one of the citizens of Nineveh!

This is the hardest challenge for us: To LOOK at the cities of the World with the EYES of GOD. We need to see the souls of the millions living in our cities from Heaven prospective. Instead of looking at the exterior actions of the people, instead of judging the city by its past history or even its present situation, we need to look at the precious souls of each and every individual in the major cities of our world today.

Abba Father, give me eyes to see and a mind to understand the pain that engulfs the refugees housed in the ghetto of Tehran, help me to feel the heartbeat of the precious children that are homeless in Lagos tonight, please break my heart over the lostness of the millions of souls in Delhi.

2.   Can we comprehend the GREATNESS of the cities in God's eyes?

God called Jonah to the GREAT City of Nineveh. That can be translated several ways:

"A very important city," or, *"A city great to GOD,"* or, *"A God-sized city,"* or, *"very big,"* or, *"exceedingly great."*

There can be much discussion among the commentaries about the meaning of the Hebrew words describing the city of Nineveh. But behind it all, we need to see the spiritual meaning of the description of the city.

"While a literal rendering 'great to God' may be unnecessary, clearly God cared deeply about the Ninevites, whom He has created in his image. Therefore he sent this prophet with a message that would ultimately lead to their turning."[4]

Phillip Cary agrees with them, when he writes, "The idiom, 'great before God' can simply mean, 'very big', or (as in the King James Version) or 'exceedingly great,' but it suggests that Nineveh is somehow a big thing in God's eyes, something that matters a great deal to him. Perhaps that is why God himself keeps calling it 'that great city'." [5] (Jonah 1:2; 3:2; 4:11)

Can we catch up with the heart of God for a moment and see how deeply He loves the Ninevites? Do they deserve any MERCY? NO! Yet, this great loving God sends Jonah to tell them that they have one more chance! Wow!

That is love! Pure love from the heart of the merciful God of all creation – even the terrible sinners in Nineveh.

The God of all Heaven and earth, who, "so loved the world that He gave his only begotten Son, and whosoever believes in Him shall not perish, but have everlasting life" (John 3:16), also loves ALL the people living in the cities of the world. WOW! Amazing love! Amazing grace!

D.J. Wiseman has noted that Scripture uses the adjective "great" of only four cities: Babylon (Daniel 4:30), Jerusalem (Jeremiah 22:8), Gibeon (Joshua 10:2), and Nineveh. For, you see GOD loves ALL the great cities of the world! [6]

I believe that ALL the cities of the world are GREAT in God's eyes because that is where the majority of the world now live. So, we must also see that the cities are GREAT in God's Master plan of the Ages to see on more great harvest before the Lord comes again!

Roger Greenway makes an observation that is so true but also so sad. He writes, "As the cities go, so go the nations. If winning the nations to Christ is our assignment, to the cities we must go. Yet, sadly we must confess that many of God's servants are in the same position as Jonah on the hillside, watching the city from a safe distance and caring little whether it lives or dies."[7]

Simply stated, and I am not sure why this is so hard to grasp – the cities are IMPORTANT to God, they are GREAT in God's plan of the Ages, because that is where the majority of the world LIVE! So, to reach the world, we <u>must</u> aggressively go to the cities and tell as many people as we can about JESUS!

According to God's law, the people of the cities may not deserve to be rescued because of their wickedness! "The stench of their sins has come all the way up to Heaven!" We may not feel like they deserve a chance to hear the love story of Jesus, and ever get a second chance. But, GOD does! And that is what matters. GOD loves the sinner and will never give up on them. That is why He was so persistent on getting Jonah to do the task He had called him to do – "Go to Nineveh and preach against that great city." Today, GOD is still the God who never gives up on anyone, let alone give up on all 10 million people in a Mega city. That is why the Call to the City is becoming louder and louder in the ears of God's people!

Let me break it down in the area of HUMAN SIN:

"Get up! Go to the great city of Nineveh, and preach against it, because their wickedness has confronted me." (Jonah 1:2)

The *wickedness* of Nineveh was *PERSONAL.*

It was personal because each one of the thousands of people personally committed sin. All the people were wrapped up and controlled by sin, which was personal in nature. Each individual decided to sin!

Yes, the city was full of witchcraft and a capital of vice. It was a very wicked place. But, it is wicked because each individual in the city chose to sin. Each one of them made a willful choice to sin! Paul tells us, "All have sinned and come short of the Glory of God" (Romans 3:23). We need to be reminded of the subtle control of sin on individual lives. Paul tells us: " For the mind-set of the flesh is death, but the mind-set of the Spirit is life is life and peace. For the mind-set of the flesh is hostile to God because it does not submit itself to God's law, for it is unable to do so. Those whose lives are in the flesh and unable to please God" (Romans 8:6-8). And, again, we must be reminded afresh of the terrible consequences of sin's control on a person's life: " For the wages of sin is death, but the gift of God is eternal life through Christ Jesus our Lord" (Romans 6:23).

Roger S. Greenway speaks straight to the church of today when he writes, "How is it that middle-class Christianity has allowed itself to settle for a watered-down comfortable notion of sin." He goes on to say, " Social wickedness for most middle-class Christian has been reduced to outward sign of antisocial behavior which shake or threaten middle-class people. But the more subtle types of sin – the deep-seated racism; the corporate violence of a society manipulated by the rich and powerful, enslaving and oppressing whole segments of the human family – are blithefully ignored. Is it no wonder that our 'success' in evangelism is only in terms of individual converts, who are often the 'marginal' people of society, whereas the great Nineveh's of our day continue in their wickedness, unchallenged by God's prophets."[8]

Among Christians and even society as a whole, their concerns for the urban world boils down to almost exclusively with the *results* of sin, that is the human misery that sin produces. The *real need* of the moment can be seen by the misery of homelessness, hunger and brokenness. And the church can put a "band-aid" on those needs, but they will keep popping up again and again, because the *cause* of the situation has not been dealt with – the real everlasting problem is SIN!

I am convinced that the Church of God will not get serious about the *lostness* of our city people until we go back to the basic truths of Scripture that tells us that man outside of Christ is a sinner and is headed to Hell. We need to believe the word of God, where it records judgment on the non-believer--"Then, he will also say to those on the left, 'Depart from Me, you are cursed into the eternal fire prepared for the devil and his angels." (Matthew 25:41)

The SIN of the city is COOPERATE SIN!

Floyd McClung gives a testimony about his experience in Amsterdam: "After walking the street of Amsterdam for six months I was overwhelmed. I passed block after block of row-houses. I walked through the high-rise apartment complexes with building hundreds of yards long that housed up to 1,500 people per building. I saw slum areas that were poverty-stricken, neighborhoods that were run down. I passed hundreds of thousands of people who did not know Jesus Christ. Church attendance was less two percent."

"I learned that Amsterdam was the sex capital of Europe, and that forty to fifty thousand homosexuals visited Amsterdam every weekend. I saw with my own eyes, the sex clubs and the child pornography. I saw hawkers standing in front of theaters calling people to watch live sex acts. I saw advertisements in magazines placed by the Board of Tourism proudly proclaiming the pleasure of Amsterdam's 'world-renowned red-light district'."[9]

Sad to say, this could be said of every major city in the world! That is what I mean by cooperate sin. SIN has penetrated and controlled the culture of the people of the city that it has become a "normal" way of life.

Individual sin has grown into cooperate sin and we have allowed SIN to control our cities more than we have allowed the Spirit of God to change our cities. "Harvie Conn calls this the 'urban tower power' syndrome and traces its roots back to the tower of Babel. Though God planned for people to live in city communities for His purposes, some rebelled and turned the city into a place to make their own names great. Cities have been spiritual battlefields ever since against the Lordship of Christ. Evil men and women have sought to turn cities into power centers of greed and corruption."[10]

This is <u>not</u> right!

So, what are we going to do about it? We <u>MUST</u> aggressively attack the *darkness* of SIN in our cities!

1. We <u>must</u> approach the city with FAITH that GOD can change the urban power structures.

God's sovereign power is great enough to change the wickedest of any and every cities.

Harvie Conn points to biblical examples of change: "A fifty-five reign - a trail of power highlighted by pride, child sacrifices, and syncretistic animism – ended with repentant Manasseh restored (2 Chronicles 33:1-13). Nebuchadnezzar, who boasted of 'Babylon the great', built by his own hand for the glory of his majesty (Daniel 4:30), turned from self-praise to 'exalt and honor the King of heaven' (Daniel 4:37). Ephesus the most important city in the Roman providence of Asia, was shaken by a movement to Christ among the religious power brokers. . . The powerful in the world of animism discarded the secret authority in order to magnify another power name, the Lord Jesus (Acts 19:17)."[11]

Throughout the history of America GOD has come through with a sweeping revival of the Christians and America desperately turning back to God with a great evangelistic outpouring! Movements of God such as the First Great Awakening starting in 1734 in Northampton, Massachusetts, where Jonathan Edwards was pastor, changed the course of America's culture and history!

Benjamin Franklin, though he stayed a confirmed agnostic even though Whitfield talked with him more than once, was impressed with what GOD was doing in Philadelphia. "It was wonderful to see the change soon made in the manners of our inhabitants, " Franklin recorded, " From being thoughtless or indifferent about religion, it seemed as if the world was growing religious, so that one could not walk through the town in an evening without hearing psalms sung in different families of every street."[12]

The Second Great Awakening came after the Revolutionary War when spiritual and morals were at a low, and God brought the people of American back to God. God used men like Charles Finney, who went from town to town to preach citywide Revival meetings. God moved so powerfully, those towns like Buffalo, New York was so thoroughly converted that all the bars were closed down. Police started Gospel quartets because there were no sinners left and no crime in the city. GOD moved powerfully through the Prayer Revival of 1861-1864 that a million souls were brought to salvation that time just before the Civil War broke out. In 1904, the Azusa Street Revival started in Los Angeles and it swept throughout the World.

GOD has been faithful to change and transform cities throughout history! Can He do it one more time? YES! Will He do one more time? YES!

But there is one aspect of the Christian life that the 21st Century Church has forgotten.

2. We <u>must</u> REPENT and HUMBLE ourselves under the mighty hand of God:

> And My people who are called by my
> Name humble themselves, pray and seek
> My face, and turn from their evil ways, then
> I will hear from Heaven,
> forgive their sin, and heal their land.
> (2 Chronicles 7:14)

Jonah got to that place the hard way. He humbled himself and sought God with a broken heart – but it was in the belly of the Fish at the bottom of the ocean! Jonah shared this testimony:

"As my life was fading away, I remembered the Lord. My prayer came to You, to your Holy Temple, Those who cling to worthless idols forsake idols forsake faithful love, but as for me, I will sacrifice to You with a voice of thanksgiving. I will fulfill what I have vowed. Salvation is from the Lord!" (3: 7-8)

George Whitfield understood this principle. He wrote, "Boston is a large populous place, and very wealthy. It has the form of religion kept up, but has lost much of its power. I have not heard of any remarkable stir for years. Ministers and people are obliged to confess that the love of many waxed cold." He goes on to lay the blame right at the feet of the ministers of the city. "I am persuaded {that} the generality of preachers talk of an unknown and unfelt Christ. The reason why congregations have been so dead is because they had dead men preaching to them. How can dead men beget living children?"[13]

It is time for God's people to humble ourselves and confess our SIN of NOT really caring what happens to the 1.75 billion poor of the world? Is it time to repent of our indifference toward the 1 billion hungry of the world? Is it time to humble ourselves and confess the sin of indifference toward the millions of homeless hurting people in the major cities of the World? Is it time to REPEBT of our callus hearts toward the fact that 22,000 children die every day in Third World cities of malnutrition or of very curable diseases? We need to fall on our faces before a HOLY RIGHTEOUS GOD and confess our SIN of NOT willing to obey the Call to the cities that King Jesus has laid upon the 21st Century Church.

Let's put 2 Chronicles 7:14 into practice in our personal life, our family life, and our church life and in our strategy to reach the World for Christ!

3. We <u>GO</u> and <u>OBEY</u> GOD'S COMMAND to preach against the city!

It is great that we can understand the significance of the City in God's Master Plan of the Ages and how critical it is to reach the cities NOW.

It is great to understand the SINFULNESS of the City and how desperately the LOSTNESS has overcome so many people in the city.

It is great to know and understand and even REPENT of our indifference and callous hearts toward the Mega-cities of the World.

But, now we must <u>do</u> something to fulfill God's plan for the cities of our world at this time in History.

We <u>MUST</u> GO!

"Then the word of the Lord came to Jonah a second time. Get up! Go to the great city of Nineveh and preach that I tell you. So Jonah got up and went to Nineveh according to the Lord's command." (3:1-3)

That is a direct command from the King of Kings and the Lord of Lords! Jonah had to obey that call the second time. Don't we need to obey that command – whether it is the first time the call has come to you or the hundredth time?

There is one thing that I have learned in the ministry: GOD DOES NOT and WILL NOT BLESS DISOBEDIANCE!

A quote from David Platt really touched my heart. In fact I read it every morning for two weeks, so I would remind myself of my arrogance in the area of disobedience. He wrote,

> We spurn our Creator's authority
> over us. God beckons storm clouds
> and they come. He tells the wind
> to blow and the rain to fall,
> and they obey immediately. He
> speaks to the mountains, 'You go there,'
> and He says to the sea, 'You stop
> here,' and they do it. Everything
> in all creation responds in obedience
> to the Creator. . . until we get to
> you and me. We have the audacity to
> look God in the face and say, "No."[14]

If, GOD has spoken to your heart and you know deep in your soul that He has called you to a specific City and place then you better do it!

Jack Rager and his family had gone overseas with the International Mission Board, SBC. They had worked in Southeast Asia among the Buddhist and Muslims for almost twenty years. Because of health reasons, they were not able to go back overseas. They went back home to Oklahoma. Jack worked in ministry there for a few years and could have been happy. But GOD had a call on his life to come to Los Angeles to see how God was going to develop a church planting movement in a Mega-city. He told me, "I have seen church planting movements overseas, but they were always in the country side. I came to Los Angeles to see God develop a movement in the city." He has been working with us for the past two years developing strategies among the 242 unreached people groups that live in Los Angeles. There is the beginning of glimpses of movement among the people groups. Please pray with us that we will see that happen soon.

B.   We <u>must</u> PREACH the Word of GOD!

Jonah began crossing the city and after traveling for a day he proclaimed. "Another forty days and Nineveh will be overthrown." (Jonah 3:4)

Leslie C. Allen explains what Jonah did with these words: " Jonah trudges for a whole day and yet he has not reached the heart of the city. He feels small, one man against a vast metropolis. Lost like a needle inside of this gigantic Vanity Fair, the Sodom of a city, the tiny figure feels he can go no further. He stops and shouts out the laconic message with which he has been entrusted. Nineveh's days are numbered: it is to be *overthrown* soon."[15]

What Roger Greenway tells us, we must put into practice. He says: "The central item in a biblical agenda is the proclamation of the gospel to saints and sinners in every part of the city. God's Word is needed in all levels of society, from the slums to society hill. It must be proclaimed in a manner that is culturally and linguistically appropriate to the hearers. It is through the teaching of the Word of God that believers are equipped for kingdom living. That is a basic premise which applies everywhere, in all cultures and among all people groups." Greenway goes on to write, " The signs of

God's kingdom takes form and shape as its citizens multiply in number and apply their faith to everyday matters, live by kingdom principles in city neighborhoods, and carry Christian values into the marketplaces, the classrooms, and all the systems by which cities operate. Only then can we expect to see better cities."[16]

We preach the Word of God to change and transform lives. Our purpose and strategy of preaching in the city is to see a great and powerful evangelistic outpouring occur.

Only as people come to Christ can a city and a world be turned around – by the power of the Resurrected Christ living in and living out through the new converts.

This has been God's plan from the beginning. It just took Jonah a little longer than it should have to catch up with God's way of changing a city toward God!

Side note: Jonah did get it – eventually. My question, my concern is: Has God's Church got it yet! We <u>must</u> go to the Major cities and Preach JESUS!

Look at what happened as soon as he OBEYED and WENT and preached God's message:

> Jonah set out on the first day
> of his walk in the city and proclaimed,
> 'In 40 days Nineveh will be overthrown!'
> The men of Nineveh believed in God.
> They proclaimed a fast and dressed
> in sackcloth – from the greatest of
> them to the least.
>
> When the word reached the king
> of Nineveh, he got up from his
> throne, took off his royal robe,
> put on sackcloth, and sat in ashes.
> Then he issued a degree.

By order of the King and his nobles:
No man or beast, heard or flock,
is to taste anything at all. They must
not eat or drink water. Furthermore,
both men and beast must be covered
with sackcloth and everyone must call
out earnestly to God. Each must turn
from his evil ways and from the violence he is doing!
Who knows? God may turn
and relent; He may turn from His
burning anger so that we will not perish. (3:4-9)

Floyd McClung says it clearly, when he writes, "The heart of authentic urban strategy is bringing people to Christ. This is the touchstone for all we do in the city. Whether we are involved with the poor or the rich, the powerless or the powerful, our presence should be motivated by the desire to see people lay down their reasons for rejecting Christ and embrace Him as their Lord and Savior."[16]

Paul understood this principle of reaching people for Christ. Paul went to the major cities of the Roman Empire. Why? Because GOD was leading him – step by step. He focused on the major cities of his day. Philippi was a major administrative center and was situated on a strategic trading route. Thessalonica was a major port for the Roman navy, located on the Ignatian Way. Corinth was provincial capital for Achaia, a port city, and a banking center. The list goes on: Rome, Ephesus, and Jerusalem.

"In these cities, Paul believed God for converts. No matter the political, social or spiritual state of affairs, he preached the Gospel; His missionary strategy was built on the bedrock of personal conversion. He stood counter to Roman emperor worship and Hellenistic syncretism; he declared that Jesus was the Christ, the long-awaited Messiah and Savior of all mankind."[17]

That strategy has worked throughout history because GOD will honor His Word being proclaimed and preached. He will honor Jesus being presented as the One and only way to heaven. He will draw people to Christ, as we preach Jesus and lift Jesus up in the cities of the World!

That is our strategy and our responsibility: To OBEY the Call of God, to GO to the cities of the world, PROCLAIM the Gospel of Jesus Christ and allow GOD to do what He does best – DRAW all men unto himself.

Did you notice what happens when God's servant humbles himself, walks in obedience and does exactly what the Heavenly Father tells him to do?

Human logic tells us that: bad behavior should bring bad things upon you. Nineveh should be judged and judged hard! The prophet wanted judgment to happen! They deserved judgment! But something happened that messed the whole thing up!

What exactly happened?

Was Jonah's message so passionate that it stirred the people? Was it the looks that Jonah had – sea weed in his hair, body probably bleached with the stomach acid of the big fish that scarred the people? Was it the living testimony of Jonah – that once he was dead, but now he is alive – that got to the people? I am sure that all the above factored into the events that occurred. But, there is something more than that cannot be explained by human logic or understanding.

There is only one explanation! GOD!

GOD TOOK OVER– miraculously, supernaturally and providentially! GOD stepped in and took over!

Jonah preached and the people heard and the message was passed on to other and eventually it got all the way to the palace. "Repent or else! You have 40 days to repent, turn from your wicked ways and turn to GOD, before it is too late!"

When God starts to do His work among a people things will happen quicker and smoother than we could ever expect. Why? Because, GOD is in the process. He is at the beginning. It was God who called Jonah out the first time. It was God who did not allow Jonah to get away with running away. He set Him up in the belly of the fish, when he deserved to just die in the sea. It was God who made the big fish just to rescue Jonah – right at the right time. It was God who put Jonah in the belly, so that Jonah could have a wakeup call, humble himself and repent. He got Jonah to a place where Jonah could get in tune with God's spirit, even if it meant wrapped up in the middle of a bunch of seaweed! It was God, who put Jonah right back where he should have been the first time – the big fish spit him out right close to Nineveh. It was God who called Jonah the second time. It was God who gave Jonah the message to preach to the people of Nineveh, "Forty days or else." "Forty Days! Turn or burn!" It was God who had prepared their hearts to repent and turn to seek God's face before it was too late!

"Forty more days! Jonah knows the biblical weight that number carries. For forty days the torrents of judgment fell in Noah's day to wipe out the wickedness of human life from the face of the earth (Genesis 7:12). Forty years in the wilderness was Israel's penalty for stiff-necked faithlessness (Numbers 14:32-35) after God delivered her from Egypt – her crime so odious that God would say, 'For forty years I loathed this generation' (Psalm 95:10). Forty strips with the whip was the God ordained penalty for a guilty man sentenced to a beating (Deuteronomy 25:1-3).[20]

Jonah knows that those forty days is all that they have left. In his opinion, that great wicked city would finally get what they deserved! But wait a minute God is still on His throne and His will is going to be fulfilled.

Charles Spurgeon pictures Jonah's proclamation this way:

> He entered the city perhaps he stood
> aghast for a moment at the multitude
> of its population, at its richness
> and splendor, but again he lifted
> up his sharp shrill voice, 'Yet
> forty days and Nineveh shall
> be overthrown.' On he went, and
> the crowds increased around him
> as he passed through each street,
> but they heard nothing but the
> solemn monotony, 'Yet forty days
> and Nineveh shall be overthrown;'
> and yet again, 'Yet forty days
> and Nineveh will be overthrown.'[21]

Did the Ninevites believe this eight-word sermon? Were they overpowered by the profoundness of the message?

The simple but majestic truth is: They BELIEVED GOD!

The scripture tells us that the Ninevites believed God! "Here a city was literally shaken by a single sermon from a foreign prophet. Even Jesus noted the contrast between the response to Jonah and that which he received from the scribes and Pharisees. Without asking for a further sign, the Ninevites believed the message of the Lord's prophet, but the scribes and Pharisees demanded that Jesus prove his identity with a sign. In fact, Jesus declared that the Ninevites will stand up in the Day of Judgment to condemn the scribes and Pharisees for their unbelief (cf. Matt. 12:41; Luke 11:30-32). The Ninevities believed after one short sermon without signs, whereas the scribes and Pharisees heard many sermons of Jesus and saw many signs yet still refused to believe."[22]

"Then God saw their actions – that they had turned from their evil ways – so God relented from the disaster to do to them. And He did not do it." (3:10)

What a wonderful God! That He would love a rotten sinful people, so much that He would send His Only Begotten Son to pay the price in full for the sins of All the people of Nineveh, plus All the people of the World! Wow! That is love and mercy!

"The turning of the Ninevites demonstrated at least a recognition of their condition before the Lord. God's compassionate heart is always sensitive to those who cry out for mercy. The truth is evidenced powerfully here in v.10. This passage speaks of the incredible mercy of God's heart, of his incredible love. Here one finds irrefutable evidence that God wishes not for the destruction of the sinner but for the redemption and reconciliation of all his creation. Even if their repentance was not thorough, God's hand of judgment was removed at least temporarily to give this frail flower of searching sufficient time to bloom." They go on to write, "Because of sin, which prevails the world, all stand condemned. Only through God's miraculous intervention in the person of Jesus Christ is there any hope."[23]

Does He want that to happen in your city? Yes! Can He do it? Yes!

Roger Greenway puts it this way: "With Nineveh, God's struggle to save cities began. Because of Nineveh, there is still hope for cities. Urban mission work started in Nineveh, and in a sense it must still begin there."[24]

Yes! Why? Because the cry of God's heart for the major cities of the World is the same cry of His heart that we read here: "Should I not be concerned about that great city?" (4:11)

Leslie C. Allen writes, "The word translated 'concerned' (*hus*) in vv.10-11 also is significant. The translation 'have compassion' would better express the emotional connotation of this word."[25]

The compassion of God for the city of Nineveh was demonstrated by His turning away from the harsh judgment that He intended to pour out on Nineveh as He had done on Sodom and Gomorrah!

4. We <u>need</u> to capture the COMPASSION that the Heavenly Father has over the cities in order that our PASSION for the cities will be driven by the COMPASSION of Christ!

"The word *compassion* is one the oddest in Scripture. The New Testament Greek lexicon says that this word means: ' to be moved as to one's bowels... (for the bowels were thought to be the seat of love and pity.' It shows a root system with *splanchnology*, the study of the visceral parts. Compassion, then is a movement deep within – a lick in the gut."[26]

Floyd McClung writes: The term 'passion' is used to describe everything from romance to hunger pangs. I don't know what it means to you, but for me passion means whatever a person is willing to suffer for. In fact, that's the root meaning of the word. It comes from the Latin *paserre* to suffer. It is what you hunger for so much that you will sacrifice anything to have it."[27]

Let's get this SIMPLE but PROFOUND TRUTH clear: The EVERLASTING LOVE of GOD is so much a part of WHO HE IS that the LOVE and COMPASSION flows out of His very being toward the sinner man of Nineveh, of Calcutta, of London, and of your city. It overflows so much that it drives His PASSION to SAVE the WORLD – no matter the COST!

Jesus demonstrated that kind of passion by giving up Heaven and all its glory and coming to earth to be born to a Virgin in a manger in the simple town of Nazareth, living and teaching as no one had before, and then going to the Cross of Calvary for you and me and everyone that lives in the major cities of the World! Hebrews 12:2 tells us:

> Keeping our eyes on Jesus, the source
> and perfecter of our faith, who for
> the joy that lay before Him endured a cross and despised
> the shame,
> and has sat down at the right hand of God.

What is the JOY of the Cross?

The JOY came out of the passion and compassion of Christ that was <u>not</u> willing that anyone of us should perish and go to Hell! Wow! That is the kind of *passion* and *compassion* that we must have if we are going to *impact* our cities for Christ!

May each of us be driven by this kind of *passion!* Floyd McClung challenges us with these words:

> If you have apostolic passion you are
> one of the most dangerous people on the
> planet. The world no longer rules your
> heart. You are no longer seduced by getting
> and gaining but devoted to spreading and
> proclaiming the glory of God in the nations.
> You live as a pilgrim, unattached to the
> cares of this world. You are not afraid of
> loss. You even dare to believe you may be
> given the privilege of dying to spread His
> fame on the earth. The Father's passions
> have become your passions. You find your
> satisfaction and significance in Him.
> You believe that He is with you always, to the
> end of life itself. You are sold out to God
> and you live for the Lamb. Satan fears you,
> and the angels applaud you."

Your greatest dream is that His name will
be praised in languages never before heard
in heaven. Your reward is the look of pure delight
you anticipate seeing in His eyes
when you lay at His feet and the just reward
of His suffering: the worship of the redeemed.[28]

In closing out this writings on God's call to the Cities I believe with all my heart that the before the Lord comes again there will be one more great revival when His church becomes a "pure and spotless bride," and a great evangelistic harvesting of precious souls before the Lord comes again in all His glory! My prayer is that such a move of God would start in the Mega Cities of the World!

Max Lucado writes:

> GOD loves the nations. He loves
> Iraqis. Somalians. Israeli's. New
> Zealanders. Hondurans. He has a
> white-hot passion to harvest his
> children from every jungle,
> neighborhood, village, and slum.
> *'All shall be filled with the glory*
> *of the Lord'*(Numbers 14:21ESV). During
> the days of Joshua, God brought his
> people into Canaan, 'so that *so that*
> *all the people of the earth* may know
> that the land of the Lord is mighty'
> (Joshua 4:24ESV). David commanded us to
> 'sing to the Lord, *all the earth!* .
> Declare his glory among the nations,
> his marvelous works among *all the*
> *peoples!'* (Psalm 96:1-3ESV). God spoke
> to us through Isaiah: 'I will make you
> a light for the nations, that my salvation
> may reach to the *ends of the earth.'*
> (Isaiah 49:6ESV). His vision for the
> end of history includes: 'people for God
> from *every* tribe, language, people, and
> nation.' (Revelation 5:9NCV)

> GOD longs to proclaim his greatness
> in all 6,909 languages that exist in
> the world today! He loves subcultures:
> the gypsies of Turkey, the hippies
> of California, the cowboys and rednecks
> of West Texas. He has a heart for bikers
> and hikers, tree huggers and academics.
> Single moms. Gray-flannelled executives.
> He loves all people groups and equips us
> to be his voice. He commissions
> common Galileans, Nebraskans, Brazilians,
> and Koreans to peak the languages of the
> people of the world. He teaches us
> vocabulary of distant land, the dialect
> of the discouraged neighbor, the vernacular
> of the lonely heart, and the idiom of the
> young student. God outfits his followers
> to cross cultures and touch hearts.[29]

TODAY – let us start with the CITIES and go out to the rest of the World!

WILL GOD BLESS THE CITY ONE MORE TIME?

FACTS:

1. The CITY is here to stay!

2. GOD LOVES THE CITY!

3. The CITY is very important in God's Redemptive plan of the Ages.

4. The Church must catch up with God and intentionally GO and PREACH in the cities of the World!

5. We <u>must</u> have:

- GREAT FAITH – believing that GOD wants to save our cities!

- We must HUMBLE ourselves so that GOD can use us.

- We must OBEY the Call to GO!

- We must PREACH the Word of GOD.

QUESTIONS:

1. When you Look at the cities of the world is your heart broken over them?

2. Do you believe by faith that God wants to reach our cities for Christ through a great evangelistic movement?

3. Will you go and preach JESUS?

FOOTNOTES:

1. Floyd McClung, <u>SEEING THE CITY WITH THE EYES OF GOD</u>, TARRYTOWN, N.Y.: Fleming H. Revell Co., 1991, p. 122.

2. Eugene H. Peterson, <u>THE MESSAGE: THE BIBLE IN CONTEMPORARY LANUGAGE</u>, Colorado Springs: NAVPRESS, 2002, pgs. 1267-1268.

3. Floyd McClung, pgs. 95-96.

4. Billy K. Smith and Frank S. Page, <u>THE NEW AMERICAN COMMENTARY: AMOS, OBADIAH, JONAH,</u> Nashville: Broadman and Holman, 1995, p. 257.

5. Phillip Cary, <u>JONAH</u>, Grand Rapids: Brazos Press, 2008, p. 108.

6. Smith and Page, p. 256.

7. Roger S. Greenway, <u>APOSTLES TO THE CITY</u>, Grand Rapids: Baker Book House, 1978, p. 27.

8. Greenway, p. 27.

9. McClung, p. 120.

10. McClung. p. 95.

11. Harvie Conn, <u>A CLARIFIED VISION FOR URBAN MISSION</u>, Grand Rapids: Zondervan, 1987, p.167.

12. Peter Marshall and David Manuel, <u>THE LIGHT AND THE GLORY</u>, Grand Rapids: Revell, 1977, 2009, p. 303.

13. Marshall and Manuel, pgs. 303-304.

14. David Platt, <u>RADICAL: TAKING BACK YOUR FAITH FROM THE AMERICAN DREAM</u>, Colorado Springs: Multnomah Books, 2010, pgs.30-31.

15. Leslie C. Allen, <u>THE BOOKS OF JOEL, OBADIAH, JONAH, AND MICH</u>, Grand Rapids: William B. Eerdmans, 1976, p. 222.

16. Roger S. Greenwat and Timothy M. Monsma, <u>CITIES: MISSIONS NEW FRONTIER</u>, Grand Rapids: Baker Book House, 1989, p. 252.

17. McClung, pgs. 145 - 146.

18. McClung, p. 145.

19. Tullian Tchividjian, <u>SURPRISED BY GRACE: GOD'S RELENTLESS PURSUIT OF REBELS</u>, Wheaton: Crossway Books, 2010, p. 94.

20. Tchividjian, p. 95.

21. Smith and Page, p. 264.

22. Smith and Page, pgs. 269 -270.

23. Greenway, <u>APOSTLES TO THE CITY</u>, p. 27

24. Allen, p. 281.

25. Max Lucado, <u>OUT LIVE YOUR LIFE: YOU WERE MADE TO MAKE A DIFFERENCE</u>, NASHVILLE: THOMAS NELSON, 2010, p. 67.

26. Floyd McClung, "Apostolic Passion," <u>PERSPECTIVES ON THE WORLD CHRISTIAN MOVEMENT</u>, Pasadena: William Carey Library, 1999, p. 185.

27. McClung, "Apostolic Passion," p. 187.

28. Max Lucado, pgs. 26-27.

CHAPTER EIGHT

RE-POTTING: RENEWING THE CHURCH IN THE CITY

"What is there about the city which has made it that awesome paradox: both the fertile field for the birth and growth of the church and the grim graveyard for the struggle and death of the church." Francis M. DuBose[1]

"Lord, I have heard the report about You; Lord, I stand in awe of your deeds. Revive your work in these years; make it known in these years. In your wrath remember mercy."
HABAKKUK 3:2

It had been a great church in the 1940's and 50's and even into the early 1960's. It had been one of the leading evangelistic churches in the Los Angeles basin. It ran one of the best Sunday school programs in the area. It had been the mother church for about fifty other churches in greater Los Angeles. Somewhere in the 1960's the world changed around them, and they did not adapt to the changing community. They didn't or couldn't or wouldn't change. Attendance started dropping. People moved away from the urban blight, people started going to other more attractive churches, and people simply started dying off.

Eight years ago, attendance was down to four people who would watch Charles Stanley's T.V. program on a portable T.V. in the auditorium every Sunday morning. There was a pastor for two years that brought a Christian school in that helped keep the church afloat. But, they were struggling – dedicated but tired, sincere but with no energy to reach out to the community.

They still had great facilities, even though they are not kept up like they should be. They had a great location – right in the middle of thousands of people. The church is paid for and there is no debt involved in their ministry. But, the church was still empty and if you drove by the church it looked like there was a Christian school there and maybe a church also.

About four years ago the church leaders came to the Los Angles Southern Baptist Association to ask for our help. After evaluating the situation and listening to the leaders hearts, we sent an intentional interim Pastor to them. His task was to help them re-dream the dream; develop a renewed Vision statement and Mission statement. He also helped them develop their core values. Here was a 75-year-old church that had lost its purpose and it direction. They were in "survival mode." In reality, they were almost dead.

The church developed a new Vision statement, a new mission statement and a new set of core values that fit with the people that were now the church. By God's grace, a new desire to reach their community was developed in their hearts. They started doing Outreach projects in the community. People started to realize that the Church was alive and well! New people started attending and others came back home to the church they grew up. People started getting and others started returning to their home church. They came back to the church where they had grown up as children.

The Church has a pastor now who fits the church and the community. The pastor and his wife grew up in the area. They know and care for the church and community. Now, the church is healthy and growing.

This is a story of one of the churches in the Los Angeles Basin. It is a little bit more extreme than most stories but it does not stand alone. Throughout the Mega cities of the United States there are hundreds of churches that find themselves in the same situation with the same struggles and discouragements.

When a community has changed, this happens quite often in major cities. Churches that were relevant 50 or 60 years ago find themselves no longer relevant. Empty seats outnumber filled seats. This is when many churches simply give up. This is when the few remaining members often decide to disband and sell property to the highest bidder. Apartment complexes, small business office space and strip mall facilities have taken the place of a once vital and evangelistic church.

The once powerful and much needed GOSPEL LIGHT HOUSE has been closed down and the witness of the Christian Church has been extinguished!

We need to be reminded that the Light of the World lives in us. Because the Light of the World lives in us, we must be reminded that: "You are the light of the world. A city set on a hill cannot be hidden, nor does anyone light a lamp and put it under a basket, but on a lampstand and it gives light to all who are in the house. Let your light shine before men in such a way that they may see your good works and glorify your Father who is in Heaven" (Matthew 5: 14-16).

We need to be reminded that the Light Houses of the Gospel have always been there – from the beginning the Gospel was first shared in the cities. The Church was first established in the city of Jerusalem. It was spread throughout the known world of their time by starting churches in the major cities of the World. Paul went to the cities.

"To trace Paul's missionary journeys is to discover a veritable catalog of cities. His pattern of ministry was to enter a city, preach and minister, gather converts, form a church with its own indigenous leaders, and move on. He kept in touch with these often fledging congregations through letters. Where possible, he visited them, usually trying to backtrack after an extended missionary tour. In some cases he was able to send others to work with them, but in most cases the churches depended upon their own connected community leaders for spiritual guidance."[2]

By the power of the Gospel and the guidance of the Holy Spirit his methods worked! The Gospel Light was planted in all the major cities of their world in his lifetime!

In the early days of the spreading of the Gospel in America the Gospel was planted in the major cities of the United States. The Old First Church was the foundation stone for all the evangelistic efforts and the spreading of the gospel to the suburbs and even around the World. It was the center point for all of society, education and religious activities. The church was an important and vital part of the city.

But, somewhere down the line it seems that the Gospel light has been snuffed out or covered over by other less important things in the activities of the City churches. Stuff or events such as:

1. The WORLD of the CITY CHURCH changed drastically around it. The church had done a great job of reaching people "just" like them. Then the cultural, social and ethnic atmosphere of the city changed drastically because of immigration and migration and the church was overwhelmed.

2. The SUBURBS became the place to be. To live and work, to shop and recreate. The city church was no longer the center of life. Once again, the church was overwhelmed and did not know how to adapt.

3. Poverty came sweeping into the once welled established neighborhoods. Flight from the city to the suburbs became a stampede. And once again, the signs of poverty, drugs and crime overwhelmed the church.

But today is a new day. Instead of looking at the very reasons the church has left the city, we need to look at them as opportunities and reasons the church needs to take the City for Christ.

In a critical time in the ministry of Paul in the city of Corinth, when spiritual and physical attack was heavy on Paul the Lord gave him a very distinct message: "And the Lord said to Paul in the night by a vision, 'Do not be afraid any longer, but going on speaking and do not be silent; for I am with you, and no man will attack you in order to harm you, for I have many people in this city." (Acts 18:9-10)

I believe that promise applies to the Churches of the cities in our time! We need to apply to our ministry.

The World is changing again and we need to see the changes as an opportunity to reach our cities for Christ. The CHURCH must realize that:

A. People are moving back into the inner city on purpose. They want to live there. The young professionals are moving back into the redeveloped condos and lofts of our cities. They also want to have recreation and church where they live. We <u>must</u> see that people group as a great mission field.

B. Many communities have changed not once, but several times over the past thirty years. People groups have changed. There are no longer an all white, all African-American, all Latino, all Chinese communities. Cities are so versatile in turns of the variety of people groups. Diversity and multi-cultural life styles is a way of life in most of the major cities. We <u>must</u> see diversity is an opportunity to reach the whole community for Christ. When we are mission-minded we don't see race, color, or creed, but what we see is a need that we are focused on meeting.

C. Many "people groups" have migrated to our cities for the first time. As they migrate to our cities they are more opened to the Gospel than ever before. The window of opportunity to share the Good News with them may shut quickly as they adjust and settle into their new world. We <u>must</u> be ready and willing to go to the ethane of the World that has come to us!

Bottom line: The need to reach and to save the Lost World of our cities <u>must</u> be the priority of the Church in the city.

Now, look at this scenario:

The church is 45 years old. It was started to reach the Southern cultured Christians that were moving to Southern California. They did a good job of doing that. They started in the garage of dedicated Christians, were able to buy land and build a very nice facility that would minister easily to 400 people.

But again, the world changed around them. Instead of a whole white Southern cultured community the city became largely Hispanic with many other cultural groups living side by side. There is a large Hindi population, strong Korean and Chinese communities and a growing Pilipino community. Add to that a mix of many other subcultures of East

Asian cultures. The original church was dying. Village Baptist Church of Norwalk, Calif., had a choice to make.

Would they continue doing the same old same thing and slowly die? Or, would they be willing to change and adapt to the community around them?

Seven years ago, they chose to do the re-potting process under the direction of the Los Angeles Southern Baptist Association. They have an intentional interim pastor who has guided into a new day of growth and evangelistic outreach. A new purpose and vision has been established. A spirit of defeat has been replaced with a spirit of victory!

The ultimate goal of every church should be to reach out to their community and *impact* that community for Christ. That is what Village Baptist Church decided to do. As you worship with this healthy congregation of 200 members you will observe a church that looks like its community. There are representatives from 15-20 different countries active in the Church. The family picture of the church is multi-cultural, multi-racial, and multi-generational. They minister to the Senior Citizen complex next to the church, to the Juvenile Correctional facility down the street, and to the young and old of the community through block parties and ministry based activities. They are also active in the planting of new churches. They have a Spanish speaking church in their facilities. They are sponsoring church starts in the Hindi population and among the Pilipino community. They have gone from being a church that was not relevant to a Church that ministers and cares about their community.

Instead of losing facilities and opportunities to reach our cities for Christ, we must change the trend of giving up and selling out and start turning around the hundreds of dying established churches in the cities of America and around the World.

This is where the Re-potting process of revitalizing our established churches must come into effect among the churches in our cities!

What is Church re-potting?

Put simply, repotting is to re-plant or re-establish churches in the existing church facilities. Repotting is a re-visiting of God's dream for a church in a particular community and location. Church repotting is taking a plateaued or dead church or church on life support systems with the plug on the floor, and taking that dead church, revitalizing it, nurturing it and systematically bringing it back to life. Repotting is bringing a church to the point where it is healthy enough to reproduce and meet the community ever-changing needs.

Why the term Re-pot?

God already planted each existing church where He wanted it, however may years ago, and like repotting a plant, sometimes you have to prune it, tend to its roots, supply nutrients, fertilizer, water, etc. Then we put it back into the same pot or same community. Basically you get a new church in an old pot of church facility.

Remember that the church is in spiritual warfare. The devil's desire is to neutralize and eradicate churches, using the excuse of the communities changing composition as the reason for decline. God's will is to establish and nurture churches.

We must remember that the established churches as well as the new churches are God's Church. Jesus' words that "Upon this ROCK I will build my church and the gates of hell will not prevail against it." applies to ALL of God's churches. That is why any discussion of church planting in the cities must include a discussion of repotting also!

Repotting a place of worship in the city eliminates any excuses the devil will try to give to the city dweller. We must take the necessary measures to provide local residents with a place to worship conveniently located in the same city they live.

Repotting helps keep JESUS in the city!

HOW TO REPOT:

(1) The first thing we do is to find out the needs of the church and community where it is potted. What is the condition of the church? Is it dad, or life support,

or starting to be re-vitalized? And, do the people really know what condition they are really in? A person cannot be helped until they realize they need help. It is the same thing with a body of people called the Church. If they do not know they need help or do not really want help our help is useless. They must be willing to commit to the long haul process also. There will be no quick fixes or simple answers to problems that have taken years to develop.

That is where relationships come into play. The leaders of the struggling churches needs to be able to trust those who what to help them. Leadership in the local association of churches must develop a healthy relationship with every church under their responsibility. That takes lots of hard work, but when the time for desperate measures come the church leaders will be comfortable in turning to the local Association.

(2) The second thing is to recruit mission – minded people that will comprise the special repot team. We look for people who want to do mission work in the major city in which they live.

A person serving in the capacity of team member must possess unique traits that the repotting church is in desperate need of. They also need ability and a distinct call for service in this effort.

The main thing that I look for in a team member is a commitment for at least two years. I am a firm believer in a sense of ownership. The missionaries must commit to become actual members of the church they are repotting. They commit to faithfully attend that church and bring the repotted church their tithes and offerings.

The team begins by performing a needs assessment, looking at the community, looking at the church, and interviewing church and community leaders. The goal of this probe is to determine the specific needs of the community. With this knowledge the ministry team then serves in needed areas after receiving necessary training.

This training includes people skills and how to draw like-minded people to this new endeavor. They start off by inviting family, friends, co-workers, and neighbors. They know better that anyone else what the church needs to do to be relevant to them. This gives the ministry team valuable insight into the needs of that people group. The needs dictate the ministries.

The cultural diversity of the team is extremely important. The repot team's "complexion" should look like the community in which they serve; each team member brings their own uniqueness or expertise to the team. Therefore a community with a large Vietnamese population needs a Vietnamese team member(s). Hispanic communities require Hispanic team members, etc. The objective in reaching the community is to provide a cultural point of reference that will initially allow the prospects in the community to feel comfortable in the re-potted congregation.

(3) Outreach events that affect and elate to the community must be a high priority for the repotting team. People in the community have watched the church slowly decline and become irreverent in their community. Now, through community events and various acts of kindness the community realizes that the Church is not dead, but alive and well and important to them and their families!

(4) The repotting team must bond with the church members that have been faithful to keep the church doors open for many years. Much team building activities and listening must be applied here. A judgmental self-righteous attitude by any of the repotting team must be avoided. The church members have struggled, done the best they could with what they had to work with, and given time, energy and money to keep the church open. They should be honored and respected for what they have done in the past.

The repotting team must work hard at incorporating the existing church members into the over all process. They need to be a part of the repotting team, not spectators to the process. This will help them to accept and adjust to the changes that will have to be made.

WARNING: There is a caution that I need to tell you about. The repotting team is not there to make the existing members comfortable or happy. They are there to make the church alive and well again. There will be struggles and even opposition to change by the "old guard." But, in love the changes must be made. So, the team must press on but it does not have to act like a bull in a China shop- running and destroying everything in their way. Remember there are some "Holy Cows" that mean a lot to the members: try to find out what they are and handle them with love.

(5) A NEW VISION and a NEW PURPOSE must be instilled into the Church.

The Vision and Purpose will be the Engine that drives the Church forward into a new direction and a new day of joy and victory. The repotting team must help the whole church understand the need for the new process and develop a plan together.

Needs and core values of the church must be connected together to allow the Church develop a strategy that will encourage the members and *impact* the community. The process of developing these goals and action plans can and will be slow and longer than the team might think necessary, but it will be worth it, as everyone buys into the process and starts putting the strategy together.

(6) Now, comes the good old HARD WORK of working out in the community, loving people and patiently staying steadfast. Then you can "stand still" and see how God is going to re-build His Church.

COUNTING THE COST:

Admittedly, repotting in an effort to revive a dying congregation takes a great deal of time, talent, money, and energy.

Well, what is the cost involved in repotting?

A. TIME.

We live in a quick fix society of instant microwave meals, a quick 30-minute show where a person falls in love, falls out of love and falls back in love – all in 30 minutes. Repotting a church does not fall into the category of quick fixes! It will take a lot of time to:

- To understand the people in the church and in the community.

- To hear the church members stories and understand where they are at in the whole process.

- To allow people, in the church and in the community, to trust you.

- To get a team consensus of what direction the team should go.

- To help the whole church get on the same page so that they can go forward.

- To start ministering in the community.

- To love people into the Kingdom of God and then into the church family.

And, to SEE LONG RANGE RESULTS!

B. TALENT.

You will have to use ALL the giftedness and talents you have within yourself and that you can find in others to get the job done. And just using that. talent once will not get the job done. It must be done over and over again until the people catch it!

C. MONEY.

Count the cost. It will add up quickly. Cost for gas, for supplies for your class, for meals and community events. Also there will be the cost of going the extra mile with needy people – providing funds for food, utilities, rent for housing and clothes. It will all add up! But, we keep things in proper order when we hear Jesus say: "Truly I say to you, to the extent that you did it to one of these brothers of Mine, even the least of them, you did it to Me"(Matthew 25:40).

D. ENERGY.

You will use up ALL the energy that you have to go knocking on doors, setting up Sunday school class rooms, picking up people for church, visiting people in the hospital and just loving on hurting people. You will have to rely on God's promise in Isaiah 40:29-31:

> He gives strength to the weary.
> And to him who lacks might He
> increases power. Though youths
> grow weary and tired, and vigorous
> young men stumble badly, yet
> those who wait for the Lord will
> gain new strength; they will mount
> up like with wings like eagles,
> they will run and not get tired,
> they will walk and not become weary.

Is it worth it? YES, because the ETERNAL COST of:

1. NOT losing the LEGACY of the Church family.

Years of sacrifice of people who sacrificed time and energy to build up a church of people but also of facilities and property and resources cannot be thrown away. Land and buildings that cost under $25,000 or less 50, 60, 70 years ago are now valued in the millions of dollars. Once lost because of a failed congregation, these valuable resources are likely to be lost to kingdom-building efforts forever. If the church can be re-potted with a new vision and a new purpose the property can be used to reach new people of various people groups and life styles. It can be a resource center to help families be healed, lives changed and transformed. It can become once again, the LIGHT HOUSE in the City!

Here is where we see the difference between Church planting and Repotting. In church starting you are starting from scratch to build a church. Repotting is like taking an old worn out car that has been discarded and making a show car out of restoring it to its original glory and potential. With the repotted church we begin with its legacy and rebuild from there. We honor the past and celebrate the future. We honor the old saints that held on and gave us a foundation to build upon.

2. The cost of One precious human soul. The witness and ministry of the Church must be kept alive so that precious souls can be reached and saved in the community.

There will be days when you wonder why you keep trying so much – to restart a dead church, to love hurting people and to go the extra mile dealing with struggling saints and totally lost sinners. But, it is worth it all when that young man that you loved and cared for comes to church and thanks you for loving then and they surrender to King Jesus!

We must always keep the same perspective that JESUS had when He told us that He came to seek and to save those who are lost!

Repotting and restoring ailing congregations is how we can demonstrate the transforming power of the Gospel in the cities. In repotting we begin restoring congregations in communities defined by difference and end with neighborhoods defined by love and service to our Lord Jesus Christ.

REPOTTING: REVIVING THE CHURCH IN THE CITY

FACTS:

1. The CHURCH in the City needs to Be REVIVED.

2. We cannot forget the LEGACY of the city church and the people that have sacrificed to keep the Church doors open in the City.

3. REPOTTING the Church is just as IMPORTANT as the starting of Churches in the cities of the world.

4. It will take hard work, but many of our churches can be saved, restored and revived!

QUESTONS:

1. Are you better built to start a church or restore a church?

2. Will you take time to explore the needs of the established churches in your city?

3. Do you understand the COST will be worth it?

FOOT NOTES:

1. Francis M. DuBose, <u>HOW CHURCHES GROW IN THE URBAN CONTEXT</u>, Nashville: Broadman Press, 1978.

2. DuBose, 46.

BIBLIOGRAPHY

COMMENTARIES:

Allen, Leslie C., THE NEW INTERNATIONAL COMMENTARY ON THE OLD TSTAMENT, THE BOOKS OF JOEL, OBADIAH, JONAH, AND MICHAH, Grand Rapids: William B. Eerdmans Publishing, 1976.

Cary, Phillip, JONAH, Grand Rapids: Brazos Press, 2008.

Green, Michael, THIRTY YEARS THAT CHANGED THE WORLD: THE BOOK OF ACTS FOR TODAY, Grand Rapids: William B. Eerdmans Publishing, 1983,2002.

Martin, Hugh, THE PROPHET JONAH: HIS CHARACTER AND MISSION TO NINEVAH, London: The Banner of the Truth Trust, 1958.

Page, Frank S. and Smith, Billy K., THE NEW AMERICAN COMMENTARY: AMOS, OBADIAH, JONAH, Nashville: Broadman and Holman, 1995.

THEOLOGY OF MISSIONS:

Anderson, Gerald H., editor, THE THEOLOGY OF THE CHRISTIAN MISSION, New York: McGraw-Hill Book Co., 1962.

Bakke, Ray, <u>A THEOLOGY AS BIG AS THE CITY</u>, Donners Grove: InterVarsity press, 1997.

Boer, Harry R., <u>PENTECOST AND MISIONS</u>, London: Litterseah Press, 1962.

DuBose, Francis M., <u>GOD WHO SENDS: A FRESH QUEST FOR BIBLICAL MISSION</u>, Nashville: Broadman Press, 1983.

Ellul, Jacques, <u>THE MEANING OF THE CITY</u>, Grand Rapids: William B. Eerdmans, 1970.

Glover, Robert Hall, <u>THE BIBLE BASIS OF MISSIONS</u>, Chicago: Moody Press, 1946, 1979.

Kane, J. Herbert, <u>CHRISTIAN MISSION IN BIBLICAL PERPECTIVE</u>, Grand Rapids: Baker Book House, 1976.

Niles, D.T., <u>UPON THE EARTH: THE MISSION OF GOD AND THE MISSIONARY ENTERPRISE OF THE CHRISTIANS</u>, London: Lutterworth Press, 1962.

Pentecost, Edward C., <u>ISSUES IN MISSIOLOGY</u>, Grand Rapids: Baker Book House, 1982.

Peters, George W., <u>A BIBLICAL THEOLOGY OF MISSIONS</u>, Chicago: Moody Press, 1972.

<u>URBAN MISSIONS:</u>

Bakke, Ray, <u>THE URBAN CHRISTIAN: EFFECTIVE MINISTRY IN TODAYS URBAN CITIES</u>, Downers Grove: InterVarsity Press, 1987.

Bakke, Ray and Roberts, Sam, <u>THE EXPANDED MISSION OF CITY CENTER CHURCHES</u>, Chicago: International Urban Association, 1998.

Bakke, Ray, <u>A BIBLICAL WORD FOR AN URBAN WORLD</u>, Valley Forge: Board of International Missions, 2000.

Bakke, Ray and Sharp, Jon, <u>STREET SIGNS: A NEW DIRECTION IN URBAN MINISTRY</u>, Birmingham: New Hope Publishers, 2008.

Barrett, David B, <u>WORLD-CLASS CITIES AND WORLD EVANGELIZATION</u>, Birmingham: New Hope Publishers, 1986.

Claerbaut, David, <u>URBAN MINISTRY</u>, Grand Rapids: Zondervan, 1983.

Conn, Harvie, <u>A CLARIFIED VISION FOR URBAN MISSION</u>, Grand Rapids: Zondervan, 1987.

Conn, Harvie and Ortiz, Manuel, <u>URBAN MINISTRY: THE KINGDOM, THE CITY AND THE PEOPLE OF GOD</u>, Downers Grove: InterVarsity, 2001.

Conn, Harvie, editor, <u>THE URBAN FACE OF MISSIONS: MINISTRING THE GOSPEL IN A DIVERSE AND CHANGING WORLD</u>, Phillipsburg, N.J.: 2002.

Cox, Harvey, <u>THE SECULAR CITY</u>, NEW YORK: Collier Books, 1965.

Cox, Harvey, <u>RELIGION IN THE SECULAR CITY</u>, New York: Simon & Schuster, 1984.

Dawson, John, <u>TAKING OUR CITIES FOR GOD</u>, Lake May, Florida: Creation House, 1989.

DuBose, Francis M., <u>HOW CHURCHES GROW IN AN URBAN WORLD</u>, NASHVILLE: BROADMAN PRESS, 19878.

DuBose, Francis, <u>MYSTIC ON MAIN STREET: REFLECTION OF A CITY SHEPHERD IN VERSE, MOSTLY FREE</u>, Chapel Hill: Professional Press, 1983.

Greenway, Roger S., <u>APOSTLES TO THE CITY,</u> Grand Rapids: Baker Books House, 1976.

Greenway, Roger S., <u>DISCIPLING THE CITY: THEOLOGICAL REFLECTIONS ON URBAN MISSIONS</u>, Grand Rapids: Baker Book House, 1979.

Greenway, Roger S. and Mensima, Timothy, <u>CITIES: MISSION'S NEW FRONTIER</u>, Grand Rapids: Baker Book House, 1990.

Grigg, Viv, <u>COMPANION TO THE POOR</u>, Monrovia: MARC, 1990.

Grigg, Viv, <u>CRY OF THE URBAN POOR</u>, Monrovia: MARC, 1992.

Gross, Craig, <u>THE GUTTER: WHERE LIFE IS MEANT TO LIVE</u>, Orange, Ct.: Relevant Books, 2005.

Hart, John Frase, <u>OUR CHANGING CITIES</u>, Baltimore: John Hopkins University Press, 1982.

Hayes, John B., <u>SUB-MERGE: LIVING DEEP IN A SHALLOW WORLD</u>, Ventura: Regal Books, 2006.

Hiebert, Paul G. and Meneses, Eloise Hiebert, <u>INCARNATIONAL MINISTRY: PLANTING CHURCHES IN BAND, TRIBAL, PEASANT AND URBAN SOCIETIES</u>, Grand Rapids: Baker Book House, 1995.

Hiebert, Paul G., <u>THE GOSPEL IN HUMAN CONTEXTS: ANTHROPOLOGICAL EXPLORATIONS FOR CONTEMPORARY MISSIONS</u>, Grand Rapids: Baker Book House, 2009.

Linthicum, Robert, <u>CITY OF GOD, CITY OF SATAN: A BIBLICAL THEOLOGY FOR THE URBAN CHURCHES</u>, Grand Rapids: Zondervan, 1991.

Linthicum, Robert, <u>TRANFORMING POWER: BIBLICAL STRATEGIES FOR MAKING A DIFFERENCE IN YOUR COMMUNITY</u>, Downers Grove: InterVarsity Press, 2003.

McClung, Floyd, <u>SEEING THE CITY WITH THE EYES OF GOD</u>, Tarrytown, N.Y.: Fleming R. Revell, 1991.

Perkins, John, <u>RESURRECTING HOPE: POWERFUL STORIES OF HOW GOD IS MOVING TO REACH OUR CITIES</u>. Ventura: Regal Books, 1995.

Van Engen, Charles and Tiersma, Timothy, editors, <u>GOD SO LOVED THE CITY</u>, Monrovia: MARC, 1994.

White, Randy, <u>JOURNEY TO THE CENTER OF THE CITY: MAKING A DIFFERENCE IN AN URBAN NEIGHBORHOOD</u>, Downers Grove: InterVarsity Pres, 1996.

<u>MISSIONS:</u>

Allen, Roland, <u>MISSIONARY METHODS: ST. PAUL'S OR OURS?</u> London: World Dominion Press, 1912, 1960.

Allen, Roland, <u>THE SPONTANEOUS EXPANSION OF THE CHURCH</u>, London: World Dominion Press, 1927.

Allen, Roland, <u>THE MINISTRY OF THE SPIRIT</u>, London: World Dominion Press, 1960.

Anderson, Rufus, <u>FOREIGN MISIONS: THEIR RELATIONS AND CLAIMS</u>, New York: Scribner, 1869.

Banks, Robert and Julia, <u>THE CHURCH COMES HOME</u>, Peabody, Mass.: Hendrickson Publishers, 1998.

Beaver, R. Pierce, <u>TO ADVANCE THE GOSPEL: SELECTIONS FROM THE WRITINGS OF RUFUS ANDERSON</u>, Grand Rapids: William B. Eerdmans, 1967.

Bergquist, Linda and Karr, Allan, <u>CHURCH TURNED INSIDE OUT: A GUIDE FOR DESIGNERS, REINERS, AND RE-ALIGNERS</u>, San Francisco: Jossy-Bass, 2010.

Bryant, David, <u>IN THE GAP: WHAT IT MEANS TO BE A WORLD CHRISTIAN</u>, Ventura: Regal Books, 1979.

Cannistraci, David, <u>THE GIFT OF APOSTLE</u>, Ventura: Regal Books, 1996.

Carey, S. Pierce, <u>WILLIAM CAREY</u>, London: Hodder and Stroughton, 1924.

Carver, William O., <u>MISSIONS IN THE PLAN OF THE AGES</u>, New York: Fleming H. Revell, 1909.

Chambers, Oswald, <u>SO SEND I YOU: A SERIES OF MISSIONARY STUDIES</u>, London: Simpkin Marshall, Ltd., 1946.

Chaney, Charles L., <u>CHURCH PLANTING AT TH END OF THE TWENTIETH CENTURY</u>, Wheaton: Tyndale House, 1991.

Coleman, Robert E. <u>THE MASTER PLAN OF EVANGELISM</u>, Grand Rapids: Fleming H. Revell, 1993.

Cole, Neil, <u>ORGANIC CHURCH</u>, Grand Rapids: Baker Book House, 2007.

Cole, Neil, <u>ORGANIC LEADERSHIP: LEADING NATURALLY, RIGHT WHERE YOU ARE</u>, Grand rapids: Baker Book House, 2009.

Dawson, John, <u>HEALING AMERICA'S WOUNDS</u>, VENTURE: REGAL BOOKS, 1994.

DuBose, Francis, <u>CLASSICS OF CHRISTIAN MISSIONS</u>, Nashville: Broadman Press, 1979.

Elliston, Edgar and Burris, Stephen E, <u>COMPLETING THE TASK, REACHING THE WORLD FOR CHRIST</u>, Joplin, Mo.: College Press, 1995.

Engel, James F. and Norton, Wilbert, <u>WHATS GONE WRONG WITH THE HARVEST?</u>, Grand Rapids: Zondervan, 1975.

Garrison, David, <u>CHURCH PLANTING MOVEMENTS</u>, Richmond: Office of Oversea Operations, International Mission Board, SBC, 2000.

Glover, Robert Hall, <u>THE PROGRESS OF WORLD-WIDE MISSIONS</u>, fourth edition, New York: Fleming H. Revell, 1930.

Gordon, A.J., <u>THE HOLY SPIRIT AND MISSIONS</u>, London: Hodder and Stroughton, 1905.

Greenway, Roger S. <u>GO AND MAKE DISCIPLES!</u> Phillipsburg, N.J.: P&R Publishing, 1999.

Hodges, Melvin, <u>THE INDIGENOUS CHURCH</u>, Springfield, Mo.: College Press, 1953, 2002.

Hodges, Melvin, <u>THE INDIGENOUS CHURCH AND THE MISSIONARY</u>, Pasadena: William Carey Library, 1978.

Harrison, Rodney, Cheyney, Tom and Overstreet, Don, <u>SPIN-OFF CHURCHES: HOW ONE CHURCH SUCCESSFULLY PLANTS ANOTHER</u>, Nashville: Broadman and Holman, 2008.

Hirsch, Alan, <u>THE FORGOTTEN: REACTIVATING THE MISSIONAL CHURCH</u>, Grand Rapids: Brazo Press, 2004.

Johnstone, Patrick, <u>THE CHURCH IS BIGGER THAN YOU THINK</u>, London: Christian Focus, 1998.

Kim, Paul K.S., with Martin, Joyce Sweeney, <u>TEAM JESUS: PLANTING CHURCHES HE MASTER'S WAY</u>, Boston: Xulon Press, 2009.

Krupp, Nate, <u>and THE CHURCH TRIUMPHANT AT THE END OF THE AGE</u>, Shippensburg, PA.: Destiny Image Publishers, 1984, 1988.

McConnell, Francis J., <u>JOHN WESLY</u>, New York: Abingdon Press, 1939.

McGavran, Donald, <u>BRIDGES OF GOD</u>, London: World Dominion Press, 1947.

McGavran, Donald, CHURCH GROWTH AND CHRISTIAN MISSIONS, New York: Harper & Row, 1965.

McGavran, Donald, editor, CHURCH GROWTH AND CHRISTIAN MISSION, Chicago: Moody Press, 1968.

McGavran, Donald, UNDERSTANDING CHURCH GROWTH, Grand Rapids: William B. Eerdmans, 1970.

McGavran, Donald, CRUCIAL ISSUES IN MISSIONS TOMORROW, Chicago: Moody Press, 1972.

Neill, Stephen, CALL TO MISSION, Philadelphia: Fortress Press, 1970.

Nevius, John, PLANTING AND DEVELOPING MISSIONARY CHURCHES, Phillipsburg, N.J.: The Presbyterian and Reformed Publishing, 1958.

Overstreet, Don, SENT OUT: THE CALLING, THE CHARACTER AND THE CHALLENGE OF THE APOSTLE MISSIONARY, Nashville: Cross Books, 2009.

Payne, J.D., DISCOVERING CHURCH PLANTING: AN INTRODUCTION TO THE WHATS, WHYS, AND HOWS OF GLOBAL CHURCH PLANTING, Colorado Springs: Pateroster, 2009.

Piper, John, LET THE NATIONS BE GLAD: THE SUPREMACY OF GOD IN MISSIONS, Grand Rapids: Baker Academic, 1993, 2003.

Richardson, Don, ETERNITY IN THEIR HEARTS, Ventura: Regal Books, 1981.

Roberts, W. Dayton, STRACHAN OF COSTA RICO: MISSIONARY INSIGHTS AND STRATEGIES, Grand Rapids: William B. Eerdmans, 1971.

Roberts, Bob, GLOCALIZATION: HOW FOLLOWERS OF JESUS CAN ENGAGE A FLAT WORLD, Grand Rapids: Zondervan, 2007.

Sills, M. David, <u>THE MISSIONARY CALL: FIND YOUR PLACE IN GOD'S PLAN FOR THE WORLD</u>, Chicago: Moody Press, 2008.

Silvoso, Ed, <u>THAT NONE SHOULD PERISH</u>, Venture: Regal, 1994.

Stearns, Richard, <u>THE HOLE IN OUR GOSPEL</u>, Nashville: Thomas Nelson, 2009.

Stetzler, Ed, <u>PLANTING MISSIONAL CHURCHES</u>, Nashville: Broadman and Holman, 2006.

Stetzler, Ed and Bird, Warren, <u>VIRAL CHRUCH: HELPING CHURCH PLANTING BECOME MOVEMENTS</u>, San Francisco: Jossy-Bass, 2010.

Terry, John Mark, Smith, Ebbie, Anderson, Justice, editors, <u>MISSIOLOGY: AN INTRODUCTION TO THE FOUNDATIONS, HISTORY AND STRATEGIES OF WORLD MISSIONS</u>, Nashville: Broadman and Holman, 1998.

Tibbett, Alan, <u>GOD, MAN AND CHRUCH GROWTH</u>, Grand Rapids: William B. Eerdmans, 1973.

Wagner, Peter, <u>CHURCH PLANTING FOR THE GREATER HARVEST</u>, Venture: Regal Books, 1990.

Wagner, Peter, <u>APOSLES AND PROPHETS: THE FOUNDATION OF THE CHURCH</u>, Venture: Regal Books, 2000.

Warren, Rick, <u>THE PURPOSE DRIVEN CHURCH</u>, Grand Rapids: Zondervan, 1995.

Winter, Ralph D. and Hawthorn, Steven C., <u>PERSPECTIVES ON THE WORLD CHRISTIAN MOVEMENT: A READER. THIRD EDITION</u>, Pasadena: William Carey Library, 1981, 1991, and 1999.

Womack, David A., <u>BREAKING THE STAIN-GLASS BARRIER</u>, New York: Harper & Row, 1971.

CHRISTIAN LIVING:

Blackaby, Henry, <u>EXPERIENCING GOD</u>, Nashville: Broadman & Holman, 1985.

Blackaby, Henry and Brandt, Henry, <u>THE POWER OF THE CALL</u>, Nashville: Broadman & Holman, 1997.

Blackaby, Henry and Blackaby, Tom, <u>THE MAN GOD USES</u>, Nashville: Broadman & Holman, 1999.

Bound, E.M., <u>POWER THROUGH PRAYER</u>, Grand Rapids: Zondervan, 1962.

Bridges, Ronald F. <u>FIRST LOVE</u>, Colorado Springs: Navpress, 1987.

Cauthen, Baker James, <u>BEYOND CALL</u>, Nashville: Broadman Press, 1973.

Colson, Charles and Pearcey, Nancy, <u>HOW NOW SHALL WE LIVE?</u>, Wheaton: Tyndale, 1999.

Cymbala, Jim, <u>FRESH WIND, FRESH FIRE</u>, Grand Rapids: Zondervan, 1997.

Dukes, Jason C., <u>LIVE SENT, YOU ARE A LETTER</u>, Tucson: Wheatmark, 2009.

Driscoll, Mark, <u>RADICAL REFORMISSION: REACHING OUT ON PURPOSE WITHOUT SELLING OUT</u>, Grand Rapids: Zondervan, 2004.

Driscoll, Mark and Bresheard, Gerry, <u>VINTAGE JESUS: TIMELESS ANSWERS TO TIMELY QUESTIONS</u>, Wheaton: Crossway Books, 2007.

Eliff, Tom, <u>A PASSION FOR PRAYER</u>, Wheaton, Crossway Books, 1998.

Groeschel, Craig, <u>IT, HOW CHURCHES AND LEADERS CAN GET IT AND KEEP IT</u>, Grand Rapids: Zondervan, 2008.

Keller, Timothy, <u>THE PRODICAL GOD: RECOVERING THE HEART OF THE CHRISTIAN FAITH</u>, New York: Dutton Press, 2008.

Lucado, Max, <u>OUT LIVE YOUR LIFE: YOU WERE MADE TO MAKE A DIFFERENCE</u>, Nashville: Thomas Nelson, 2010.

Platt, David, <u>RADICAL: TAKING BACK YOUR FAITH FROM THE AMERICAM DREAM</u>, Colorado Springs: Multnomah Books, 2010.

Tchividjian, Tullian, <u>SURPRISED BY GRACE: GOD'S RELENTLES PURSUIT OF REBELS</u>, Wheaton: Crossway Books, 2010.

Warren, Kay, <u>DANGEROUS SURRENDERED: WHAT HAPPENED WHEN YOU SAY YES TO GOD</u>, Grand Rapids: Zondervan, 2007.

Warren, Rick, <u>THE PURPOSE DRIVEN LIFE,</u> Grand Rapids: Zondervan, 2002.

URBAN STUDIES:

Bunton, John, <u>L.A. NOIR: THE STRUGGLE FOR THE SOUL OF AMERICAS MOST SEDUCTIVE CITY</u>, New York: Haring Books, 2007.

Barth, Gunther, <u>CITY PEOPLE: THE RISING MODERN CITY CULTURE IN NINETEENTH CENTURY AMERICA</u>, New York: Oxford Press, 1980.

Carr, Harry, <u>LOS ANGELES: CITY OF DREAMS</u>, New York: Grosstt and Dunlap, 1935.

Caughey, John and LaRee, <u>LOS ANGELES: BIOGRAPHY OF A CITY</u>, Berkley: University of California Press, 1977.

Davis, Mike, CITY IF QUARTZ: EXCAVATING THE FUTURE IN LOS ANGELES, New York: Random House, 1992.

Davis, Mike, ECOLOGY OF FEAR: LOS ANGELES AND THE IMAGE OF DEATH, New York: Henry Holt, 1998.

Deverall, William, WHIEWASHED ADOBE: THE RISE OF LOS ANGELES WITH THE REALIGNMENT OF THE MEXICAN PEASANT, Berkeley: University of California Press, 2004.

Fogelson, Robert M., DOWNTOWN: THE RISE AND FALL, 1880 – 1950, New Haven: Yale University Press, 2001.

Fulton, William, THE RELUCTANT METROPOLIS: THE POLITICS OF URBAN GROWTH IN LOS ANGELES, Point Arana, Ca.: Solano Press, 1997.

Isenhert, Alison, DOWNTOWN AMERICA: A HISTORY OF THE PLACE AN THE PEOPLE WHO MADE IT, Chicago: The University of Chicago Press, 2004.

Hall, Peter, CITIES IN CIVILIZATION, New York: Pantheon Books, 1998.

Kotkin, Joel, TRIBES: HOW RACE, RELIGION, AND IDEALS DETERMINE SUCCESS WITHIN THE NEW GLOBAL ECOLOGY, New York: Random House, 1993.

Kramer, Paul and Holborn, editors, THE CITY IN AMERICAN LIFE; FROM COLONIAL TIMES TO THE PRESENT, New York: Caprtcorn Books, 1970

Kunstler, James Howard, THE CITY IN MIND:NOTES ON THE URBAN CONDITION, New York: Free Press, 2001.

Munford, Lewis, THE CITY IN HISTORY: ITS ORIGEN, ITS TRANSFORMATION AND ITS PROPECTS, New York: Harcourt, Brace, Jonovich, 1961.

Rieff, David, <u>LOS ANGELES: CAPITAL OF THE THIRD WORLD</u>, New York: Simon & Schuster, 1991.

Robinson, W.W., <u>LOS ANGELES: A PROFILE</u>, Norman: University of Oklahoma Press, 1968.

Sawhaney, Deepak Narang, editor, <u>UNMASKING L.A.: THIRD WORLD AND THE CITY</u>, New York: Palgrave, 2006.

CPSIA information can be obtained at www.ICGtesting.com

228759LV00002B/18/P

DEDICATIONS

THERESA'S

To First Baptist, Bridge City, Texas, my home church. Thank you for nurturing a missions zeal that has weathered the years.

To my family: Mac, Amy, and Derrick who live with my missions zeal and love me in spite of it.

To all those to whom I've said, "No, not until the book is finished."

LOLA MAE'S

To the Christian educators who minister at Howard Payne University—especially for those who ministered to me: Dr. Cleo McChristy, Dr. M. E. Davis, Dr. O. E. Winbrenner, and Dr. Thomas H. Taylor.

To the First Baptist Church, Ozona, Texas, for all their love, prayers, and material support.

Contents

Preface

Lola Mae came into my life in the winter of 1986. It had been less than a year since the death of my feisty missions-minded mother. I was immediately drawn to this determined, energetic missionary. Once I heard her story, I knew that it should be shared.

Her story is one of faithfulness to early commitment, but there is also another story within this book. It is the story of another young woman who surrendered for special service. She did not become a career missionary, but she found that if she submitted to God's will, He could find a special use for her talents. This book fulfills my commitment for special service; it was written to encourage, to inspire, and to motivate.

Much gratitude is given to those who saved letters, Audrey Glynn and Margaret Coates; to Gene Allison for providing his home for interviews; to Dr. Roger Roberts for marketing advice; to Mary Ann Ward for passing on the manuscript. A special thanks to my 11-year-old daughter who ran down the stairs with the first four chapters in her hand yelling, ''Mom, this is one of the best books I've ever read. You've just got to finish it.''

1

Voices from the Past

The scorching summer sun hit the wings of the large plane as it sat on the sweltering concrete runway of the Austin, Texas, airport. It was August 19, 1962. Austin was not the sprawling megalopolis it is today. Although it was the state capital, there was still a small-town atmosphere about the central Texas city. The Flower Children of the 1960s had not yet appeared on the campus of the University of Texas, and since it was summer, between school semesters and legislative sessions, the airport was relatively quiet.

Outside the plane a small group of people hovered around a dignified woman whose dark brown hair was showing its first signs of gray. A feeling of intense emotion hung in the air. Hidden below the surface conversations was much love and concern kept in check by a family who had learned words were not always necessary.

"Behave yourself, Aunt Lola Mae," whispered one of her nieces. The niece, in her 30s, giggled to herself at the strangeness of the words coming from her lips when her aunt had spoken those very words countless times to her.

"Yes, remember those Chinese people may not be ready for a five-foot three-inch ball of Texas dynamite," exclaimed another family member as telltale tears threatened to slide down her cheek.

The oldest members of the group, two women, em-

1

braced. Then the dignified woman began to climb quickly up the airplane steps. "Good-bye, Lola Mae. We love you," yelled the group in unison.

"Take care and God bless," Lola Mae murmured in her thick Texas drawl.

No one would have guessed the woman entering the plane was only a few weeks shy of her 60th birthday. No one but the family standing at the foot of the steps realized that Lola Mae Daniel had taken 42 years to climb those airplane steps that would take her on the first leg of a trip to Taiwan and her heart's dream.

Winding her way down the aisle toward her seat and away from the watchful eyes of family, Lola Mae emitted a loud sigh. She had operated the past four weeks on nervous energy as she readied herself to fulfill this lifelong dream to work among the Chinese people. It had been a long road, but finally she had been approved as an associate missionary in Taiwan working for the Foreign Mission Board of the Southern Baptist Convention. Lola Mae Daniel, single schoolteacher from Texas, was on her way to Taichung, Taiwan.

Slipping gracefully into the padded seat, she smiled cheerfully at the lady seated next to her.

"Where you headed?" asked the woman with a beehive hairdo heavily lacquered in hair spray.

"To fulfill a dream!" exclaimed Lola Mae.

With a puzzled look on her face, the tired traveler turned toward the window and assumed a posture of sleep. Lola Mae understood that the lady with the beehive hairdo must think she had been sentenced to ride to San Francisco with a bona fide loony.

At that moment, Lola Mae did not care to try to change her seatmate's opinion. Perhaps, after all, she was a little loony. People had said that much and more off and on for the majority of her life. In fact, those voices from her past echoed in stereo as the plane's engines roared and vibrated beneath her. Even as the plane taxied for takeoff those voices spoke in her memory from across the decades.

"Lola Mae, you're crazy to want to start classes at Howard Payne University when classes have already been in session over a week and you are registered at Oklahoma Baptist in Shawnee," the voice of her father echoed.

"You're sure you can handle the pressures of being a school principal at 24?" whispered another voice.

"You're just flab-dab crazy not to marry that Brooks boy now. He's a real catch! You know a guy like that can't afford to wait forever."

"Really, lady, isn't it time to give up this dream of being a foreign missionary? You know the Board will not accept anyone over the age of 35."

Lola Mae chuckled as the plane lifted off the central Texas soil. "Thank you, Lord, for giving me this dream, this vision. Thank you, Lord, for making this part of my dream come true." She mouthed the prayer, certain that the lady in the adjoining seat was watching her through half-closed eyes, and not caring that she was confirming the other traveler's belief that Lola Mae was a little crazy.

She was on her way to Taiwan—it seemed that the years of waiting were finally behind her. Could it be that she would lose the feeling she was marking time with her life while she watched others march forward to the foreign missions field? Lola Mae sank back in her seat allowing her mind the luxury of wandering. There had been little time for reflection as she packed, received necessary immunizations, and said good-byes to friends and family. Finally she had time to think! Lola Mae wanted to sift slowly through the years, praising God for the people who had played a part in the development of her character.

As the plane journeyed west across the American continent, her mind journeyed into the past. The memories washed over her, caressing her tired yet happy spirit. Thoughts of early childhood occupied her mind, and she smiled as the stewardess reminded the passengers that they were safely en route to California—a stepping stone closer to Taiwan.

3

2

A Rich Heritage of Faith

"I am not going to play dolls with you anymore. Do you hear me, Lola Mae? Never, ever again. I'm sick of this dumb game," exclaimed Billie, a vivacious brunette not quite two years older than the four-year-old at her side.

The two girls had been playing on the porch of their white duplex. Through the screen door their mother maintained a watchful eye on her preschoolers. Across the road stood Baylor University. Its red-brick buildings and white-pillared columns rose in Lola Mae's childhood memories of Texas. What a rich heritage to remember playing in the shadow of Baylor where her father was in school studying for the ministry.

Each morning the girls, Lola Mae and Billie, watched their father walk across the road to attend classes. Evenings were spent playing at his feet on the living room floor while he studied. Their lives had changed drastically in a short time. Only six months ago the family had moved to Waco and left a comfortable existence in Stephenville where her father had worked at the general store.

As the youngest Lola Mae lowered her large brown eyes and smiled sheepishly as she explained, "But Billie, you know it is my favorite game."

"Sure, I know. Every day it's the same stupid game.

Your doll gets big and goes to China. Don't you ever think of dolls doing anything but serving as missionaries? Couldn't our dolls get married and have a family like regular people?'' Billie chided.

"Listen, meanie, you can play anything you want with your doll, but my doll wants to play going to China,'' Lola Mae declared.

Billie shook her brown curls and smiled. Even at five she was old enough to understand that once her younger sister made up her mind there was no use trying to argue with her. Billie knew that Lola Mae and China were two of the things in life that she was going to have to accept. Billie loved her sister, her sister loved China, and that was that.

After their father's graduation the family moved to Dublin, Texas, a town that boasted a rich legacy of missions zeal thanks to Mina Everett, the first corresponding secretary for the Baptist Women Mission Workers in Texas.

Six-year-old Lola Mae accompanied her mother to the church one afternoon where the ladies from the missionary union were readying a box for missionaries. Surprising all the ladies except her mother, little Lola Mae announced, "You might as well start packing a box for me, 'cause someday I'm going to China to be a missionary.''

Two years later, Lola Mae and Billie were diligently working on homework at the kitchen table. Lola Mae's geography book was opened to the chapter on China. In a deliberate elementary scrawl was written above the chapter title, "I'm going here.''

Billie glanced up from her math to see her sister writing on the map of China, "Going here.''

"Momma, come here,'' screamed Billie. "Look, Momma, Lola Mae's writing in her geography book. She's written right over Shanghai. Betcha we're gonna hafta pay for that book,'' scolded Billie.

"Betcha I don't. Betcha I go here, right where I've said,

someday. Betcha I mail you a postcard right from China," retorted the spunky youngster, who was more than a little afraid that she would be punished for writing in her book.

"Lola Mae," said her mother, "when you get to China, do send your dad and me a postcard, and do remember to tell your students not to write in their books." Mrs. Daniel had kept the book. She felt that it was significant that a child so young already knew the direction her life would take.

A short time later Mr. Daniel moved his family to Electra where he served as the district missionary. His job was to help with new churches and to fill pulpits of established churches when the need arose. While living in Electra, the youngest Daniel had a life-changing experience. On a Friday night in June 1913 ten-year-old Lola Mae publicly professed Jesus Christ as her personal Saviour.

Early in her Christian experience, Lola Mae learned the power of prayer and personal witnessing. Immediately upon acknowledging Jesus, she felt an overwhelming burden for her best friend, Rachael, who was unsaved. Her prayers were answered when Rachael walked down the aisle the following night. The two girls were baptized together, and Lola Mae had her first taste of the joy that comes from seeing someone embrace the Christian life. That joy would be repeated many times in the year that followed.

Lola Mae's family moved again: this time to Oklahoma. Being a minister's family meant moving almost as much as a military family. In Oklahoma they lived in a rural farmhouse surrounded by wheat fields. Lola Mae's days were spent in school and her evenings were spent playing missionary in the wheat field. Dividing the field into sections representing the various districts in China, she would walk to each district and preach to the golden stalks of grain. Her sermons were the ones she had heard her daddy preach the Sunday before.

"Really, Mom," said the maturing Billie, "Don't you

6

get tired of Lola Mae's talk of China? She's old enough to give up playing China.''

Mother chuckled and said, ''Lola Mae has a mind of her own. She's determined about China, and she thinks if she plays going there often enough, her dream will come true. It's a worthy dream. Let's not discourage her by not believing with her in the dream.''

The happy days in Oklahoma passed too quickly. Before the Daniels knew it, their daughters were teenagers. When Mr. Daniel had a revival meeting to preach, both girls would accompany him. Billie would play the piano for services, Lola Mae would sing the special music, and Daddy would preach the good news.

While preparing for one of many trips, their mother commented, ''Each of you has a special job to do for the Lord, and my job is seeing that you have clean clothes ready to wear, hot meals to keep you goin', and prayin' that you will give your best efforts and the Lord will bless them.''

Both girls laughed, and kissing their mother said, ''Don't forget the other important thing you do for us— you're our favorite and best audience!''

During Lola Mae's junior year in high school, Billie married. Her new husband worked in another city so Billie was not close enough to visit regularly. The quietness of the house without her lifelong companion left Lola Mae lonely and depressed. Wisely her parents decided to send her to a secondary boarding school on the grounds of Oklahoma Baptist University. There she would complete her senior year of high school.

The first Sunday night of January 1920, on one of her frequent weekend trips home, Lola Mae attended worship service at the church her father was pastoring. Mr. Daniel preached a stirring message on commitment and church membership. The words about commitment touched the attractive 17-year-old. She realized it was time to make a real commitment to the dream of becoming a missionary to China. Her call was specific—she felt a strong pull to the China of her childhood games.

Even before the sermon concluded, Lola Mae decided she must share this commitment with her church family. As the piano struck the opening chords of the invitation hymn, a beaming young lady rushed down the aisle. "Dad," she said softly, "I am surrendering to go to China. God has called me to the foreign missions field."

A tearful grin broke across the familiar face, and she felt the slightest tremble from the large hand that lay gently across her back. As her father raised his head, turning to speak to the congregation, tears rolled down his face.

"Friends," he began in a voice that quivered, "my prayers have been answered. Long ago I asked God to send me to foreign soil. His answer for me was no. I was called to remain in service here, but tonight He has called Lola Mae to China."

Lola Mae looked across the faces of that small rural congregation and understood why God had not called her father to a place across the sea. Mr. Daniel had served God well planting churches in rural Oklahoma and Texas. His talents had been put to worthy service here. Lola Mae was glad she had made that decision that night because at the end of her senior year, her grandfather died, and Lola Mae moved away from the church family she loved.

In order to be near his mother, Mr. Daniel accepted another church in Texas. The family returned to their native state, and Lola Mae spent the summer counting the days until college would start in the fall. She looked forward to being a freshman at Oklahoma Baptist University (OBU).

Mr. Daniel did not feel the excitement his youngest child felt. OBU was a long way from their Texas home. He had given up Billie, and it would not be easy to watch Lola Mae leave for a college so far away.

Midway through the summer, knowing the fine reputation of Mary Hardin Baylor University (MHB) in Bel-

8

ton, which was an all-female school, Mr. Daniel persuaded Lola Mae to go along with him for a weekend revival. On the way to the revival, he detoured by the campus of MHB.

"Lola Mae," he explained, "I have just a little surprise for you. I have made arrangements for you to spend the weekend with the girls at the dormitory here. They will show you around and introduce you to some of the professors. Maybe you would like it here if you gave it half a chance. I'll be here late Sunday night to pick you up."

"Dad, we've been through this before. I'm already registered at Oklahoma Baptist."

"Please, just give it a chance. If you went to school here, you could come home weekends. That would please your mother and me very much."

Assuring her he would be back, he proceeded to unload her bags. Lola Mae stood on the dormitory steps surrounded by girls who were convinced MHB was the greatest college on earth. She shook her head as she watched her daddy drive away in their old Model T. Certainly, she understood how she so rightly came by the stubborn streak in her personality. Her dad was surely determined to keep her from school in Oklahoma.

After a tour of the campus, Lola Mae began to make plans for her great escape. Calling the bus station she discovered she could go home by bus. Explaining politely to the girls that she had her heart set on OBU, she caught the first bus back home. When Mr. Daniel returned to his room that night he received a phone message that Lola Mae had already beat him home.

Resigned to his daughter's dogged determination, W. L. Daniel dropped his finagling. He prayed as September approached that Lola Mae would change her mind.

One evening shortly before Lola Mae was to leave for OBU, Mr. Daniel mentioned, "I need to attend an associational meeting tonight and drop off these items. Would you go with me?" Lola Mae's mother smiled, implying

9

that this would be the least their college-bound daughter could do to humor her father.

As they walked into the meeting that night, the bright eyes of family friends turned to greet them. A man was delivering a rather dry report. As the meeting progressed, Lola Mae had to pinch herself to stay awake. "It's no wonder I want to get away. No telling how many more of these meetings I might have to tolerate if I stay in Texas," she thought.

Then her own name caught her ear and snapped her body erect. "Yes, ladies and gentlemen, our association is pleased to announce that Lola Mae Daniel has won the associational scholarship for one year of college."

She could not believe her ears. Although she had worried about the expense of the family relocating, about the necessity of accepting responsibility for her widowed grandmother, and meeting the financial requirements of higher education, the Lord had all the while worked out a way for her needs to be met. She understood why her father had insisted she accompany him. Walking down the aisle to accept the scholarship, Lola Mae was so proud to be a part of the associational Baptist family. The scholarship would have been an impossibility for one church to provide, but by pooling their money, the association made her first year of college much easier.

At that meeting was Dr. Hornburg, acting president of Howard Payne College, a small Baptist school in Brownwood. After the announcement, he stopped by to congratulate her. "You know, Howard Payne could use a young person like you."

That night Dr. Hornburg's words were a catalyst for her. Riding home that evening, staring at the night expanse of Texas sky and stars, Lola Mae considered carefully Dr. Hornburg's words. She also thought about leaving her parents and grandmother. Her dad turned and spoke softly. "I was very proud of you tonight. We're going to miss you very much."

10

"No, you're not, Dad," came the swift reply. "I have decided to stay right here in Texas. Tonight I felt pulled to attend Howard Payne. It's a fine college, and you simply can't beat the location."

"But, you're crazy; classes have already begun at Howard Payne and you haven't even been approved for registration. You're registered to go to OBU. Your suitcases are packed to leave in the morning for Shawnee."

"Great. The same packed suitcases will go to Brownwood."

Mr. Daniel smiled broadly. Actually he wanted to shout. He had learned long ago his brown-eyed daughter rarely wavered from her course once her mind was made up, and her mind certainly seemed to be turned toward Howard Payne.

Lola Mae snapped out of her 1920s daydream when the plane hit a rough spot. The captain's voice calmed the passengers and reminded them to fasten their seatbelts until the plane cleared the turbulent weather. How quickly the mind was capable of moving. Lola Mae had been thinking of an age when airplanes were new, and here she was in 1962 riding in a plane.

After a brief time, the seatbelt light flashed off. The lady in the seat next to her commented, "I hate these rough times. It gives me a queasy feeling when I think I have no control over my life."

Lola Mae grinned, understanding the woman's feeling. But unlike this lady, she had learned that the greatest time of growth for any human being was when they realized God was in control, and He knew best. Aloud she said, "I know God is in control and He will not bring me this close to Taiwan and let this plane crash."

"Oh, yes, I forgot," said her new friend. "You're on your way to fulfill a dream."

The 59-year-old teacher lowered the back of her seat and returned to her daydreams. Where was she? "Oh, yes, Howard Payne in the west Texas town of Brownwood." The thoughts of her alma mater caused her to smile.

The college was just a small school those many years ago in 1923 when she walked into the registrar's office and signed up for school a week after fall classes had already begun. "It will not be easy to catch up," said the secretary who was helping her fill out the mountains of forms, "but at least you won't have to work and go to school. This scholarship from the Erath Baptist Association pays for your tuition, room, board, and textbooks. You are set for your first year of college."

"Thank you, Lord!" mouthed the excited freshman. Her decision to enter Howard Payne had been affirmed. At OBU, the money would only have covered tuition and books. She would have needed to work for room and board. Certainly the Lord was good. Besides, she needed the extra time for studying, because on the very day Lola Mae enrolled with a full college load at Howard Payne, she also signed up to take seminary correspondence courses from Southwestern Seminary in Fort Worth. The seminary courses were a necessity if she intended to be accepted as a Southern Baptist foreign missionary. China was still beckoning, and time was a cruel taskmaster.

Plenty of practical training or on-the-job training was available at Howard Payne where she majored in English and minored in Bible. The campus volunteer missions band was formed, and students found numerous projects in the community to keep them busy after class. Friendships with teachers and students were cemented for a lifetime. Throughout the years that followed her teachers from Howard Payne maintained correspondence with her. Each time there was a triumph or difficulty, she knew she could count on receiving a letter of exhortation from one of her former instructors. As Lola Mae taught others, she tried to follow in the footsteps of those dedicated instructors. One of them had often quoted a Scripture verse that had become a source of strength throughout the years:

"God hath not given us the spirit of fear; but of power, and of love, and of a sound mind" (2 Tim. 1:7).

As the voices from her past accused her of being half-crazy, Lola Mae claimed that Scripture verse again. Knowing she had a sound mind was quite a comfort as the plane taxied into the San Francisco airport.

3

Ordered Steps

After changing planes at the San Francisco airport, Lola Mae finally began crossing the last barrier to the Orient—the Pacific Ocean. There was something unsettling about flying across a vast body of water for the first time. Lola Mae exchanged courtesies with the young military man in blue beside her.

"Boy, I'm tired," he said. "I stayed up most of last night with my buddies. Hope you don't mind if I get some sleep. I am going to a new base in Taiwan, which has a new commander, and I'm not so sure what to expect. I'll be in a lot better shape to face whatever I find if I get sleep now."

"Certainly," said Lola Mae trying to stifle a chuckle, "you go right ahead and get some rest. I am going to a new base, but I have the same commander, and I'm not so sure what to expect either."

The young man in his air force blues appeared content with her answer. The military was one way to get overseas that Lola Mae had never tried—she had applied with a fellow teacher, Gene Allison, to work at a Department of Defense school in Europe, but she had never considered enlisting in the military. Unfortunately, like the other alternatives she had tried, she probably would have been too old to meet the age requirements for military service.

When she had first spied the military uniform, she had

been afraid that her new seatmate might need to talk. As the airman fell into a gentle sleep beside her, she rejoiced, realizing they were both satisfied with silence. She had longed to return to her 1920s daydreams. His breath came in soft purrings. "Let's hope he doesn't snore," she thought as her mind drifted back to the year 1926.

The 1920s had been tough for the Farm Belt of the United States. The land cried for rain, the sun was merciless, and Texas crops continued to fail. West Texas was part of the American Dust Bowl. Families pulled up roots and headed on little more than faith to California.

Although Lola Mae had already worked two years with a teaching certificate, she did not graduate from college until May 26, 1926. How proud she was that she was able to finish college when so many classmates were dropping out because their families could not afford to finance their studies, and part-time jobs as well as full-time jobs were scarce. Higher education was a luxury for the students as well as the instructors. Lola Mae remembered the time Howard Payne professors had voted unanimously to stay through lean years, although salaries could not be guaranteed.

As pastor of a small church in Bangs, Texas, part of Mr. Daniel's salary was often paid in produce. Lola Mae, still living at home, worked at a four-teacher school nearby. After receiving her diploma, the school promoted her to principal.

"You must be crazy to think you can be a principal and continue to teach full-time; you're only 24," said a well-meaning girlfriend.

"Times are tough. We need the money, and I don't have time to wonder if I can handle the job. When God dumps a job in your lap, He equips you to do it," explained Lola Mae in confidence and faith.

Teachers had to be a special breed in those years. Home visits were expected. In fact, occasionally a teacher was given room and board in the home of a pupil as part of

15

her salary package. Teachers were also expected to take part in all community activities. It was certainly no surprise when one of her young pupils, one of the Brooks girls, slipped a note on her desk early one morning. The note was an invitation to supper. Artie's father was a deacon in the church her father pastored, and Lola Mae did not have to think twice about accepting the Brooks's invitation.

"Artie, you may tell your mother that I'd be pleased to be there for supper," said the pretty young teacher-principal, blushing.

The blush was brought on by the thought of the oldest Brooks son who had been sitting with the family last Sunday. From her vantage point in the choir loft, she had caught him giving her the eye several times during her dad's sermon. It had become a matter of self-discipline to keep her mind on her father's message.

That night in her upstairs room dressing for dinner, Lola Mae found herself wondering if the oldest Brooks son would eat dinner at home. A girlfriend in town heard from the Bangs grapevine that Ennis Brooks had returned home from a short military stint at Annapolis to purchase a ranch and find a wife.

"Just watch your thoughts," Lola Mae chastised herself. "You have a commitment to the Lord and to China, and here you are considering marrying a rancher when you haven't even been properly introduced." Still, she took extra time with her hair and donned her prettiest dress. How she did love to dress up and look nice!

As soon as Lola Mae entered the Brooks's home, she noticed the handsome young man that had the Bangs grapevine buzzing. "Miss Daniel, I'd like you to meet my son Ennis," said Mrs. Brooks with a twinkle in her eye, indicating that the purpose of the visit was more than a chance to discuss the younger Brooks children's progress in school.

"Pleased to meet you, Miss Daniel. Too bad we didn't

16

have teachers pretty as you when I went to school," Ennis said.

"Artie, you didn't tell me your big brother was such a charmer," replied the young teacher-principal as she felt a slow blush begin at her neck and move upwards.

"How's my kid sister doing in school?" asked Ennis, skillfully changing the subject. "She better be the smartest girl in the room."

"Come on, Ennis, you know I'm doing fine," said Artie, getting in on the act. "What kid wouldn't want to be good for Miss Daniel?"

The supper conversation focused on the weather, the poor economy, and ranching. (Lola Mae momentarily came back to the present and chuckled, thinking that those subjects were just as important in Texas today as they were that night in 1926.) She had watched Ennis behind her thick eyelashes hoping he was not opposed to a girl with glasses and a brain. Noting how caring and courteous he was with his mother and sisters earned him a high rating in her book. The evening went smoothly, and Lola Mae earned more than the approval of the parents of the child she taught.

As soon as Artie entered the classroom the next day, she ran up to her teacher and said, "My brother thinks you're pretty. He said he wasn't quite as old as you, but you were the first girl he'd gotten interested enough in to marry."

In the weeks that followed, Ennis rarely missed a church service. Soon he began to phone asking to accompany her to church functions. Several months later over a soda at the drugstore, Ennis mustered the courage to ask, "Lola Mae, would you consider living in Bangs on a permanent basis? Would you consider being a rancher's wife?"

"Ennis, six years ago, before I even knew Bangs or the Brooks family existed, I made a commitment to go to China. As soon as I get enough seminary hours and the Foreign Mission Board's approval, I must go. I might consider being your wife, but living in Bangs isn't a possibility for me."

"Honey, if I told you I'd go to China, would you marry me?" was his only reply.

"If God calls you to China, I'd be happy to be your wife."

He gave her a shiny gold band with a solitaire diamond. On a drugstore stool they made a commitment to each other and to China.

A few years passed. Lola Mae continued working on her seminary correspondence courses and teaching. Then one year, the Daniel family weathered a major crisis. Billie returned home with her three young daughters. They were welcomed home with open arms.

Needing to help provide for her girls, Billie found a job with Harvey House Restaurants, a chain that operated in railroad stations. Because jobs were so scarce, the Daniels felt fortunate to have a pastorate and both daughters working. Unfortunately, Billie's job required that she move from town to town helping set up new restaurants. Mr. and Mrs. Daniel insisted on having the three girls stay with them; the girls did not need to move from school to school as demanded by their mother's job. The Daniels could provide a safe, stable environment for the girls while their mother worked.

Those three beautiful little girls pulled at the strings of Lola Mae's heart. They were Billie's children, and having them close was almost as good as having Billie home once again.

These were the depression years, and the Daniel family, like most other families, weathered those turbulent times as a closely knit unit. Billie worked sending money and coming home at every opportunity, hungry to see and hold her babies. Lola Mae continued to teach and she helped with the girls and household responsibilities. Mr. Daniel pastored the church, ministering to his flock, who

18

also faced hard times. The decade passed slowly, and Ennis waited.

Being a man with strong family ties, Ennis loved Lola Mae all the more for her dedication to her own family. He, like Lola Mae, hoped that the Foreign Mission Board would call. Lola Mae corresponded with the Board regularly, hoping to keep her name fresh on their memories. But the Southern Baptist Convention Foreign Mission Board was in dire straits. In 1927 it was discovered that the treasurer had embezzled $103,772. For a time it appeared that foreign missionaries might have to be called home.

In the years that followed Woman's Missionary Union (WMU), the missions education organization, Auxiliary to SBC, appealed to women to give more to the Lottie Moon Christmas Offering. Those gifts enabled the Foreign Mission Board to return some missionaries to the field, but only a handful of new missionaries were appointed, with preference given to graduates of the Woman's Missionary Union Training School. Then, of course, the depression hit and few new missionaries could be appointed. All of this might have been a bitter pill to swallow for someone less determined than Lola Mae Daniel.

Although she continued to hope and pray that any day might bring a letter saying there were funds available to send her to China, she was too busy with teaching and her family commitments to allow herself to become angry or bitter. Almost a decade passed, and Ennis, the patient man, began to grow weary of waiting on his fiancée to become his bride.

"Ennis, if we married now, you and I would become a family. We'd have children and put down roots, and I would never fulfill my commitment to God and full-time missions. We simply must wait a little longer."

"Look," said her fiancé of a decade, "I'm going to join the navy. While we're waiting to marry, I might as well be working and saving some money. Truth is I can't sit still patiently any longer.''

As the 1940s rolled in, Lola Mae and Ennis finally set a wedding date for the Christmas holidays of 1941. Fifteen years after Ennis first proposed, they were to be married. Wedding preparations kept Lola Mae so busy that she had little time to worry about the tense feelings developing in Europe and Japan. Letters arrived regularly from Ennis, who served aboard the USS *West Virginia.*

Eighteen days before they were to be married, Ennis Brooks, the handsome rancher from Bangs, perished aboard that ship as it lay docked at Pearl Harbor. Lola Mae never heard exactly how he died, but history recorded that many of the sailors were killed while they lay in their bunks early that ill-fated Sunday morning. A tear threatened to slide down her cheek, and moved her forward 20 years in time.

Lola Mae, en route to Taiwan, glanced down at the ring on her finger. During speeches she often said, ''I'm a monument to man's stupidity. I'm single.'' The truth was Lola Mae had continued to honor that commitment made on a drugstore stool so many years before. The engagement ring still shone on her finger warming the memory of the man who had waited all those years for her to be his bride.

Ennis's death had been hard to accept. The Brooks family had called, relaying the grim news from the War Department telegram. Given the perspective of 20 years, she could now see God's hand guiding each step of her life.

Several years after Ennis's death, Mr. Brooks had phoned to say, ''Ennis had never felt the commitment you felt to China. The truth, Lola Mae, is he loved you, and you loved China. If you had married Ennis, you could not have fulfilled your first commitment to God.''

''Surely,'' thought the 59-year-old Lola Mae, ''the Word

20

of the Lord is true." She remembered, "The steps of a good man are ordered by the Lord: and He delighteth in his way. Though he fall, he shall not be hurled utterly cast down: for the Lord upholdeth him with his hand" (Psalm 37:23-24 KJV).

Through those dark December days of 1941, Lola Mae had known Who held her hand. Having helped with Billie's girls was the closest she would come to having children. They had made good Christian women, and she took special pride in their families. She had experienced the commitment of a fine Christian man, and in 1962, she was on her way to Taichung, Taiwan, knowing that "her steps" were ordered by the Lord.

4

A Drink from the Fountain of Youth

By 1941 Lola Mae had passed the cut-off age for missionary appointment. She finished out the school year after Ennis's death.

Seeking God's will at this point in her life was not an easy process. For one of the first times in her life, Lola Mae was depressed. The loneliness and grief over losing Ennis would periodically wash over her like a wave. During this time she received notes from former teachers at Howard Payne. They reminded her that grief and depression are often absolved by immersing oneself in others. Lola Mae knew the remedy would work, but she searched and prayed that God would give her just the right place, custom-made for her.

That summer her dad was preaching at the Baptist encampment in Lueders, Texas. Lola Mae joined him there. After a service, Roy Kay, who was president of San Marcos Baptist Academy, introduced himself. "I need a teacher. Are you interested? Your father seems to think that you need a job for the fall."

Lola Mae had heard of the Baptist school in the hill country of Texas. "The job would demand physical stamina, emotional strength, and spiritual preparedness," Mr. Kay continued.

Feeling again the hand of God, Lola Mae boldly stated, "Then I'm the teacher you need."

President Kay stifled a laugh and said, "Then pick up your belongings and your spirits, and I'll see you in San Marcos just before school starts."

There at San Marcos Baptist Academy, nestled in the hills once populated by Indians who sought water at the bubbling springs that form the headwaters of the San Marcos River, this single lady became the dean of approximately 100 energetic and sometimes lonely elementary schoolboys. Their energy and zest for life in the face of the looming war years would be her cup of water from the spring of youth.

"Who would have thought," Lola Mae whispered to herself, "that a single schoolteacher would become mother to dozens of young boys?"

Lola Mae parked her car on the steep street and walked across the lush green lawn up the multitudes of steps onto the cool porch that stretched the entire length of red-bricked Carroll Hall. Entering through the double front doors her heels clicked on the shiny wooden floors of the spacious foyer. She was on the ground floor of the rambling building. A young cadet approached and directed her to the office of the head administrator.

Later, after her contract was signed, Lola Mae was escorted by the same young cadet, who wore a uniform that resembled army fatigues, to her bedroom and office on the first floor of the building. Her escort, as well mannered as he was meticulous, explained as they clicked together down the wide hallway, "The junior boys are housed on this floor. Most of the offices and a few classrooms are here as well. This gets the smaller boys easily into the mess, I mean dining hall, at the end of the corridor."

"I see," was her only reply. Of course, she had been given the same instructions during her time in the office.

"The main chapel, which also serves as our auditorium,

is on the second floor. That's where the girls are housed. There are additional classrooms there, and at the end of the hall you will find another entrance." Winking slyly he continued, "Sometimes rumor has it that the girls slip out that entrance. It's the second floor fire escape. Of course, I don't know for sure, but that fire escape usually managed to appear in our yearbook. Since we haven't had a fire, it must have some importance to the graduating seniors."

Lola Mae smiled. She was always amazed at the wealth of information you could gain when you listened instead of talked to young people.

"How many students are at this school?" asked Lola Mae.

As if he had memorized it for an initiation, the young man spit out the words, "We have approximately 310 students from 16 states and 6 countries. Miss Daniel, why are you smiling? Have I said something funny?"

"Oh, no. You see I have been waiting for years to go to the foreign missions field, and it just occurred to me when you answered that the foreign missions field has come to me."

"Well, Ma'am, the way I see it is, you are a lot safer here at the academy than you would be on any foreign missions field today. I can't wait to graduate and enlist. I hope the war isn't over before I have my chance to fight."

The young man's attitude was so like the patriotic streak that had run deep in Ennis Brooks. She immediately liked the young man and hoped that the junior boys in her care would prove just as polite and eager as her escort.

As she opened the door to her suite, the young man helped with her luggage. He went back to the office leaving her to unpack. The heat had caused a bead of sweat to roll down her forehead. She removed the white gloves from her hands and grabbed a handkerchief to remedy the mess the powder and sweat had made of her face. The first order of business would be to open her screened window and turn on the fan.

24

Her room was spacious with its high ceiling and Lola Mae was determined to make it as homey as possible. Most of the junior boys would find their way into her quarters at some time or another for additional mothering. Lola Mae wanted them to feel at home when they needed to see her. Although fully aware that God had provided this place of service, she could not at this point, fall 1942, fully comprehend how God would use this time among youngsters from six countries to mold her for future service.

Quickly settling into the regimented life that was the pattern at the academy, Lola Mae discovered there was a multitude of "boy things" she had to learn. Assisting in the care of her nieces and being reared with a sister had not fully prepared her for life with a rowdy group of boys. Besides teaching math, she broke up pillow fights, rescued countless insects and reptiles, and planned more birthday celebrations in her first year than she would have as a lifelong mother to Ennis's children.

Among her tasks was a monthly letter to the parents of each junior boy. She realized how important it was for the academy and the parents to communicate. She often returned to her room late at night to record personal anecdotes about the boys, so that her letters would express the depth of love and concern she held for each child entrusted in her care. It was easier to write in the peaceful stillness that enwrapped the campus only during "lights out" time.

Serving at the academy during the war years was a unique experience. The faculty and students melded into a family. The world was embroiled in hostile conflict, yet at the academy children from many nations lived and worked peacefully together. Lola Mae especially enjoyed the foreign children. She worked at learning about the cultural backgrounds of these children. Most were eager to share about their homelands; and her interest in them became a communication bridge to show her love of Jesus.

Each day began with the sound of her boys, grades 1-6, scurrying to dress, brush their teeth, and leave their rooms orderly before marching to the dining hall for breakfast. Teachers were required to eat at the tables with their students. After breakfast Lola Mae would begin her workday with the same prayer, "Lord, I still want to go to China, but I accept with gladness the foreign missions field you've given me here in Texas. Help me to be an example of Christ to these boys. Help me to teach them to love one another as Christ loved us. Amen."

Classes were held after breakfast. Then there was lunch, time for cleanup, and sports activities on the playing fields. Occasionally a student found his way into the cool fountain in front of Carroll Hall. After supper there would be study time, and nightly devotionals for which Lola Mae was responsible. Teachers were expected to attend First Baptist Church, San Marcos, with their students. Teaching at the academy was a 24-hour-a-day job with no reprieve on the weekends.

"Why on earth," one friend from town had asked, "would an unmarried woman rapidly approaching middle age want to spend her days amid gym socks, military uniforms, and rock collections?"

"There isn't an earthly answer," remarked Lola Mae while straightening an earring which was threatening to slip off. "I'm here because this is the job God gave me to do. If I'm meant to marry, God will give the lucky fellow a road map to San Marcos. Until God sends me to the foreign missions field, or sends a guy to accompany me to China, I'll stay here and mother these boys because this is where I'm needed."

Of all the precious boys whose lives touched hers, the one most vivid in her memory was Aizic Sechter. Aizic's love and trust in her had brought assurance when doubts of her own sanity plagued her.

One day her supervisor instructed her to drive to the San Antonio airport to pick up a small boy who would be arriving from Maracaibo, Venezuela. She coerced several other boys to drive with her to the San Antonio airport to greet him. In her full-skirted dress which modestly covered her knees, and fashionably padded shoulders, she guided three little boys in uniforms across the airport lobby. They must have given the impression of a family arriving to welcome a soldier husband on leave. Instead, she and the boys greeted a young Jewish boy from Venezuela.

As the passengers filed off the plane and into the terminal waiting area, Aizic was easily located. He was the olive complexioned boy with dark hair and lonely, scared eyes. Lola Mae had been told his grandparents had fled Russia during the Revolution and moved to South America. She thanked the Lord for San Marcos Academy. Where else would she have the opportunity to minister to a Russian Jew who was a native of Venezuela?

As she and the boys rushed over to greet Aizic, his eyes widened as he realized that these were new friends. "Well, young man," said the pretty teacher, "are you ready to get in the car and travel to your new home?"

There was a look of puzzlement. "No," he replied. The reality of the grim situation was almost funny. This young man did not speak English. In complete faith, he placed his tiny hand in the hand of his teacher's and followed her and the boys out to her car.

The awkward silence in the car was difficult for all of them. "Paul, you reach into my purse and get that package of gum," instructed Miss Daniel. When Paul pulled out the bright green package of gum, Aizic's eyes glowed. He recognized the packaging. "Gum," said the teacher, offering him a slice.

"Gum," replied the boy. His pronunciation of the word sent the other boys into peals of laughter, but her mission was accomplished—the silence had been broken. Taking her cue, the boys began to point to objects in the car and name them for Aizic. He was an eager learner.

Before Aizic arrived the administration had decided he should room with an American student so he would be forced to learn English as quickly as possible. After they arrived on campus, Lola Mae placed his bags in the assigned room. Sitting with him through supper, Lola Mae watched him smile agreeably at the children who came to introduce themselves to him. Behind that smile she could sense his loneliness; the poor child was homesick for his parents.

After dinner she directed him to his room, and communicated with her hands that he must bathe and get ready for bed. Sensing his need to communicate with someone, she found another child, an older boy who spoke Spanish. The boy explained to Aizic that Miss Daniel would allow them to room together a few days until his homesickness ebbed and he had fallen into academy routines. As she shut the door to their room, she stopped a moment to hear Aizic talking nonstop. She sensed he would be content with his newest friend.

That night a thunderstorm struck. Lightening flashed across the sky illuminating the rooms for brief seconds. She could hear windows slamming shut all over the building. Then she heard the patter of bare feet in the hall outside her room. Her door opened and the emergency exit light in the hall outlined the form of Aizic whose eyes were wide with fright. "Momma," he cried. Lola Mae scooped up the tiny first-grader and took him to the divan in her room.

In soothing tones, she said, "You're afraid and homesick. This couch can be your bed only tonight."

The next morning a happy, rested boy who was determined to learn English emerged from his couch cocoon. From that point on he did not call her Miss Daniel; she was to remain his "American mother."

Years later after his family had moved to Israel, he had written that his favorite memories of San Marcos Academy were of the nightly devotionals led by his American mother. There he first heard about the Christian Messiah, and he admitted that he had learned more about the history of his own people, the Jews, through their Bible studies.

Toward the end of her fifth year at San Marcos Academy, tragedy once again struck the Daniel family. Her father called to say that Mrs. Daniel was very sick and not expected to live much longer. As school drew to a close, Lola Mae once more honored commitments to her closely knit family. Her parents had moved to Kilgore to be close to Billie. Lola Mae resigned from the academy and obtained a clerical job with a Fort Worth insurance company. She drove to Kilgore on weekends. It was not an easy decision to make, but after her mother's death, she felt it had been the right choice.

The family house was in Lueders. Not wanting her father to be alone, Lola Mae accepted a teaching position there and kept house for her father, who had retired from preaching. Although her job in Lueders did not hold the same challenge that her academy position had mandated, she was glad to be with her father who felt the loss of his lifelong partner so intensely. If she had married, her first commitment would have been to her own family. Since she lacked those ties, she felt a strong need to care for this man who had played such an important role in her life. After all, Lola Mae had always been a woman who took commitments seriously.

5

On to Ozona

Lueders was empty for her once her father died in 1953. In his last years, he had driven a school bus, and had made such a place for himself with the children that the children had been bused to the church for his funeral. That was certainly one way life had changed in the ten years from Lueders to Taiwan, she mused. American parents seemed to want to shield their children from death. In the mid-1950s children could understand that dying was a part of the process of living.

Her father's death had broken her closest family ties. Billie was now happily married, the nieces were married, and Lola Mae realized that she was free to pursue her dreams of finding a way to the missions field. She and a young friend applied for Department of Defense teaching jobs. The friend, 30 years her junior, had been accepted. Lola Mae was too old!

"Lola Mae," said Gene as she drove him to the airport for his adventure overseas, "what you need is a vacation. If you aren't happy in Lueders, get in your car and drive to Del Rio. Apply at every school district along the way."

"That's crazy, and you know it. School will start in three weeks. Everybody's already contracted their teachers for this school year."

"Look who's calling who crazy. You're the one that's still trying to find a way overseas after 30-plus years. You

30

sound like sour grapes. This is just another setback. You'd better take the advice you're always dishing out and 'bloom where you're planted,' " Gene advised.

The words were harsh but they were what she needed to hear. With much determination, she phoned friends in Del Rio, loaded up her tan Chrysler, and headed by way of San Angelo to Del Rio.

West Texas is like an inferno in August. Her car seem to part the waves of steam rising from the asphalt highway. As she drove the backroads through small towns, the words of her friend rang in her ears.

Then she noticed a road sign to Ozona. Her father had always jokingly said, "I'd go wherever the Lord calls me to preach, but I hope He doesn't call me to Ozona." He always concluded the joke by explaining that, "Ozona is the only town in all of Crockett County. Named after the hero of the Alamo, it covers about 3,000 square miles of ranch and oil land. Can you imagine living in the only town in a county that covers that many miles?"

Wondering if the town would live up to family stories, Lola Mae veered off her mapped route and headed into Ozona. The town, located in the Edwards Plateau region, was hilly terrain barren of anything but scrub oak and mesquites. It possessed a stark beauty that delighted her. Occasionally she would pass a ranch house and see cattle grazing beside a working oil well.

Entering from the north side of town on Highway 163, she passed several brick buildings on her left that were surrounded by a fine rock fence. Thinking that this must be a small junior college, she stopped in front of a house near the campus.

She walked confidently up to the porch and knocked on the door. When no one answered, she shrugged her shoulders and said, "OK, Lord, obviously this is not the place for me."

As she started the motor, a woman came running wildly from the house, her hair in pincurls, her robe hastily thrown over her shoulders. She was shouting, "Wait, lady,

31

wait!'' in a voice loud enough to alarm the entire town. ''Are you a teacher?'' she asked as Lola Mae cautiously rolled down her window.

''Yes,'' was the quick reply.

''Good, then you're at the right place. My husband is the superintendent of this district, and we need a teacher.''

''This isn't a junior college?''

''Oh, no, that's the junior and senior high facility. When you're the only town in the county you can have some of the best facilities in the state. We pay real good too.''

''I see,'' said Lola Mae beginning to see that she had been led to this town by more than curiosity.

With pincurls bobbing, the lady gave her directions to her husband's office. The school grounds were spotless, and the purple sage was in bloom. Later she learned that the old-timers said that the purple blooms signaled rain, a needed factor in the life of the county.

Lola Mae felt a sense of peace and belonging as she entered the office. She had decided only to accept an elementary position.

The usual questioning followed. ''Miss Daniel, I need a first-grade teacher,'' the superintendent explained.

''One who pushes phonics?'' she asked.

''Just what I've hoped for. If you want the job and your references check out, it's yours.''

''What kind of salary do you offer? A single lady has to know that she can support herself.''

''We offer $300, which is over the monthly state minimum and a teacherage, a furnished apartment or house. Yours would be across the street from the elementary school,'' he said.

Certainly God was marvelous. She had not accumulated many household furnishings, and the extra money would allow her to save for the summer missions experiences she had already begun planning.

''Sir, before I accept your offer, I need to talk to my supervisor in Lueders and make certain they can find someone to take my place. If all that works out, I'll be here in a week.'' She could hardly suppress the excitement in her voice. Lueders had been good to her, but the town was full of painful memories of her father.

Returning briefly to 1962, Lola Mae downed her lunch before the stewardess could return for her tray. It's a miracle how daydreaming can make time pass so quickly, she thought. She had managed to move from her childhood to the fall of 1956 in less than two days as she traveled to Taiwan. ''Actually,'' thought Lola Mae, ''perhaps, that's how quickly my life has flashed from the Lord's perspective. All this waiting might be to Him as the bat of an eye.'' The air force friend beside her gulped down his dinner, grabbed a pillow, and returned to his dreams.

Words from Proverbs 16:9 ran on the recorder of her brain, ''A man's heart deviseth his way: but the Lord directeth his steps.'' The Lord had surely determined that her life would become woven into the tapestry of Ozona.

Lueders had released her from her contract, and Lola Mae began a love affair with the Ozona first-graders. The Pacific Ocean was still beneath the silver plane when she returned to her humorous memories of Ozona. It was there that she had begun saying that no one was truly educated until they had taught first-graders.

She remembered that after the first reporting period one of her less scholarly students returned with his report card in hand. As he walked through the door, he stared straight in her face and said, ''Miss Daniel, I have something to tell you, but don't you be scared.''

''Well, son, I don't scare easily. What's bothering you?''

''It's this. My dad said if anyone came home with this bad of marks again, someone was going to get a whippin'. Since I'm not the one that writes these marks, I thought you might like to know.''

As early as 1946, children seemed to be learning that their failures were someone else's responsibility, Lola Mae mused.

"Well, young man," replied Miss Daniel, "I've been teaching more years than you've been on this earth, and I've yet to be whipped by a parent. Seems to me like you need to work very hard this six weeks to bring up your marks."

Another child was consistently tardy to class. She always reminded him that he must learn to be punctual because punctuality was a virtue needed to be successful in life. Finally one day she had said, "Tomorrow, if you are late, you will have to be punished."

Sure enough the child was late again. "Why were you late?" she demanded in her most authoritative voice.

"Miss Daniel," he replied with the slightest whine, "you always tell us to watch traffic signs and obey them."

"Yes, that's true."

"I can't read them all, but that one out front says, *SLOW—SCHOOL*. So when I get to that sign I always walk real, real slow."

She didn't have the heart to punish him when he demonstrated how he had walked very slowly past the sign.

At the end of each day she would walk across the street to her apartment, a white stucco bungalow, and plan for the end of the school year. It seemed unbelievable that she would have an entire summer to pursue her greatest love—missions.

Although she had helped Audrey Glynn with the Girls' Auxiliary (GA), a missions education organization for young girls, at First Baptist Church, Ozona, she still wanted to do more than educate and prepare others for missions opportunities. She was still certain God had called her to China. Even in 1949 when the Communists had driven Chiang Kai-shek and his followers to Taiwan, she clung to the idea that someday she would go to China.

She shared her burden for mission service with the people of First Baptist, Ozona. While they prayed and waited, Lola Mae began to seek opportunities in missions endeavors to fill her summers. She did not have to look very hard.

34

6

Preparing While Marking Time

When school closed, Lola Mae left for New York City with a group of friends. These younger teachers were planning to enroll for graduate summer courses. Lola Mae had other plans. She had decided to tag along with the others, after she learned Billy Graham was conducting a crusade in New York City that summer.

"You go on down to the university and get registered," Lola Mae instructed her friends, "I'll just go over to the Billy Graham headquarters at Madison Square Garden and get a job."

When she entered the office, she asked to see the person in charge. The office aide led her through cubicles until they reached the one with the appropriate markings. The office buzzed with activity.

"Ma'am," said the charming young man in charge, "what brings you to New York City to spend your summer?"

"The Lord," answered Lola Mae, not blinking an eye.

"We usually don't have many women your age who appear from Texas ready to go to work. Most women your age have family responsibilities," he noted.

Lola Mae was temporarily offended by the reference to her age. At times she grew painfully aware that it had been years since her "missionary call." Most people questioned her intense assurance that the call had been clear and specific—to China. She knew this young man before her would question too if she wasted time telling her story. She also knew he was totally unaware his remarks about her age had cut deeply. He was merely making a truthful observation.

"Yes," she replied, "most women my age are home with families, but I am not most women, and I am ready to go to work. Don't you have something I could do to help?"

"The truth is one of our workers quit yesterday. Not minutes before you came through that door we held an office devotion and prayed together that the Lord would send us a replacement."

Leading her toward a large machine, he spoke again. "This is a flexowriter. If you can operate this machine, we'll not only put you to work for the summer—we'll pay you also."

Seeing the look of uncertainty in her eyes, he asked, "You can operate this machine, can't you?"

Mustering up the determination that had been one of her strongest character traits, she reminded herself she was not most women and gamely replied, "If anybody can work this machine, I can. Just give me a quick lesson, and I think you will find me an able learner."

"OK," replied this new friend, "I am going to show you how to operate this machine, and then I'll give you a few hours of practice. At the end of the morning, if you can master the job, it's yours."

The flexowriter was used to type lists of names and addresses of persons making decisions at crusade meetings. In addition to a printed list, a tape was made. The tape was forwarded to the headquarters in Minnesota. Lola Mae breathed a silent prayer and tackled the machine. By the end of the morning, she had landed a paying job for the summer.

Evenings were spent in crusade meetings where she sang in the choir and counseled persons coming forward to make decisions. That summer she learned to enjoy Yankees; she conquered the flexowriter; and she convinced the office personnel that a middle-aged first-grade schoolteacher could be an asset to their organization. The excitement she felt during the services when she witnessed the miracle of hardened young people become willing servants of the kingdom made the experience so worthwhile that the following summer she volunteered to go with the team to San Francisco.

By her third year in Ozona, she had decided to try a new missions experience. Alaska was the newest pioneer missions territory. She and her students from Ozona had spent the year dreaming of what it would be like to go north for the summer.

Through her WMU-GA affiliation, she had read in the missions magazines about the Tentmaker program being used at that time. Volunteers were assigned to help home missionaries. She began to correspond with the Home Mission Board. The program, named after the apostle Paul who had supported his ministry by making tents, accepted Lola Mae for summer work in Alaska.

Shortly before school was out she sold a few of her household goods to help finance her trip. "Miss Daniel," said a man from Ozona who was purchasing her television set, "are you certain you want to part with this?"

"Look," she said with her dogged determination, "this summer I am leaving for three months, but sooner or later when I get my teacher's retirement I am going to the foreign missions field so you'll be doing me a favor by taking it off my hands now."

That first summer in Alaska she helped start five new churches; wore out two pairs of shoes walking door to door conducting neighborhood surveys; taught Vacation Bible School so many times that she had memorized the curriculum; and promised the Lord that she would return the following summer to help again. She also pledged she would use every opportunity in Ozona to promote mission support, prayer, and giving. She prayed that the people would catch her vision for missions. Indeed, they did!

At some point in this period, Lola Mae and her missions work and projects became a line budget item for First Baptist Church, Ozona. The church already gave generously to the Cooperative Program, but they wanted to be a part of Lola Mae's ministry as well. They became convinced that through the Cooperative Program and Lola Mae's ministry that their small church could reach beyond the 3,000 square miles of Crockett County—they could reach the world beginning with Alaska.

The following summer she returned to the "cold North," but this time she was determined to see more of the wilderness beauty than the town of Anchorage. She was assigned to help Ollie and Ellie Marson who were home missionaries to the Canadian Indians on the Yukon River.

Flying into the area, she could see the homes of the Indians. As she drove to the Marson's two-story log house, she asked, "What are those mounted small log buildings behind the homes of the Indians?"

"Those are caches. Meat is stored high in them. Then the ladders are removed. By keeping the meat high and away from the house, it is protected from bears."

"Hungry bears?" asked Lola Mae.

"Sure," answered Mr. Marson, "a Texas farm girl like you isn't afraid of bears?"

"Sure," replied Lola Mae with more confidence than she felt, "if I get scared, I'll just climb up in one of those caches and sleep."

"Just make sure you pull the ladder up after you," laughed Ollie.

Lola Mae had to admit Southern Baptists had accurately tagged Alaska as a pioneer missions field. Certainly this was as close to being a pioneer as she wanted to come.

38

Besides living in a log cabin, groceries had to be brought once a year by boat up the Yukon River. "How do you ever manage to remember what you'll need?" Lola Mae asked.

Ellie took Lola Mae over to a kitchen drawer. She pulled out a list that was several pages thick. "I don't remember," admitted Ellie. "I keep adding to the list until the last day for it to be sent. Then I pray that whatever has been forgotten won't be an essential item. I will say this—my organizational skills have improved since we've come to Fort Yukon."

Lola Mae slept in a room located in the new mission. Blankets had to be hung over the windows that first night. Lola Mae had almost forgotten the sun shone most of the day and night during the summer months.

The problem of learning to sleep in sunlight was solved after her second full day there. She understood why the Marsons had adjusted so well; missionaries were so tired by the end of a day that they had no trouble falling into a deep sleep.

Besides helping to organize GA and other WMU organizations she helped paint the brand-new church. The church was attached to the Marson's garage for heating purposes, and could only be entered by walking through the garage entrance.

Summer camp consisted of loading as many children as possible into the Marson's large truck and driving over rough backroads to a wilderness campsite. At this summer camp they actually slept in sleeping bags on the ground. It had been years since Lola Mae awakened feeling so stiff. Her nights were spent in restless sleep, waking occasionally to make certain someone was guarding the campsite. Ollie's opening remark about bears was imprinted on her mind.

As the wonderful summer drew to a close, she decided to join a tour group to Point Barrows, Alaska, which was known as the Top of the World. Even in the summer the cold was intense, but the rugged scenery was beautiful!

When she arrived, the local Presbyterians were conducting a Bible school and they needed help. She chuckled, thinking what a blessed thing it was to be in obedience to God's will. Each day He directed her steps to new opportunities of service. Here she had spent most of her life trying to serve overseas, and she found herself at the Top of the World working in a Presbyterian Bible school.

When describing the experience to friends she remarked, "Well, it was a Presbyterian Bible school with a great deal of Baptist doctrine."

During one of her classes, word came that the Eskimos had killed a whale and were butchering it on the shore. Seeing everything as a living and learning experience, Lola Mae walked her class down to the shore. Someone in the group flashed a picture of her standing beside the beached whale. Just as luck would have it, the picture turned up later on a travel brochure, and still later in the Ozona city newspaper.

She had to endure much teasing about combining missionary experience with whale killing. "Well," explained Lola Mae, "God said that we would be fishers of men. I did a little of both this summer, fishing for whales and fishing for lost men, women, boys, and girls."

In the winter of the next school year, she received a call from one of the faculty members of Wayland Baptist University in the panhandle of Texas. He explained that a group of young people was planning a summer tour of missions experiences in California. They had secured the finances, a station wagon, and a U-Haul, but they had not found a chaperon. "Would you be interested in helping us, Miss Daniel?"

"When do we leave?" replied Lola Mae.

The college students had prepared a drama to be presented in churches along the tour route. She soon discovered her job of chaperoning included a role in the play. The play was a missions drama focusing on the part of Christians in God's message of salvation for a lost world.

40

During the summer performances, Lola Mae became even more convinced that her time for foreign mission service was rapidly approaching.

She had been corresponding with Dr. and Mrs. Charles Culpepper, missionaries to the Chinese in Taiwan, having met them while they were speaking at Lueders Baptist Encampment. When they returned to the States on furlough, she visited with them. It seemed with the doors closed to China, Taiwan was as close as she would get to the Mainland. The Culpeppers had encouraged her to continue teaching until she could draw retirement, and join them in Taiwan.

When she returned from her summer trip, she was convinced she should retire at the end of the 1962 school year. In November she had gone forward in a Sunday morning service to ask her pastor, Dr. Harry Trulove, and her church to pray she would find a way to Taiwan and the millions of Chinese who had fled for freedom to that country. Dr. Trulove and Lola Mae agreed they would not discuss the possibility of her going to Taiwan until they had prayed privately about the matter for six weeks.

The people of Ozona prayed. It seemed that the entire town knew their first-grade teacher might leave at the end of the school year. At the gas station, at the grocery store, at the bank, and at church, she would find loving people who offered words of encouragement and ended their inquiries by stating, ''You know, we've been praying for you.''

Baker James Cauthen, then executive secretary of the Foreign Mission Board, was contacted. Although there was a gracious response, no real encouragement was given. Following several unsuccessful attempts to generate interest from Richmond, headquarters of the Foreign Mission Board, Dr. Trulove made contact with a pastor on leave from a church in West Germany. The German church he pastored was growing and was in need of an additional staff person. Lola Mae was qualified, and the pastor was interested in meeting her.

"Lola Mae," said Dr. Trulove well into the fourth week of their agreement, "you know your doctor has indicated from a health standpoint that Germany would be a better choice."

"Don't forget, Pastor," said Lola Mae, "we're not going to discuss the matter for six weeks!"

While Lola Mae maintained her prayer vigil, Dr. Trulove was busy. First Baptist Church, Ozona, agreed they would help with moving costs to Germany. The church in Germany agreed to pay a salary she could live on if she would only give up her magnificent obsession for the Chinese people. "From a human standpoint," Dr. Trulove told his wife, "the church in Germany is the wisest course for her to take."

Still he and Lola Mae held to their initial agreement and continued to pray. Dr. Trulove received the *Christian Index,* the Georgia state Baptist paper. Normally the *Index* carried Southern Baptist Convention news a week ahead of the Texas Baptist paper, the *Baptist Standard.* The sixth week, the *Index* carried a news release on a new program, the Missionary Associate Program, which would allow persons over 35 to qualify for English-language positions overseas. In addition, there was a smaller article calling for teachers in English schools in Taiwan. "There's Lola Mae's answer," said the pastor's wife.

Dr. Trulove later admitted that, faithful to their agreement, he had decided not to tell Lola Mae what he and his wife had discovered.

That same day Lola Mae closed the door to her tidy classroom, waved good-bye to the school secretary, and drove over to the post office to pick up her mail. Her daily ritual was to drive home, brew a cup of coffee, and avidly read her mail. It was Wednesday, *Baptist Standard* day; she couldn't wait to get home and read it.

As she slid into her faithful tan Chrysler, her eyes caught the headlines, "Foreign Mission Board Approves Missionary Associate Program." Sitting in the post office parking lot, she devoured the story that followed. The 35-

age limit had been extended. Lola Mae whooped with joy!

Two pages over another headline read, "Teachers Needed in Taiwan." Rivers of tears flowed down her face. Lola Mae at 59 years of age had marching orders from God. She was certain of it.

She drove at breakneck speed to Dr. Trulove's office. It was time to talk. "Dr. Trulove, I have my answer," she exclaimed as she opened his office door.

"Yes, Lola Mae," said her good friend, "I had read the information earlier, but still felt you would be better off in West Germany. Normally you would not have known until next week. The *Standard* has carried the story earlier than I expected. You're right. I believe that this is your answer."

Of course, Lola Mae had no confirmation from the Foreign Mission Board that she would be one of the associates chosen. That seemed a minor point, teachers were needed and she could retire, financing her own way if necessary.

By mid-January she had been interviewed by a Foreign Mission Board representative who stressed that Lola Mae would need a physical checkup before any definite plans could be made. "If only my birthdate did not need to be included on the physical and application," Lola Mae thought. Her missionary biography was written and mailed, and she and her first-graders waited daily for news.

"Why are you worried?" asked the doctor who gave her the exam, "You hardly look a day over 40."

It was true she weighed little more than she had as a 30-year-old, and her hair had only a little gray. It was also true that at least once a year some widower felt an obligation to remove her from spinsterhood and would propose marriage. Lola Mae laughed, "Unfortunately, none of them would agree to follow me overseas."

Lola Mae decided to ship a large box of goods on to Dr. and Mrs. Culpepper in Taipei. One Sunday after church Dr. Trulove stopped her and said, "If you'll drop by my office after work tomorrow, I think I've found just the size box you need."

The next day she followed his directions. They pulled in front of one of the stores of a church member. It was a furniture store, but the owner also carried a line of coffins. More than a little suspicious, Lola Mae parked and followed him to the back of the store.

The owner, with eyes twinkling, said, "Come on in, Lola Mae; I have just the box you need."

He led her over to a large wooden crate, a shipping box for caskets. Both men were grinning broadly. It was obvious they thought they had a good gag going.

"You know, gentlemen, this is a great idea. Just think, my goods can be shipped over there, and even if the worst happens to me, I'll always have a way to be shipped home," she crowed.

So it was that Lola Mae shipped her household goods to Dr. Culpepper in a casket box, long before she had the slightest bit of encouragement from the Foreign Mission Board. "If I wait until they tell me I'm not too old to go, my household goods will take months to arrive. By sending them now, I'll have them when I step off the plane," she explained to friends.

When school ended, she bid good-bye to her Ozona family and moved what household goods she had left to Billie's home for the summer. Soon a notice came that she should attend a ten-day orientation in Mars Hill, North Carolina. "Does this mean that I'm accepted?" she asked during a phone call to the FMB.

"No, it means you come to orientation and then we'll give you an answer," the Board official replied.

Returning to Austin after the orientation, she stewed for a few days trying to decide what she would do if she turned 60 before the Board gave her confirmation. Her birthday was only a few weeks away, and she had discovered the cutoff for the new program would be 60.

One morning after a relatively sleepless night, she hurried into the kitchen where Billie was preparing breakfast. "I've prayed most of the night, Billie, and I've decided."

"Have you decided to fly right over the Great Wall of China and evangelize the Communists?" joked Billie.

"No, but I have decided to get my passport and ticket to Taiwan. If I don't get there by September 20, someone will decide I'm too old to go, again." Lola Mae did not stop that day until she had made arrangements for both a passport and a ticket.

A few weeks later, she received a phone call from a man at the Foreign Mission Board. "Miss Daniel, we would like for you to attend a commissioning service next week at Glorieta. At the end of that meeting we will hold a business session and you will be told whether or not you can go to Taiwan."

"Sir," said Lola Mae, "I won't be able to attend that meeting."

"Why," he exclaimed, "we were told you were anxious to get to Taiwan."

"Because I'm scheduled to leave for Taiwan the day after your service. I simply won't have time to get back and catch my plane."

The man was too flabbergasted to speak so Lola Mae continued, "Would you please have someone call me the morning after the service so that I'll know if I'm going officially."

"Certainly, I'd be afraid not to!" he added, laughing.

7

At Last—Taiwan!

The night before she was to leave Lola Mae had warned all the family who had come to see her off, "When the phone rings in the morning, please let me answer it. I've been waiting on this call for 42 years."

Rrring, Rrring—the phone sounded like a chorus of angels. "Lola Mae, if you don't move a little faster, we're going to answer it," teased the assembled family members.

"Hello, Miss Daniel, you go ahead and fly on your own ticket. The Foreign Mission Board will refund your money. It is my pleasure to tell you that you'll officially go to Taiwan as an associate missionary," the Foreign Mission Board official said.

Many directions followed. Lola Mae obediently wrote them down. She was too excited to remember them otherwise. The family cheered, acting as if they had witnessed a miracle.

"We can't stand around here gawking and bawling all day," she lovingly chided. "You've got to get this missionary to the Austin airport."

"Miss Daniel, we're circling over Taiwan," came a voice from the seat next to her.

"My goodness," said Lola Mae, "I guess I've dreamed my life away since we left the airport. Let me get my camera."

Pressing the camera close to the window, she began taking pictures. Full of emotion, her hands began to shake, and tears slid down her face making tiny highways in her face powder. She dropped the camera.

The stewardess was checking to see that their seatbelts were snugly fastened. She handed Lola Mae the dropped camera. "You're crying. Are you all right?"

"Of course. This is the happiest day of my life." As the plane touched the ground, her heart beat so quickly. "Surely, Lord," she said to herself, "You've not brought me this far to have a heart attack on the plane before I touch the soil."

The young military man helped her with her carry-on items. "Someone to meet you?" he asked.

"I'm certain someone from our Baptist mission office will be here."

Lola Mae's certainties became less certain as she descended the steps. Expecting to see a friendly face at any time, she picked up her luggage and waited near the front entrance. After 30 minutes, no one had come to claim her.

"Are you lost, Ma'am?" a well-groomed air force officer asked.

"I'm saved, thank you," said Lola Mae. She could not see anyone that appeared to be looking for an incoming missionary. "But there must have been a mix-up. There's no one here to meet me. Can you tell me where there's a good place to eat and a telephone? I need to call the Baptist mission office."

The officer was amused at this American woman with the strange answers. He also knew that she should not be without a friend in a strange city where people spoke a new language. "I'm going over to the Grand Hotel to get a room. Why don't you go along with me? I'll see that you get a bite to eat and find a phone to call your friends."

By phoning the Baptist mission office, Lola Mae was greatly relieved to discover that a group of missionaries had been sent to meet her, but she had been expected earlier. The office had been trying to call the States to get her exact arrival time, or report her missing.

A group of missionaries drove over to get her and took her back to the Baptist mission office building. "Well, Miss Daniel, I was worried about you, but it appears that you're a survivor. You'll do just fine here," one missionary told her.

The details of her assignment were explained. She was booked on a morning flight to Taichung, where she would be working at a school for missionaries' children called Morrison Academy. "Would you like to be paid your first month's wages before you leave? You might have need of money to set up housekeeping," the missionary said.

"Thanks," said Lola Mae, "that's very considerate of you."

"Check or cash?"

Thinking she might not be able to cash a check, she replied, "Cash, please."

"This is only the equivalent of 100 US dollars, which is your monthly salary." Lola Mae took the large, heavy envelope and tried stuffing it into her purse.

"This is the first time in my life that my purse runneth over," she said.

That evening she had her first Chinese cuisine, sweet and sour pork. Driving through the city, she could not believe how crowded the streets were. The traffic was worse than it had been in New York City. "I'm going to drive as little as possible," she said.

They drove out to see a large Buddhist temple. Lola Mae had read books on Buddhism or Taoism in preparation for her trip. She knew that at that time there were approximately 1,400 Buddhist and 1,800 Taoist temples scattered on the tiny island of Taiwan. She had seen small statues of Buddha, but nothing had prepared her for the shock she was to feel as she stood looking up at the statue of Buddha, watching men and women kneel in prayer before the idol. She watched them toss chips into an open

48

fire. They would purchase the chips from the priests, and read the way they fell to determine whether their prayers would be answered.

Silently she prayed, "Lord, use me to teach these people about the Living God, not one made of concrete and clay."

The next morning she journeyed by plane to her new home in Taichung. The plane flew low enough that she could see the panorama of terraced mountains, rice fields, rivers, and innumerable villages and cities. She understood why material she had read called Taiwan, the *Ilha Formosa* (Beautiful Island).

This time when her plane landed she was met by missionaries who would come to seem as close as sisters. They drove her to the home of Mary Sampson with whom she would stay temporarily. Lola Mae's apartment was under construction.

That night all the missionaries from Taichung drove over for supper. The Chinese cook made fried chicken and mashed potatoes in her honor. "Are you homesick?" someone asked.

"No," she said speaking honestly and directly as was her habit, "I feel as if I am at home."

The following morning was Sunday. Lola Mae was given a choice. She could attend an English-speaking church or one where Mandarin was spoken. "I prefer to worship with the Chinese," she firmly stated.

At the church, wanting so desperately to belong, she picked up her hymnal and opened it as the congregation began singing a favorite hymn, "How Firm a Foundation." Thrilled with the experience, she sang loudly along in English. Shyly a young woman edged near her and gently reached over, took the hymnbook, and turned it right-side-up. Lola Mae learned quickly that she would make cultural mistakes, but Chinese Christians would forgive and love unconditionally.

That morning during the invitation, Lola Mae went forward to join the church. The pastor understood her decision and greeted her with smiles and strings of Mandarin phrases. In addition to moving her membership, Lola Mae promised God that she would study diligently to learn the language so she might be a more useful tool in His service.

Several weeks after she had settled in to her job teaching English-speaking children at Morrison Academy, a delivery man arrived with a large box. The Chinese cook came after Lola Mae. "Man bring box, Miss Daniel," he said. The cook looked as if he had seen a ghost.

"Won't you help me unload it?" she asked. When she opened the door, she recognized the coffin crate sitting on the delivery truck and understood the cook's hesitation. Only when she attempted to help the driver unload it did the cook rush to help.

They moved the box out onto the back porch. After it was unloaded, Lola Mae stood it on end and used it as a closet. When anyone questioned its position on the porch, Lola Mae would reply, "My friends back home wanted to make certain that I could return home, 'dead or alive.' "

Lola Mae had only been on the island two months when she became elementary principal of the academy. When the principal returned to the States on furlough, she was asked to replace him. Because of her promotion, she needed to live closer to the academy. She found a small house to rent while her apartment was finished, and hired a Chinese girl to help with housework. Although it was difficult to communicate, the experience was a blessing because she began to pick up phrases of Mandarin even before her official language training began.

Lola Mae worked in the Morrison school by day. As soon as school dismissed, she would attend a two-hour language class. Later she would go to a Baptist mission church and teach the Bible in English. The evening Bible classes were the highlight of her day. Young Chinese professionals would attend the Bible class simply to learn English.

50

The work among the Chinese was slow. Many hours of Bible teaching had to be done before they would make a decision. Lola Mae was amazed when in November of that first fall 20 decisions were made at one revival. That was the affirmation she needed to continue the grueling schedule she had established.

The weather the first winter was damp and cold. Much to her dismay, many of the buildings were not heated. At school, at church, and at home, she wore several layers of clothing. Noting that she was blessed to own several layers of clothing, she resolved not to complain. There were so many Taiwanese who did not have the luxury of overshoes or gloves.

Writing frequently to Ozona, she rarely mentioned the hardships, choosing instead to focus on the spiritual blessing and the positive aspects of her life on this crowded island. Once she mentioned the difficulty of adjusting to the food:

"There is an abundance of fruits and vegetables grown here which we can get at reasonable prices. But they must be thoroughly cooked before eating because of the fertilizer used. These are very frugal people using even the strips of land along the highway to produce beautiful vegetable gardens. Pray that I am as diligent and resourceful as they are in using every minute in productive service."

Midway through that first year her apartment near campus was completed. A missionary family lived above her.

Mike Wilson, a teacher and the missionary assigned to oversee the building of the apartments, came by one evening shortly before the apartments were to be completed. "Lola Mae, I've got both good and bad news. Remember when we attended those meetings in Taipei last week?"

"Yes," said Lola Mae anxious to hear the rest of the news.

"The good news is that your apartment is almost finished. The bad news is that the Chinese aren't accustomed to the way our bathrooms are plumbed. In our absence, they installed the shower plumbing in the center of your bathroom. You will have to walk through the shower stall to reach the toilet.''

''Don't worry, Mike. That's a minor inconvenience that I can live with,'' she calmly assured him.

''Well, you'll certainly have the most unique bathroom on the island,'' he added.

Plumbing was the least of Lola Mae's concerns. The language as she had feared was the most difficult challenge she would have to hurdle. Language classes lasted two hours. She discovered that each word had four different meanings and tones. The way a word was pronounced changed the meaning.

Her Mandarin instructor had challenged the women. ''You must be brave and courageous if you are to master this language. Each day in addition to your class time, you must practice the language among our people. You can count on making mistakes, but it is the only way to learn.''

Certain of the truth in what her teacher had said, Lola Mae determined to spend a portion of each day practicing. One day she attempted to buy a cooking utensil and instead she said, ''I want to buy a small child.''

''What?'' exclaimed the shocked storekeeper.

With confidence she continued, ''Yes, I want to buy a small child.''

To be courteous, the shopkeeper excused himself and hurried behind a partition. Lola Mae could hear his muffled laughter. It was then she realized the mistake. Collecting herself, she returned home to listen again to the language tapes.

A few weeks later she ventured out alone on a city bus. As they neared her stop, she moved forward through the throngs of people crammed tightly on the bus. Loudly, in order to be heard above the noise, she instructed in what she thought was flawless Mandarin, ''Let me out at the next corner.''

52

Seeing the shock on the driver's face, Lola Mae knew something was wrong. He repeated the phrase exactly the way she had spoken it. What she had emphatically told him was, "Please, kill me at the next corner."

The laughing man slowed the bus and let the "crazy lady" exit. "Really, I must be crazy," Lola Mae said. "Here I am almost 61, in a strange country learning one of the world's most difficult languages, and begging bus drivers to kill me."

By the summer months Lola Mae had made progress with the language. She had learned to buy sugar on the first try instead of purchasing two or three unneeded products before she could make herself understood. She had even learned to make her way around Taichung on public transportation. What she was not prepared for was the heat.

"Really, Mary," she said, "you'd think a lady from Texas could handle the heat."

"It's the combination of heat and humidity that bothers you. Even Houston does not prepare a body for Taiwan summers," Mary explained.

Had there not been so many revival meetings and summer camps to help organize, Lola Mae would have gladly spent those months in her bed in front of the fan.

After a short two-week vacation, she had an unforgettable experience. One of the missionaries had been working with a devout Buddhist family in a little town 30 miles outside of Taichung. The elderly father had become quite ill. Finding his own faith insufficient, the missionary was summoned. After many visits and countless hours of prayer, the father and mother had been led to the Lord.

The elderly couple had invited all the area missionaries to their home one Sunday afternoon for a special service. Lola Mae wrote to her Ozona family about the event:

"We sang songs, Scripture was read aloud, and prayers were offered. After the service, idols and scrolls were removed from this humble home. It was a joy to watch those idols burned and to see the radiant look of happiness on the faces of those new Christians.''

It was a wonderful way to close her first year on Taiwan. She looked forward to the years that would follow.

As her second year began, she remarked to Mary, ''If we could only have a little break from this heat.''

''That's a dangerous statement,'' remarked Mary, who had served on the island a long while. ''One of the fastest ways to break up the heat is to have a typhoon.''

''In Texas our heat waves are broken by hurricanes. I imagine I can survive a typhoon,'' Lola Mae quipped.

A few weeks later Lola Mae had the opportunity to survive her first typhoon. Because her apartment was high, she had only a few inches of water inside. Her worst damage was in mildewing linens and clothes. Many Chinese families were not so fortunate. They flocked to the school and Baptist missions seeking food and clothing. Using this as an opportunity to meet both physical and spiritual needs, the missionaries exhausted the supplies on hand.

''I know what to do,'' remarked Lola Mae as the last of the clothing was distributed. ''The people in Ozona will respond if they know of the need.''

And so late that night she penned a letter asking her friends for help:

''I am thankful that the house and school were not damaged to any great extent. We have shared already with those less fortunate.

''I hesitate to ask any of you to send packages out here because the postage and the duty is so high, but if anyone could send used clothing or new clothing of any size, I could give it to the many who have lost everything.''

Before Christmas a large box arrived. All the missionaries in the compound gathered to open the box and sort the items by size.

''You know, Mary, touching these clothes and knowing that they were sent because of love by my Ozona friends

54

makes me feel so close to the people at home. How right God was the day He directed my steps to Ozona, Texas.''

"Just think about our many friends here who your friends will help. Think about the face of our newest Chinese pastor when he receives this fine suit. Think about the young student who visits the student center and has no winter coat. Won't he be overwhelmed when he sees this warm beauty?'' Mary asked as she held up a brand-new coat. "If you think about the faces of the many these clothes will reach, you won't have time to be homesick for your friends in Ozona.''

"I think I must feel what Paul felt when he wrote to the church at Philippi, 'I thank my God upon every remembrance of you.' Now let's go through that list we made of the names who were most in need and get these sized in boxes for each family,'' Lola Mae said.

Several nights later Lola Mae penned another letter to Ozona. This time it was a letter of exultation:

"You had a large part in making many people warm and happy. It was hard for many of them to understand why you would go to so much trouble to help someone you had never seen. This gave me the opportunity to tell them how much Christ loves them and how a Christian person, no matter how far away, has the desire to help people who are in need.

"Several of these people were in our classes this morning, and I am confident there will be rewarding results because of your gifts.''

Countless times this scenario was repeated during the decade Lola Mae remained on the island. First Baptist Church, Ozona, bought pianos, Bibles, literature for the Chinese kindergarten, and paid for scholarships at the Baptist seminary in Taipei. Lola Mae knew she remained in their prayers daily, and she pressed on being the frontline warrior while they stayed by the stuff at home, as did those in 1 Samuel 30:24.

8

Blessings Too Numerous to Count

As Lola Mae began her third year on the island, her supervisor suggested, "There's a village near here where the local schools are so crowded that many children were unable to be enrolled in the kindergarten. You know that the Chinese place a heavy emphasis on education. They are gravely disappointed that their children will not receive the same help that many others will receive. We have a small mission church in that area, and I see this as a real opportunity to provide a needed service that should open doors to many more homes."

"Yes," Lola Mae responded, struggling to hide a grin. She already knew where the conversation was headed, but she was not going to make it too easy.

"Would you sponsor this project?"

"In addition to my job at Morrison? Will my missionary salary increase or will this be yet another jewel in my heavenly crown?" she asked, unable to hold back the smile that had spread from her eyes to her mouth.

"Lola Mae, this will be a diamond in your crown; I'm sure of it," the supervisor responded.

The little Chinese kindergarten project opened in the fall of 1964 with two Chinese teachers; 55 lively students; and a director who ordered materials, held teacher's meetings, and wrote curriculum guidelines after her own teaching day was completed. As sponsor, Lola Mae insisted that prayer and songs of praise be included in the daily activities. She told the Chinese Christian teachers, "Sing often the songs of Jesus; insist on prayer before snacks and lunch. These songs and prayer habits will find their way into Buddhist homes on the lips of these children."

She discovered how prophetic her words had been when a few weeks later an irate Chinese father knocked on the door of her home.

"Tell me, why is it my daughter prays, even when I tell her not to, before meals? Why does she sing about this Jesus Who loves her? Even when I forbid her to sing, she slips, and I catch her singing as she plays. Must she lose her heritage to attend a Baptist kindergarten?"

Lola Mae had the father right where she wanted him. Education was highly valued in Taiwan. Children attended school longer each day than American children. At that time they were given an exit exam at the end of the elementary years. The test results were posted for everyone to see. Much shame was brought to a family when a child failed. Lola Mae knew how important it was for this man to have his daughter in kindergarten—her future might be hampered if she could not attend. Calmly yet firmly, Lola Mae explained that the children would pray and sing if they attended the mission school. "Why don't you come one day and observe her class? Don't make a decision to withdraw her until you've seen how our teachers work with your child."

The man turned and left as angrily as he had come.

Several days later one of the Chinese teachers ran to meet Lola Mae as she walked into the yard of the school. "Miss Daniel, Miss Daniel," the lady spoke excitedly, "the angry dad came today."

"Did he cause you trouble or disrupt the class?"

"Oh, no, he only nodded when he entered and watched from the back of the class. He would not sit down!"

For several days the story was the same. Each afternoon the teacher explained that he quietly watched. "Has he taken his daughter out of the school?" asked Lola Mae.

"Oh, no," was the teacher's reply. One afternoon the father waited for Lola Mae.

"My daughter will be staying at your school. It is a good place to learn. She may sing and pray at home. The songs slip out of her mouth. The teachers are good, and she likes this church school."

Lola Mae invited the father to stay for the English Bible classes. He declined, but that night her students noticed that their usually tired teacher taught with more zest. The encounter with the young father had renewed her sense of purpose for the kindergarten that was to be the diamond in her heavenly crown. Although the man was not ready to make a decision, his heart had softened. There was evidence the Holy Spirit was at work.

"Even a child shall lead them," she thought that night as she crawled into bed. Lola Mae knew this Buddhist father would not be the last father to be touched by a praying, praising child who would boldly sing as she played, "Yes, Jesus loves me. The Bible tells me so."

The years at Morrison Academy in Taichung seemed to speed by. In December 1967 the entire Baptist community on Taiwan bought Chinese Bibles to send to Mainland China. The missionaries and Chinese Christians met to launch hundreds of balloons, with Bibles attached, in time to reach the Mainland by Christmas.

"How will we know if any of them reach the Mainland?" asked a small Chinese GA.

"Every now and then someone makes their way to Taiwan from Mainland China. Eventually we will receive word that some of these Bibles have reached their destination," explained Lucille Dawdy, another missionary associate who was about to complete her first term of service.

"The sight of those balloons launching will remain in

my mind,'' Lola Mae told Lucille a few days later. "It is terrific to know that although I may never have reached Shanghai, China, that one of my Bibles may touch down on that soil.''

By May 1968, Lola Mae knew that her time was short. She had completed one full term as a missionary, but she had also reached the age of 65. Cards and letters from home asked the question that was on her mind. Would she be allowed to return to serve yet another term as a missionary associate, or would she be forced to retire?

That summer she tried to cram witnessing and teaching into every hour of the day. When she left that fall, she prayed it would not be the last time she would see the missionary friends and Chinese friends she had grown to love. Although she was willing to return, she knew much of the decision would depend on the physical exam and doctors' reports that would be scheduled once she was back in the States.

While on furlough, she met with a GA group from Ozona. "What do you do on vacation in Taiwan?'' asked a brown-haired beauty who was fresh from a family vacation.

"Who vacations?'' responded Lola Mae. "We teach Vacation Bible Schools, hold youth camps, crusades, revivals in missions, and get ready for school the next fall.''

Realizing that it was an adventure tale the girls wanted to hear, Lola Mae proceeded to tell them of one summer trip she had taken to Green Island in 1965.

"Where's Green Island?'' asked another girl.

"On the east coast of Taiwan. You must travel by boat to get there.''

On that trip, she and Lucille Dawdy had accompanied the O. J. Quicks to lead evangelistic meetings. On that trip she had had her first experience with seasickness.

"Girls, you understand that the Pacific Ocean is known for being calm. But on that particular summer day it was anything but calm. Massive waves swelled, and our boat was heaving. At first Lucille and Mrs. Quick became ill. It was almost funny to see them run for the railing, but just about the time I found humor in their predicament, I had to join them at the rail. Living through that small storm gave me a renewed understanding of the reasons why the men in Jonah's story were so willing to throw him overboard. Previously, I had judged them rather harshly, but I can assure you if I had thought someone on board that day was responsible for the storm, I would have gladly tossed the culprit overboard.

"The island is very small, yet it is crowded with people. Our evangelistic work was some of the first on the island. The people came out of curiosity the first night, but they continued to come back because they were anxious to hear about a Living God Who loved them. In most of the meetings we had standing room only."

"Oh," said one of the girls, "I can't imagine our church being that full. That must have been very exciting."

"Yes," said Lola Mae, "but the most exciting part was becoming a singing celebrity."

"What do you mean?" asked a blonde who was dressed in the GA uniform of the 1960s, consisting of a green skirt and white blouse.

"Well, Lucille and I helped with one meeting that was held at a prison on the island. Before we went that night, the evangelist had asked us to sing a duet. Not having much time to practice, Lucille and I decided on some of our most traditional hymns. We were both a little afraid; we had never sung before prisoners. What a delight! At the end of our songs, they clapped and asked us to sing again. Many asked for us to sing the following night. Actually, girls, they were the most grateful audience I've ever had."

"You might say Miss Daniel had a captive audience," declared the GA director, Mrs. Glynn.

The GAs hooted. "Oh, no," said one of the sharpest girls sitting on the front row, "that's not the only captive audience Miss Daniel ever had. Remember she is a schoolteacher.''

Lola Mae winked at the child. She had always appreciated precocious children. Then she turned the discussion toward more serious matters. "There is something else that is very important that I must share with you. Do you remember when I came home that summer four years ago?''

"Most of us were not old enough for GA then," one girl reminded her.

"I know most of you know Mrs. Glynn's daughter Ginger," Lola Mae prompted.

"Sure, the one in senior high school."

"Four years ago when I came home to Ozona for a brief visit, I spoke to the GAs. Ginger was a GA at that time. I had been talking about the importance of giving yourself and all that you have to be used by the Lord. Ginger asked that night what a GA could do for missions. I had reminded her that her prayers and the prayers of this church had meant so much to me. Then I said that a GA could also give whatever money she might have to be used in missions causes."

"Ginger said, 'But Miss Daniel, I have only this silver dollar. What can you do with a silver dollar?' When I told her that a Chinese/English Bible in Taiwan could be purchased with a silver dollar, she gave me her dollar. Girls, I want you to know that I took Ginger's dollar back to Taiwan and bought a Bible. I gave the Bible to a young Chinese man that was attending my English Bible class. He began to read Ginger's Bible. Soon he accepted Jesus as his Saviour, and now he is attending our Baptist seminary in Taipei to become a minister.

"Ginger, a GA just like you, made a difference in that man's life. Never doubt that God can use you just as He used Ginger; you must understand how important it is for each of us to do our part."

When Lola Mae returned again to Taiwan, she carried

many dollars from GAs back with her to purchase Bibles. She knew that the lives touched and changed would become blessings too numerous to count. Those blessings would seem very important in the difficult days that lay ahead.

"Lola Mae, Lola Mae." Across the semiconscious valley of fatigue, she heard the screams outside her apartment. Clinging to the top of the refrigerator, she breathed a prayer of gratitude. She could not remember how long she had hung on to her perch. The lapping of the water which had risen so quickly had been frightening at first, but she had eventually dozed off, lulled to sleep even in the midst of the crisis.

The sounds of her apartment door being pushed open was like the first harbinger of spring. She knew she would be safe; relief washed over her leaving her exhausted but joyous. A missionary couple who lived nearby made their way through the chest-deep water toward her. Already stains on the walls indicated that the water had reached the pictures hanging there. Although it had begun to recede, the filthy water still swirled in her home.

"We missed you, and began to ask the other missionaries and people near the school. They said they had seen you earlier at the school, and someone said he had seen you coming back to this area in a cart pulled by a Chinese man," her friend said.

The events of the day began to come back to her as she was carried between her friends back to their dry home to change clothes and be guided to a safe, dry bed. "This feels so good," whispered Lola Mae. "I had doubted whether I would ever feel dry again."

Events had occurred so quickly since she had returned to Taiwan after her year's furlough. The doctor had given her a clean bill of health, and the Foreign Mission Board had approved her staying until her 70th birthday. Although past the age of retirement, she had excitedly returned to this beautiful island to serve again among the Chinese people whom she had always loved. This time she had been assigned to teach at a branch of Morrison Academy in Taipei.

The second fall after her return, word had come that the largest typhoon in 20 years was headed for Taiwan. Lola Mae listened to the reports and readied her apartment. Linens, towels, and clothes were placed high enough to avoid several inches of water.

The rains had begun. Sitting there listening to the wind and rain, Lola Mae became concerned about the files in her room at school. School records, years of lesson ideas, and other important papers were stored in a cabinet that she knew would receive water damage if the school building flooded. With deliberation, she made her way to the school and managed to drag the small filing cabinet up one flight of stairs. Knowing that it would be safe, she made her way back into the street. A passing stranger informed her the area ahead of her had already flooded.

"Where are you going?" asked the strong young man.

"I need to return to my home and move more of my household items to a higher area. I'm a missionary here, and those possessions are all I have." Seeing she was determined to press on in the water, the young man asked her to wait.

He returned several minutes later with a cart. "Climb on," he instructed. "I can get you to your apartment; you'll never make it by foot. You already look exhausted."

When Lola Mae reached the apartment, water was several inches deep. Quickly she began piling small appliances high on the closet shelves. The water was waist high when she used a step ladder to cling to the refrigerator top. Much to her surprise, the water washed away the ladder. Somehow she managed to pull herself high enough on the refrigerator to balance precariously on its top. "Lord," she said loudly over the roar of the rain, "Give me peace in the midst of this storm." Then she drifted into a semiconscious daze resting in the strength of the Lord and waiting.

The local doctors ordered bed rest after her friends found her. "You are much too old for such adventures," one doctor gently chided as he administered one of several shots as a precaution for diseases that accompany dirty water. Not an obedient patient, Lola Mae borrowed a dress and wore a pair of houseshoes to church the next morning.

"I just feel the need to thank the Lord for the blessing of life," said Lola Mae.

Lola Mae returned a few days later to salvage what she could from her apartment. All her furniture was ruined; the refrigerator that had saved her life was beyond repair; and her clothes, linens, and towels were filthy. Other missionaries began to share, and the Ozona church deposited money into her missions account to help replace ruined furniture. Lola Mae, surveying the damage, thanked God that her life had been spared, even though most of those perishable items in her life had been lost.

The winter before the typhoon hit, a young man from Mainland China had escaped on a refugee boat to Hong Kong. Word came through him as well as others who had filtered out over the years since 1949 that Christianity had survived Communist oppression. Small groups of Christians had even survived the cultural revolution and were meeting underground. He had also brought word of persecutions of preachers. In some provinces, offenders were given punishment such as sweeping streets. In others, ministers and those caught with Bibles had been sent to labor camps, where some had not survived. Others, yet, were paraded through city streets after having half their heads shaved. He told of hiding the family Bible under broken pottery when Communist soldiers had searched their home. Missionaries on Taiwan read the story in the Hong Kong paper and rejoiced. Several of them served on Mainland China before the Communist takeover.

None who read the clipping were more excited than

Lola Mae. "Mary," she said one day after the typhoon, "I still believe that China will open up. Just look at the reports that continue to come to us. Do you suppose God spared my life so that I can still fulfill my call to the Mainland?"

"Lola Mae," replied Mary laughing, "there are two forces on this earth that never cease to amaze me. God, of course, has not abandoned those people who have been faithful in persecution. He can open the doors to China. I've also learned not to underestimate this obsession you have for the Chinese. I pray I might live long enough to receive a letter from China with your name on the return address."

After those two years in Taipei she returned to Taichung and her many friends there to finish the last two years of her second term. In 1971, when China was admitted to the United Nations, American missionaries were told to keep their passports on them at all times. In addition, they were to keep a small suitcase packed in the event circumstances mandated a hasty departure. Lola Mae was not concerned; they had many friends on the island. Many Chinese were angry, but their hostilities were not vented on the missionaries.

Work was begun at another church near a factory. The first evening only nonbelievers attended. Most had never heard the Bible read aloud before.

That spring in 1971, Lola Mae had to be hospitalized a few days for tests.

"Look, you must slow down some," said the doctor. "How many nights a week are you teaching Bible studies in addition to your regular work week at the academy?"

"Most weeks, five. Then, of course, I attend church on Sunday evenings."

"Six nights a week going until 10:00 or 11:00 P.M. is too much. If you don't slow down, you won't live to see your 70th birthday. You must keep at least two nights open for rest," the doctor ordered.

Reluctantly, she agreed to try. She had always believed that you needed to be sensible, and she knew if she became ill, she wouldn't be able to continue teaching at the school.

In a letter to the Ozona church a few nights later, she said, "I'm perfectly happy right here, but just hope I can stay long enough on this side of the world to see the doors open to Mainland China."

"Just read this," said Audrey Glynn to her friend, Ann. "That woman's obsession with China beats anything I've ever seen. The doctor wants her to slow down. And Lola Mae isn't content with trying to win the Chinese on Taiwan. She still feels compelled to go to China."

Later that same month Lola Mae wrote again:

"The political situation doesn't look good for Americans on Taiwan because of Nixon's trip to China. Just hope and pray that it will not cause the missionaries to have to leave, unless it's to go to the Mainland again. I would love that, and this could be God's way of opening that field again. There are more than 800 million Chinese on the Mainland, with few Christians in the group. What a harvest field is waiting. Nothing is impossible with God, so we are going to be ready if and when the time comes."

Even as she penned those words to the GAs in Ozona, she began to pray at her kitchen table that the Lord would open doors to China within her lifetime. "Oh, Lord, how I am blessed to have been used here on Taiwan, but I have not forgotten my clear call to the Mainland. Knowing You do not make mistakes, let me trust You for the outcome."

The words to a favorite Scripture verse ran through her mind bringing contentment and promise: "Trust in the Lord with all thine heart; and lean not unto thine own understanding. In all ways acknowledge him, and He shall direct thy paths" (Prov. 3:5-7 KJV).

Lola Mae returned home when her second term expired. After passing her physical, she spent precious time catching up on family business with Billie in Austin. "We're so glad to have you finally home," said Billie as they sipped a cup of coffee together.

Lola Mae's lack of immediate response told Billie much more than she wanted to know. "I've seen that look in your eyes before. You're not here to stay this time either, are you?"

"A teacher has left on furlough. I feel I'm still needed. Although too old for the Board to send me, if I can raise the funds, I'll go back," Lola Mae responded.

After a speaking engagement in Ozona, the church wrote the Foreign Mission Board offering to guarantee her living expenses, her medical bills, and responsibility for seeing she could go home if she needed care unavailable on the island. "That about takes care of it, all of it, even the perishable container," said Lola Mae. She returned to the island to serve two more years at the expense of the Ozona church.

By the end of the second school year, Lola Mae was beginning to feel her age, or at least 60. Although there was still much to do on Taiwan, much had been accomplished in the 12 years she had served. Baptist churches dotted the island. There was an encampment, schools, student centers, and a seminary. Five new missionaries were in language school, and she commented to Mary Sampson, "I think that I will be ready this time to go home. At 72, I need to be situated closer to my family."

"You're finally retiring, are you?" asked Mary with a broad smile on her face, knowing full-well that Lola Mae did not include the word *retire* in her vocabulary.

"You might say I'm temporarily retiring from Taiwan, but we never reach the age of retirement as far as God is concerned. Christians are hired for eternity," Lola Mae said emphatically.

9

More On-the-Job Training

When Lola Mae returned to the States, she took a year away from teaching to get settled in the Rebekhah Baines Retirement Center in Austin, Texas. This multistoried apartment complex overlooking the Colorado River and the Austin skyline, which had changed much in the decade since she had left, would be her nest. Although the one-bedroom apartment was small, the rent was moderate, the building was secure, and the missions field, as usual, was great. There were senior citizens living in the complex who needed to know the Lord, and there were those that needed to be reminded that although society classified them as elderly, they could still be an asset to others.

After catching up on all the family history that had unfolded while she was in Taiwan, Lola Mae began a grueling schedule of speaking engagements. She would never turn down an offer to speak at a church regardless of its size. Churches without Woman's Missionary Union organizations were especially important. She would accept the opportunity and then hammer home the necessity of an active missions organization, especially for children.

"Most of the missionaries at home and abroad stress the importance of Girls in Action and Royal Ambassadors in their lives. Your church needs to be helping train future workers today," she would say with heartfelt conviction.

While visiting friends in San Antonio, she received a

phone call from a military wife whose child she had taught when the couple had been stationed in Taiwan. "Miss Daniel," said the voice, "Our church school, Gateway Christian School, is looking for a first-grade teacher. I've sung your praises, and they have said they'd hire you sight unseen if you're really as good as I say."

After a brief telephone interview she was hired. "It's a good thing they didn't see you," said Gene. "They would be afraid to hire someone as old as air and water."

After only a year in retirement, Lola Mae began a five-year career with Gateway Christian School. Each year she would say, "Maybe next year I should retire."

Then the parents would beg, "My child starts first grade next year. Won't you stay to see that he has a good foundation? Just one more year, please?"

Then an invitation arrived from a church in Taiwan that she helped start shortly before she left. They wanted her to be on hand for the dedication of their new building, a brick and stone facility, which was a vast improvement over the original bamboo hut. "Would you please speak at our dedication service, Miss Daniel?" the letter asked.

Once again, First Baptist Church, Ozona, aided in her adventure. When she left at the end of five years at Gateway, she had never missed a day of work because of illness. "Quite a feat for such an old lady," said Lola Mae at one of several retirement parties given in her honor.

As most of her friends and family predicted, Lola Mae discovered an opening at the academy where a missionary had left on furlough. Arriving by boat in Keelung, she practiced her Chinese as she made her way across the island to Taipei, where she obtained a room at the YWCA. Boarding at the YWCA afforded her multitudes of opportunities to share Jesus with curious young women who had flocked to their capital city seeking work. Almost nightly girls gathered in her room to learn more about America and the Bible.

At the end of that year, when she returned home to

Texas, she had the feeling she would not work again among the Chinese on Taiwan. But she was determined not to forget the Mandarin language that had taken her so long to learn. Wherever she would go, she sought out Chinese—at the University of Texas where she volunteered to tutor, and with the International Relations Club in San Antonio. Lola Mae was still counting on making it to China, and she was going to converse with the Chinese once she got there.

Needing more than speaking engagements to occupy her time, she again sought work in private schools, teaching first at Lackland Baptist Church kindergarten. When she heard that another church school had an opening that was closer, she told her friend Gene, "I'm just going down to that church and get a job."

Understanding that she would use her usual tactic, which was to interview first and give them the application second, Gene merely said, "OK, and good luck."

This time Lola Mae tried a new tactic. She failed to put her date of birth on the application. The school principal and the pastor of Northwest Hills Baptist Church interviewed her. They could see she appeared to be near retirement age, but her credentials were outstanding, and her experience and spiritual depth impressed them greatly.

After she answered their questions, Mr. Bob Clontz nodded and said, "Let's sign her up!"

Several days later the teachers went together to the Health Department for blood tests and health cards. One of the teachers glanced down at Lola Mae's application.

"Your birthdate, please?" said the woman at the desk.

"September 20, 1902," stated Lola Mae. "1902!" exclaimed the principal, "We knew you were past retirement age, but not *that* past retirement age!"

As the school days clicked off the calendar both the pastor and principal agreed that their initial impression had been a good guide. Lola Mae worked magic with her students, knowledgeable in her subject matter and firm but loving in her discipline. They agreed that the "lady knew her stuff."

At the beginning of her second year, the school and the church relocated to new facilities. Because of an unfortunate set of circumstances, gas pipes had not been laid all the way to the church. Lola Mae taught that entire winter with only a small space heater.

"Gene, it's just like teaching in Taiwan," she said.

Not a complainer, she was wise enough to understand that God was using even this unfortunate inconvenience to prepare her for something else.

Lola Mae's employers at Northwest Hills understood that she had begun corresponding with agencies who were supplying English teachers for Mainland China. At home she devoured the newspapers and newsmagazines, and prayed. In 1984-85, it became obvious that China was not only opening to tourists but to businesspeople and teachers as well.

As soon as Lola Mae heard that Cooperative Services International (CSI), a division of the Foreign Mission Board, was recruiting teachers to go to China, she resigned effective at the end of that school year. Each night she prayed 1986 would be the year she would be able to answer God's call to China.

That summer was probably the busiest summer of Lola Mae's life. Through correspondence with the Foreign Mission Board, she learned that a group of volunteers were going to China in the fall to teach English at schools, colleges, and technical centers throughout the country.

Every time she contacted the CSI office she was told, "Yes, you are qualified; yes, the national language is Mandarin; yes, we know you speak Mandarin; yes, we'll send you the forms, but we cannot offer you anything beyond a sliver of hope because of your age."

Lola Mae checked the mailbox daily for the forms. When they arrived, she scheduled a physical. The night before her appointment, she became so excited she was certain that her blood pressure would be too high. She spent time quietly reading the Bible and praying. This time of meditation brought peace and the usual abiding trust that the decision was God's and not hers alone.

After passing the physical, the doctor gently reminded her of her age. "But you've been determined to go to China ever since I've known you. I suppose any warnings I give won't matter much anyway," he sighed.

Word leaked that there would be a CSI orientation in Dallas. Lola Mae called everyone of any importance she knew and asked them to help her by calling the CSI offices. She received an invitation to attend the orientation.

Even before the orientation Lola Mae began to prepare her friends and family for the inevitability of her acceptance. "How can you be so sure?" asked a young lady who was interviewing her for an article. "Always before external circumstances or the decisions of boards or nations have blocked your call."

With faith, Lola Mae answered, "When God calls you to do something, men nor governments can prevail against you forever. You just go ahead and prepare, using all the in-between time as a training ground. At some point in your life it becomes crystal clear that all the circumstances have prepared you for the job."

"But why this time? How do you know this time it will happen?" the interviewer persisted.

"At 83, soon to be 84, I just know that I don't have much time left to train. God doesn't make mistakes when He calls, and I didn't hear wrong. I was called to China."

Finally Lola Mae flew to orientation. At the meeting were three couples; a young man; a 78-year-old man; Addie B. Choate, 72, whose parents had been missionaries to China; and Lola Mae. The Chinese woman helping with orientation had them introduce themselves and give their experience and ages. Lola was last. "I am a month shy of 84," she said.

An audible sigh of disbelief could be heard. When she

72

told the story of her desire to work in China, the group was obviously touched. Then she spoke in Mandarin to the Chinese lady.

James Cecil, who was the Foreign Mission Board representative, offered her little hope. He glumly reminded her of her age, and said, "We'll call you in a few days and let you know."

The sweet Chinese lady took her aside and assured her she would try to find a place where they would accept a teacher who was "around the age of 65."

She continued, "Our teachers are forced to retire much earlier than that. I can offer you very little hope. Yet, there are some places in China where it is more difficult to obtain an English teacher. If you are willing to accept whatever I can find, perhaps I can find you a school."

Lola Mae had had her heart turned toward Shanghai since she was an elementary child, but she calmly said, "I'll go wherever you find me a place."

10

At Last—China!

Returning to Austin with no firm assurance except her
faith, Lola Mae began gathering the essentials she would
need. They had been instructed to carry everything in two
suitcases. Although it was a typical August day in Texas,
and it was difficult to think of Chinese winters, she began
to assemble a warm winter wardrobe. They were told they
could take a Bible in each suitcase. The lady insisted they
dress casually, not flashy. With a woman's vanity, Lola
Mae selected her more demure earrings. "How would
anyone recognize me in pictures sent to the States without
those earrings?" Lola Mae asked.

Finally, when she could stand the anxiety of waiting no
longer, the phone rang. "Pack your bags, Miss Daniel,
you've been accepted," the voice on the phone said.

"My bags are packed," came her quick reply between
tears of happiness. The Austin telephone company made
a huge profit that day; she simply had to call everyone
who had prayed with her over this decision.

Once again her family met at the airport to bid her
good-bye as she moved toward the fulfillment of her ultimate dream. This time Billie was not in the group. The
family had lost her three years before. Lola Mae imagined
that her father, mother, and Billie were rejoicing together
in Heaven. The thought warmed her and almost brought
on the tears she was fighting to hold in check.

"But where will you be?" asked one of the nieces.

"All I know is China, and that's enough for me. I will write as soon as I have an address," answered Lola Mae.

The CSI group stopped briefly in Hong Kong to spend a day shopping for last-minute essentials and paperwork.

"Addie B.," said Lola Mae to her new friend, "this is just a waste of time. I've waited 66 years, and we're in meetings and shopping."

"Be patient a few more days," chided Addie B. Their first stop in China was Guangzhou, formerly Canton. The university there was well equipped, and they were told there was lovely housing for teachers.

"Wouldn't it be nice if we could be assigned here," said Lola Mae. She knew the warm southern climate would be a blessing. The openness of the city amazed her. Across the Pearl River were hotels and restaurants, many of which were American chains. Although the people spoke Cantonese, she knew she would fare well.

The Chinese woman assured them that all of China was not like Guangzhou, that there were open and closed cities and the living conditions were best in those which were open.

Soon the assignments were made. Lola Mae and Addie B. were delighted to hear they were to live together. Unfortunately, they were not assigned to Guangzhou.

With optimism, they left the city and traveled with their friend from orientation northeast to the city of Zhangzhou. "I will see if the principal of the technical school will hire you. You will be teaching teachers who will instruct their students in English. It is important that we learn English so that we may be prepared for tourism and trade."

Lola Mae had to laugh, "I wish more of our students were as serious about the need to learn our language."

Later their Chinese friend returned. "The president of the school will see you."

By that evening Lola Mae and Addie B. had a job for

the semester. "Wonder why we didn't sign a contract for the whole year," remarked Addie B.

"Well, the lady told us we were the first Americans he'd ever employed. Don't you think he wanted us to be put on a sort of probation until he saw if we were worth our pay?"

"Yes, and weren't you lucky, he never even asked your age," Addie B. chimed in.

Before leaving them in the ten-story guest house, their friend cautioned, "This is not as open as Guangzhou. You mustn't say anything about teaching in Taiwan, or mention God while you teach."

Lola Mae and Addie B. were happy to see that the hotel, or guest house, had electricity, especially since they were housed on the ninth floor. Their meals were taken on the first floor in a dining room; and their quarters consisted of one room, a bath, and twin beds. "This is like having to share a room with a sister again," teased Lola Mae.

Their classes were full of students eager to learn. "How did you decide to teach?" Lola Mae asked one of the more verbal students.

"In China, we are selected to teach," explained the thin young man.

The second day, Lola Mae and Addie B. made a startling discovery. They left their bedroom to go down to classes. Lola Mae pressed the elevator button and nothing happened—no light, no noise.

"What do you suppose has happened to the elevator?" asked Addie B.

"Guess we don't have much choice. Let's take the stairs," Lola Mae said.

Since Addie B. did not speak Mandarin, Lola Mae quizzed one of the young men on the first floor. He kindly explained that due to a shortage of fuel for generators the electricity only worked sporadically. Lola Mae did not have to translate this to Addie B. The look on her face told enough. Quickly they calculated the trips to the classroom and the dining hall. They would make five trips a day up nine flights of stairs. "Well," joked Lola Mae, "we will certainly be in shape after several weeks of this."

A few days later, a young man lingered in the classroom after the other students had departed. "You're a Christian aren't you?"

"Yes, I am. Are you?"

"No," he said, "my grandmother was a Bible woman. I remember her. I would like to learn more of what it is to be a Christian."

Lola Mae invited the young man to her room. She had already decided that if they weren't allowed to mention God in school, she would host small groups of students for Bible study in her room just as she had her last year in Taiwan.

That night the curious young man came to their room, and Lola Mae explained God had given the world, through the gift of His Son Jesus, the only means to have fellowship with Him. She explained about the birth and life of Christ and about His Crucifixion on the cross as atonement for our sins.

She marked passages in her Bible for the young man to read. After the third visit, the young man accepted the free gift of salvation. The next night he returned for more Bible study, bringing with him two friends.

Lola Mae and Addie B. cautioned the men that they must keep the group small by rotating newcomers, and those making decisions must drop out.

Eventually she and Addie B. were relocated to another facility, and they each received a blessing—rooms on the second floor. By mid-October it had begun to grow cold. Although they had a radiator in their room, it did not work due to the lack of fuel. By the next month winter had definitely arrived in Zhangzhou. They wore two, three, and finally four layers of clothes.

Because the dining hall was on the north side of the

building, they decided to take their meals in their rooms. Each morning two girls delivered four thermoses of hot water and broth for rice that would be served at lunch. Lola Mae and Addie B. discovered a place where they could purchase bread. They had brought instant tea and coffee. Using three of the thermoses, they saved one for hot instant coffee for breakfast. They ate bread, fruits, jam, and coffee instead of the rice broth.

One day the girls asked, "Do you like green peppers and pork for supper?"

"Oh, yes," exclaimed Lola Mae in Mandarin. For four weeks their evening meal consisted of peppers and pork. Addie B. eventually warned, "The next time they ask you if we like something, you tell them we like it, but only for a few days at a time."

"OK," promised Lola Mae as she forced down yet another dinner of peppers and pork.

On a holiday, Lola Mae traveled by train to the town that once had been marked in her elementary geography book. In one of her letters of correspondence the Foreign Mission Board had mentioned the Grace Baptist Church. That was the church she had dreamed of serving in so many years before as a young girl enrolled at Howard Payne. While in Shanghai, Lola Mae found the building and attended a worship service. This was an open city, and people were permitted to go to church.

Although there was a speaker, Lola Mae noticed that the majority of the worshippers did not appear to be listening. They were praying intensely with heads bowed and lips silently moving. After the service, an elderly woman made her way toward Lola Mae. "You're a Southern Baptist," she said.

"Yes, I'm a Southern Baptist."

"You go home and tell your friends that they did not waste their money building churches. Some of the buildings have been converted into factories, but the real church is in here," she said as she pointed toward her heart. "Here is the real temple of God."

Their special bond that moment was so keen that Lola Mae wanted to wrap her arms around the tiny, wrinkled woman. "Only Christians can know what it is to be in one spirit with another whose culture, life, and heritage were so different. Certainly in Christ, there is no difference!" she said as she hugged the woman.

A while after her return to Zhangzhou, Addie B. became ill. After a week at home, she had to be hospitalized. During the four weeks that she was ill, Lola Mae combined their classes. "Why, Lola Mae, that will make you sick doing so much work," warned Addie B.

"I'm not going to have them send me home. Since we're the first Americans this man has employed, I've got to prove that we can handle this."

On one visit to the hospital, Addie B. shared, "I've decided to go home. The cold is just too intense. I can't take the -25°F without heat. My children are concerned and want me home. I don't want to leave you here; won't you come too?"

"No, not as long as I'm healthy," Lola Mae answered.

At the semester's close, all the CSI volunteers gathered in Hong Kong. Lola Mae was examined by a doctor. "Lola Mae, you've suffered damage to your legs. You just don't need to stay," warned the physician who examined her.

"I'll be fine after I've spent a few days in heated buildings and catch up on my rest," she responded.

The night before she was to leave for the States, Addie B. and Lola Mae had devotional time together. As they prayed, Addie B. said, "Lord, let Lola Mae come home with me, but if she won't come, please send her to a warmer area."

After they prayed, Addie B. tried to persuade her, "The Lord told me you need to go home."

Firmly, but in love, Lola Mae answered, "When He tells me, I'll go."

While attending church the next day, Lola Mae could

not help but think of Addie B.'s prayer. She added her own, "Lord, I know I said I'd go wherever, but I'm tired of the cold, and I've lost 18 pounds; I need a warmer place."

After the service, two men approached her. "Are you Miss Daniel?" one asked.

"Yes, who are you?"

"We are with the University of Ghangzhou. Would you be interested in teaching beginning this semester with our system?"

Lola Mae broke out in a good case of Texas-sized goose bumps. After spending a few hours talking to the gentlemen, she assured them she would be interested in transferring if she could have the blessing of the president at the technical school in Zhangzhou. It dawned on her how miraculous it was they had not signed a contract for more than one semester.

When she returned to Zhangzhou, she spoke to the president. She explained that at 84 she needed a warmer climate.

"Eighty-four! Oh, Miss Daniel, if I had known that you were 84, I would have encouraged you to seek a warmer climate."

The day that she went to the station the school van was loaded with students wishing to say good-bye. One slipped her a note as she left. It read, "There are 57 contacts." Lola Mae knew that he meant 57 Chinese had accepted Jesus because of the semester she and Addie B. roughed it out in Zhangzhou. The hardships, the cold, and the poor food were minor compared to this number. She knew too the number would multiply as the teachers returned to "teach" their students. How many lives would be influenced through the years because the Lord had sent her to a school to teach teachers?

In Ghangzhou, the same pattern followed. Students would stay after English class with questions, and Lola Mae would invite them to her apartment where she would share the Bible and her testimony. "We knew you were a Christian," they would say, "because you are so kind."

She had often told children, "It isn't what you say so much as what you do." Certainly one of her living principles had borne true in her work with the Chinese.

Several weeks after classes had begun, and she had been having Bible study in her room, one man asked if he could borrow her Bible. "But I only brought two. If you do not return this Bible, I will only be left with one to study. I won't have one to lend."

"Trust me to return the Bible, please," he pleaded.

After three weeks, Lola Mae had seen the man only in class. In front of the other students, she was afraid to ask him what had become of her Bible. One day as he left the room, he said simply, "Soon."

The next day he returned to class with a folded newspaper. At break he laid the newspaper on her desk. Seeing that the Bible had been folded inside, Lola Mae slipped the entire newspaper inside her schoolbag. That night he came to her apartment for Bible study.

"But where have you been?" she asked, concerned that he had missed many nights of Bible study.

Without looking up, he murmured, "Three friends and I have spent nights copying the New Testament in three-hour shifts. We have a Bible now too!"

When Lola Mae thought about his sacrifice and the bookshelves full of Bibles in many American Christian homes she almost became sick. She committed to pray that once again presses would roll in China with Bibles that would not be illegal. "In the meantime, Lord," she prayed, "send me Bibles."

Almost a week later, Lola Mae had gone to one of the open churches for Sunday services. A tour bus was parked outside. At the close of the service, she made her way to a young man who stood out from the tour group. By the proximity of the bus, she guessed he was a tourist.

"What's the matter, son?"

Looking startled, but pleased to see an American lady, he spilled his secret. "Listen, lady, I've got some Bibles in my suitcase, and I don't know what to do with them."

"I know what to do with them," said Lola Mae, trying to suppress a smile that wanted to spread across her face. "I need those Bibles."

As she and the young man talked, she discovered that he had indeed had her name written all over him. He was from University Hills Baptist Church in Austin, Texas.

As the young man rejoined the tourists, Lola Mae shouted, "You call my pastor at Hyde Park Baptist Church when you get back home and tell him he ought to keep better track of his members, since you found one of them in China."

"For some reason," the young man said shaking his head, "I don't think he'll be at all surprised."

A new twist to her experiences at Ghangzhou came when school authorities asked her to go to several of the public schools and speak about the customs and life-styles of Americans. Each time a student would ask, "But why would you come so far to tell us about America?"

"Because," she would say, "I've spent 66 years of my life trying to come to China."

"But why?"

"Because God has given me a love for Chinese people. I did not want any generation of Chinese to die without hearing that Jesus loves them."

By the look on their faces, Lola Mae could see that many of them understood about a love that would weather six decades of on-the-job training. She also understood that many of them could not begin to fathom that God would love them so much that He would burden a capitalist heart for their salvation.

By the end of the spring semester, Lola Mae had made 38 successful contacts. "Perhaps," she wondered, "there were fewer saved because the people had a better way of life. They were less in need of a personal God."

Several weeks before school was out, Lola Mae had gone to the head of the school and asked, "How old were you told that I am?"

"Somewhere around 65," answered her employer.

"Well, I'm way out around 65. I'm 84 years old, and I thought it only right that you know."

A little later, Lola Mae was told that she would not be renewed for the fall semester. Since she had failed to regain the weight lost in Zhangzhou, she had already resigned herself to the fact that she would be unable to stay another year.

As the students came to see her off at the pier, one asked, "But what will you do? In America you are too old to teach."

With tears in her eyes, Lola Mae answered, "Some day the doors to China will open again for missionaries. I'm going home to tell them how hungry you are for the gospel. Our Baptist young people need to train now in order to be prepared to come when the doors open."

Lola Mae boarded the boat. Turning one last time, she waved a hasty good-bye to the Chinese people she had waited a lifetime to serve. Moving away from the rail, she found a place to sit. Her mind was full of so many wonderful thoughts. How glorious it was to worship the God of creation and the Fulfiller of dreams. "Yes, I'll go home, but I won't retire. And if my health holds out, I just might find my way back."

The boat whistle blew, the boat lurched forward, and Lola Mae began plotting to return.

About the author

Theresa (Terry) grew up in a Christian missions-minded home. She is a product of a Southern Baptist missions heritage. This heritage has led her to teach in public schools in both Texas and Ohio and to serve as a house parent in a home for unwanted boys.

Married to Marion (Mac), a military officer, their formula for transplanting their children Amy and Derrick is to immediately become active in a local church fellowship. With her husband's support, Theresa manages to write for missions publications, work as a writing instructor at the University of Texas at San Antonio, and serve as Baptist Women director of the San Antonio Baptist Association.